faith first

Legacy Edition
SCHOOL

Grade Five

RCL Benziger

Cincinnati, Ohio

This book reflects the
new revision of the

ROMAN MISSAL
THIRD EDITION

W9-CMZ-946

"The Ad Hoc Committee to Oversee the
Use of the Catechism, United States Conference
of Catholic Bishops, has found this catechetical
series, copyright 2007, to be in conformity with
the *Catechism of the Catholic Church.*"

NIHIL OBSTAT
Rev. Msgr. Robert M. Coerver
Censor Librorum
IMPRIMATUR
† Most Rev. Charles V. Grahmann
Bishop of Dallas
September 30, 2005

The Nihil Obstat and Imprimatur are official declarations
that the material reviewed is free of doctrinal or moral error.
No implication is contained therein that those granting the
Nihil Obstat and Imprimatur agree with the contents,
opinions, or statements expressed.

Send all inquiries to:
RCL Benziger
8805 Governor's Hill Drive
Suite 400
Cincinnati, Ohio 45249

Toll Free   877-275-4725
Fax   800-688-8356

Visit us at www.RCLBenziger.com
         www.FaithFirst.com

20535   ISBN 978-0-7829-1120-6 (Student Book)
20545   ISBN 978-0-7829-1126-8 (Teacher Guide)

5th printing.
Manufactured for RCL Benziger in Cincinnati, OH, USA.
March 2012.

ACKNOWLEDGMENTS

Scripture excerpts are taken or adapted from the *New
American Bible with Revised New Testament and Psalms*
Copyright © 1991, 1986, 1970, Confraternity of Christian
Doctrine, Washington, DC. Used with permission. All rights
reserved. No part of the *New American Bible* may be
reproduced by any means without the permission of the
copyright owner.

Excerpts are taken or adapted from the English translation
of *Rite of Baptism for Children* © 1969, International
Committee on English in the Liturgy, Inc. (ICEL); *Rite of
Marriage* © 1969, ICEL; the English translation of the
Roman Missal © 2010, ICEL; the English translation of the
Act of Contrition from *Rite of Penance* © 1974, ICEL; the
English translation of *A Book of Prayers* © 1982, ICEL; the
English translation of *Book of Blessings* © 1988, ICEL;
Catholic Household Blessings and Prayers (revised edition)
© 2007, United States Conference of Catholic Bishops,
Washington, D.C. All rights reserved.

Excerpts are taken or adapted from English translation of
Gloria Patri, *Kyrie Eleison, Nicene Creed, Apostles' Creed,
Sanctus, Benedictus, Agnus Dei,* and *Te Deum Laudamus* by
the International Consultation on English Texts (ICET).

Faith First Legacy Edition

Developing a religion program requires the gifts and
talents of many individuals working together as a team.
RCL Benziger is proud to acknowledge the
contributions of these dedicated people.

Program Theology Consultants
Reverend Louis J. Cameli, S.T.D.
Reverend Robert D. Duggan, S.T.D.

Advisory Board
Judith Deckers, M.Ed.
Elaine McCarron, SCN, M.Div.
Marina Herrera, Ph.D.
Reverend Frank McNulty, S.T.D.
Reverend Ronald J. Nuzzi, Ph.D.

Contributing Writers
Student Book and Teacher Guide
Reverend Louis J. Cameli
Christina DeCamp
Judith Deckers
Jack Gargiulo
Mary Beth Jambor
Michele Norfleet
Marie Raffio
Susan Stark

Catechetical Specialist	*National Catechetical Consultant*	*Managing Editor*
Jo Rotuno	Kate Sweeney Ristow	Susan Smith

Art & Design Director	*Electronic Page Makeup*	*Production Director*
Lisa Brent	Laura Fremder, *Manager*	Jenna Nelson
	Marti Ewing	

Designers	*Project Editors*	*Web Site Producers*
Pat Bracken	Patricia A. Classick	Joseph Crisalli
Tricia Legault	Steven M. Ellair	A. C. Ware
	Craig W. O'Neil	

General Editor	*President/Publisher*
Ed DeStefano	Maryann Nead

Contents

We Celebrate: The Liturgical Seasons

We Pray

Dear God,
We can't believe we are finally in fifth grade! We are thankful for all the gifts you have given us. Help us learn more about you this year and to be good followers of your Son, Jesus. We promise to love you and to treat your world and your people with care and respect. Amen.

A Snapshot of Me

My name is _____.

The sacraments I have celebrated are _____ _____.

As a Christian, one thing I believe is _____ _____.

My Favorites

Animal _____

Bible story _____

Book _____

Snack _____

Music _____

Hobby _____

Movie _____

Celebrating Our Faith

Every year the Church helps us learn more about Jesus and his teachings. This year in fifth grade we will explore many ways that the Church celebrates the good news of our faith—the Resurrection of Jesus, the Light of the world.

Solve the Puzzle

This puzzle is a little bit like a crossword puzzle. Begin by solving the four clues in the boxes on page 9. Then transfer the letters of the answers into the puzzle squares with the corresponding numbers. The solution is a sentence that tells the main theme of the Gospel.

		9	14		20	8	5		16	1	19	3	8	1	12	
13	25	19	20	5	18	25		10	5	19	21	19				
16	1	19	19	5	4		6	18	15	13		12	9	6	5
	20	8	18	15	21	7	8		4	5	1	20	8		
9	14	20	15		1		14	5	23		1	14	4		
7	12	15	18	9	15	21	19		12	9	6	5			

1. We Believe

This year in Unit 1 you will learn about the section of the Gospel that tells about a very important event in Jesus' life. The section is called the

___ ___ ___ ___ ___ ___ ___ narrative (see page 88).
16 1 19 19 9 15 14

2. We Worship

In Unit 2 you will learn much more about the Church's liturgy. The liturgy is the "work of the people" that we do when we worship God. The yearly cycle of the Church's celebration of the liturgy is called the

___ ___ ___ ___ ___ ___ ___ ___ ___ ___ year (see page 142).
12 9 20 21 18 7 9 3 1 12

3. We Live

The seven sacraments celebrate God's love for us. The Bible tells us how to respond to God's love. In the First Letter of

___ ___ ___ ___ we read,
10 15 8 14

" ___ ___ ___ ___ ___ ___ ___ ___ ___ ___ ___ ___
23 8 15 5 22 5 18   12 15 22 5 19

___ ___ ___ ___ ___ ___ ___ ___ ___ ___ ___ love
7 15 4 13 21 19 20   1 12 19 15

___ ___ ___ ___ ___ ___ ___ ___ ___ " (see page 268).
8 9 19   2 18 15 20 8 5 18

4. We Pray

Because of all the gifts God has given us, Christians have a reason to celebrate every day. A way that the Church prays together around the clock every day of the year is called

___ ___ ___ ___ ___ ___ ___ ___ ___ ___ ___ ___ ___
20 8 5   12 9 20 21 18 7 25   15 6

___ ___ ___ ___ ___ ___ ___ ___ (see page 321).
20 8 5   8 15 21 18 19

9

Your Word Is Light

LEADER: *Walk at the head of a procession to the prayer area, holding the Bible high for all to see.*

ALL: *Make the Sign of the Cross together.*

LEADER: Lord, we gather today to honor you and to thank you for the gift of your word.

ALL: Your word is a light for our path.

LEADER: A reading from the holy Gospel according to Matthew.

ALL: Glory to you, O Lord.

LEADER: *Proclaim Matthew 5:3–12.*
The Gospel of the Lord.

ALL: Praise to you, Lord Jesus Christ.

LEADER: Lord Jesus, whenever we gather to hear your word, you are here with us. You are light for our path and food for our spirit. Guide us as we continue our journey of faith this year.

ALL: Amen.
All come forward and bow before the Bible.

What does the Church ask us to believe?

Getting Ready

What I Have Learned

What is something you already know about these faith terms?

Divine Revelation

_____

_____

Old Testament

_____

_____

Marks of the Church

_____

_____

Words to Know

Put an X next to the faith terms you know. Put a ? next to the faith terms you need to know more about.

Faith Vocabulary

_____ faith

_____ Holy Trinity

_____ Gospel

_____ miracle

_____ Lord

_____ Paschal Mystery

_____ Evangelists

_____ charisms

_____ Sacred Tradition

_____ Kingdom of God

Questions I Have

What questions would you like to ask about the work of the Holy Spirit in the Church?

_____

_____

_____

_____

A Scripture Story

Jesus and the disciples at sea

Why did Jesus perform miracles?

Speak, Lord

We Pray

Hallelujah!
Praise the LORD from
    the heavens;
  give praise in the
    heights.

Praise the LORD from
    the earth. PSALM 148:1, 7

**We believe in one God.
We believe in one
    Lord, Jesus Christ.
We believe in the
    Holy Spirit.   Amen.**

*What are some of the ways
you come to know people
better?*

Sometimes the more you
learn about people, the
more there is to know. The
Holy Spirit continuously
invites us to know and
believe in God the Father,
the Son, and the Holy
Spirit.

*What have you learned
about God?*

Divine Revelation

Faith Vocabulary

Divine Revelation. God making himself known over time and the divine plan of creation and salvation.

We Are Looking for God

There is a desire inside every person that makes us realize there is Someone much greater than we are. That Someone is God. That desire is part of who we are as human beings. Each of us is looking for God, and he is looking for us.

One of the people in history who taught about God was Saint Augustine of Hippo. He was a bishop in North Africa from A.D. 396 to A.D. 430. Before he became a Christian, Augustine tried to find happiness in many ways, but he was never satisfied. Finally, Augustine realized that he had kept God out of his life. He realized that he was really searching for God. Saint Augustine wrote:

You, O God, have made us for yourself, and our hearts are restless until they rest in you.

FROM *CONFESSIONS*

God's love for us is so great that he comes to us and invites us to know him, hope in him, and love him. It is the very reason God created us.

Saint Augustine's search for happiness helps us learn something about ourselves. We too are looking for God, and he is looking for us.

God Reveals Himself

How does God help us get to know him? The answer is: God reveals himself, or makes himself known, to us.

Revelation is showing or sharing something that is not clear or that we cannot come to see or know on our own. The word *reveal* means "to take the veil off something." When you take the veil off something, you uncover something that is hidden.

Divine Revelation is God making himself and his plan of creation and salvation known. We cannot see God. We cannot know what is in his mind. We cannot, on our own, come to know who he is and his plan of goodness for us and for the world. So God, out of love, revealed himself.

God has revealed that he created us. He is always inviting us to share in his life and love. Making God part of our lives, learning about him, and coming to know him bring us happiness. God wants us to be completely happy with him not only forever in heaven, but also now on earth. That is why he created us.

 What does it tell us about God that he reveals himself to us?

Helping Others Come to Know God

Describe how you can help others come to know God.

_____

_____

_____

_____

_____

_____

_____

_____

Faith Vocabulary

Israelites. The Old Testament people to whom God revealed himself and with whom he made the Covenant.

Pentateuch. A word meaning "five containers"; the first five books of the Old Testament.

God Speaks to Us Through Creation

One way God speaks to us is through creation. God is the Creator who tells us about himself through the world in which we live. The sky, the stars, and the galaxies sing God's love for us. The beauty of animals galloping on dry land, dolphins gliding through the waters, and eagles soaring in the skies all reflect God's goodness, beauty, and love for us. Through watching these creatures, we can come to know God who created them. They are all signs of his love.

In the Bible, we read:
Praise [the LORD], sun and
    moon;
  give praise, all shining
    stars.

You mountains and all hills,
  fruit trees and all cedars;
You animals wild and tame,
  you creatures that crawl
    and fly. . . .
Let them all praise the
  LORD's name,
  for his name alone is
    exalted,
  majestic above earth
    and heaven.
          PSALM 148:3, 9–10, 13

Psalm 148 puts into words what we sometimes feel inside. When we look at creation, we realize how wonderful and good God really is. All creation gives honor and glory to God.

God Speaks to Us Through People

One of the best ways that we get to know God is through people. God loves everyone. Throughout the ages God has chosen special people through whom he revealed himself. In the Bible God tells us that the **Israelites** were the first people he chose. They would be his people, and he would be their God. In the Book of Deuteronomy, the fifth book of the **Pentateuch,** we read:

"For you are a people sacred to the LORD, your God; he has chosen you from all the nations on the face of the earth to be a people peculiarly his own." DEUTERONOMY 7:6

God spoke lovingly to the Israelites. Again and again, he invited them to believe and trust in his love. He was no stranger to his people. He revealed that he was always present with them. Through the Israelites God told us about his love for all people.

 What does God reveal about himself through creation?

PEOPLE OF GOD · PRAISE THE LORD

Look at the seal above. Design your own seal. Give praise to God.

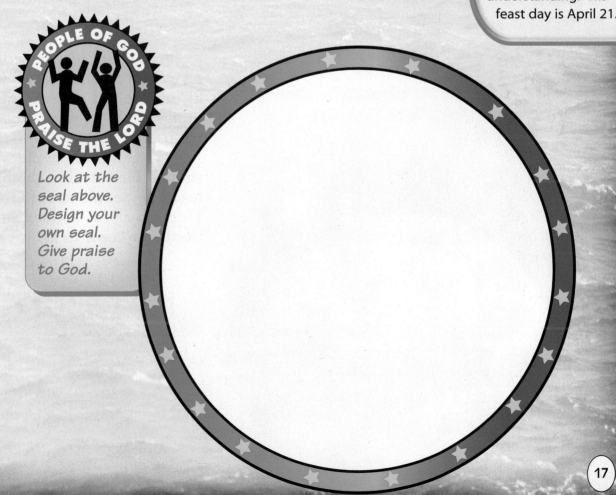

Faith Vocabulary

Word of God. Title given to Jesus, the Son of God; the Bible, which is the inspired word of God.

faith. A supernatural gift and power from God inviting us to know and believe in him and our free response to that invitation.

Jesus Is the Word of God

God revealed himself most fully in Jesus Christ. Jesus Christ is the Son of God who became one of us without giving up being God. He is true God and true man. All that Jesus said and did revealed God to us.

Jesus is the **Word of God.** In John's Gospel we read:

In the beginning was
the Word,
and the Word was
with God,
and the Word was God.
And the Word became
flesh
and made his dwelling

The Risen Lord, stained glass

among us. . . .
No one has ever seen God.
The only Son, God, who is
at the Father's side, has
revealed him. JOHN 1:1, 14, 18

Jesus spent his whole life on earth revealing God's love for us. He did and said many things while he was on earth. He healed people who were sick. He forgave people who sinned. He traveled about teaching people about God. Through all his actions and words, we come to know God.

Earth, Mars,
Venus, and Saturn

The Gift of Faith

God is always inviting us to come to know him and believe in him and love him. He also helps us listen to and say yes to that invitation. He gives us the gift of **faith**. Faith is a supernatural gift and power that helps us respond to God's invitation with all our heart, mind, soul, and strength.

God helps us accept the gift of faith. As people of faith, we are the Church, the community of believers in Jesus Christ. When we accept and live the gift of faith, God works through us to help others come to know, love, and serve him.

 What does it mean to say that Jesus is the Word of God?

Councils of the Church

The councils of the Church help us understand and live the faith of the Church. The pope sometimes calls a meeting of all the bishops to help the Church better understand and live what God has revealed. These meetings are called ecumenical, or worldwide, councils of the Church. The last ecumenical council of the Church was the Second Vatican Council. It began in 1962 and ended in 1965.

Jesus, the Word of God

Create a cinquain about Jesus Christ.
A cinquain is a five-line verse.

Title: <u>Jesus</u>

Write two words that describe the title.

_____ _____

Write three action words that describe the title.

_____ _____ _____

Write four words that describe a feeling about the title.

_____ _____

_____ _____

Write another word for Jesus.

_____

Pope John XXIII recording a radio and television address

Pope John XXIII died on June 3, 1963. Pope Paul VI continued the Council, which ended in 1965. On September 3, 2000, Pope John Paul II named Pope John XXIII Blessed John XXIII. The title *Blessed* is the final step before naming a person a saint of the Church. Blessed John XXIII continues to inspire people to place their faith, hope, and love in God.

Blessed John XXIII

The Catholic Church from her very beginning has had pastors who have guided the Church and others in the search for God. Blessed Pope John XXIII was one of those pastors.

QUESTION *Who helps you better understand God's Revelation? Who helps you live as a follower of Jesus Christ?*

Reproduction of 1,200-lire (60-cent) stamp commemorating the beatification of Pope John XXIII

Pope John XXIII called the bishops of the Church together for the Second Vatican Council in 1962. He called the Council to help the whole Church and the whole world better understand the meaning of God's Revelation. He wanted the Church to be a clear and powerful sign of God's love in the world.

CITTA' DEL VATICANO 1200

Pope John XXIII at prayer, Saint Peter's Basilica, Vatican City, Rome, Italy

What Difference Does Faith Make in My Life?

Every day the Holy Spirit is helping you come to know, love, and serve God better. Learning what the Catholic Church teaches will help you understand and live what God has revealed. It will help you grow as a child of God.

Place a check in the box next to the things you are doing to grow in your faith. Then write down other things you can do to come to know God better.

Learning More About God

☐ Reading the Bible

☐ Learning the teachings of the Catholic Church

☐ Praying to the Holy Spirit

☐ Thinking about God's gift of creation

Other things I can do are _____

_____.

Some people who can help me are _____

_____

_____

_____.

My Faith Choice

This week I will try to come to know God better. I will

_____

_____.

Lord, Help Us Believe

Leader: God gives us the gift of faith. Let us listen to God's word and accept that gift.

Reader: A reading from the Letter of James.
Be doers of the word and not hearers only, deluding yourselves. For if anyone is a hearer of the word and not a doer, he is like a man who looks at his own face in a mirror. He sees himself, then goes off and promptly forgets what he looked like. But the one who peers into the perfect law of freedom and perseveres, and is not a hearer who forgets but a doer who acts, such a one shall be blessed in what he does. JAMES 1:22–25
The word of the Lord.

All: **Thanks be to God.**

Leader: Let us ask God to help us come to know, love, and serve him better.

All: **"Speak, LORD, for your servant is listening."** 1 SAMUEL 3:9

Leader: Lord, help me come to know you better.

All: **"Speak, LORD, for your servant is listening."** 1 SAMUEL 3:9

Leader: Lord, help me listen and say yes to your gift of faith.

All: **"Speak, LORD, for your servant is listening."** 1 SAMUEL 3:9

Leader: Lord, help me love and serve you more and more.

All: **"Speak, LORD, for your servant is listening."** 1 SAMUEL 3:9
Amen.

We Remember

What I Have Learned

1. Use the faith terms in the word bank to describe Divine Revelation.

> creation   people
>
> Jesus Christ   faith   Church

_____

_____

_____

_____

Answer the following.

2. Explain what our desire for happiness tells us about ourselves.

_____

_____

3. Explain the role of Jesus in Divine Revelation.

_____

_____

_____

4. Describe faith as both a gift and an invitation.

_____

_____

_____

To Help You Remember

1. Divine Revelation is God making himself and his plan of creation and salvation known.

2. We can come to know God through creation and through people.

3. God most fully reveals himself in Jesus Christ, the Son of God who became one of us and lived among us.

Growing in Faith

One important thing I learned this week is

_____

_____

_____.

This is important because

_____

_____

_____.

What will people see me doing as I live my faith choice this week?

_____

_____

_____

This Week . . .

In chapter 1, "Speak, Lord," your child learned that there is a longing and a desire for God inside every person. God has revealed himself and gives us the gift of faith to know and believe in him and in all he has revealed and to respond to that desire. Creation points to the existence of a wise and loving and all-powerful God. Through the ages God has chosen special people through whom others can come to know, love, and serve him. Through his people God has revealed his love for all people. In Jesus Christ, the Son of God who became one of us and lived among us, God is revealed most fully.

For more on the teachings of the Catholic Church on the mysteries of Divine Revelation and the gift of faith, see *Catechism of the Catholic Church* paragraph numbers 50–67, 142–175, and 185–197.

Sharing God's Word

Invite all family members to share their favorite Bible story. Then talk about what each Bible story tells about God. Emphasize that the Holy Spirit helps us know and believe in God.

Praying

In this chapter your child prayed an act of faith. Read and pray together this prayer on page 22.

Making a Difference

Choose one of the following activities to do as a family or design a similar activity of your own.

- Invite each person to share the names of people who have helped them come to know God. Share how these people have helped. You might like to send notes thanking these people.

- Watch TV or look through magazines. Talk about what the commercials and advertisements tell us about happiness. Compare the happiness that commercials and advertisements describe to the happiness God brings us.

- Blessed Pope John XXIII is remembered for his great love and compassion for all people. Choose one thing you can do to show your love and compassion for others.

For more ideas on ways your family can live your faith, visit the "Faith First for Families" page at **www.FaithFirst.com**. You will find the "About Your Child" page helpful as your child begins a new year.

The Word of God

2

We Pray

For the LORD's word
  is true;
  all his works are
  trustworthy. PSALM 33:4

Lord God,
send the Holy Spirit
to open my heart
  and mind
to your holy word.
                    Amen.

What is your favorite kind of book?

There are many kinds of books. The Bible is the most widely read book in the world. It is God's word.

What is your favorite story in the Bible?

Sacred Scripture

Faith Focus

What does it mean to say the Bible is the word of God?

Faith Vocabulary

Sacred Scripture.
Two words that mean "holy writings"; the writing the Holy Spirit inspired the people of God to write and that have been collected by the Church in the Bible.

inspiration of the Bible. The Holy Spirit guiding the human writers of Sacred Scripture to faithfully and accurately communicate God's word.

The Holy Writings of God

Books tell stories of happiness and sadness, successes and failures. The Bible tells the story of God's love for his people and their response to his love. The Bible is God's own word to us. He speaks through the Bible.

Sacred Scripture is another name for the Bible. It is a name that means "holy writings."

And for this reason we too give thanks to God unceasingly, that, in receiving the word of God from hearing us, you received not a human word but, as it truly is, the word of God, which is now at work in you who believe.

1 THESSALONIANS 2:13

The Bible is really more than one book. It is a collection of many books. Some of the books in the Bible tell wonderful stories, such as the story of Moses. Others are history. There are also songs and poetry. But while there are different types of writings in the Bible, they all, in their own way, tell the story of God's love for us.

The Canon of Scripture

The Holy Spirit inspired, or helped, the human writers of the Bible to faithfully and accurately communicate God's word. We call this truth of our faith the **inspiration of the Bible.**

Guided by the Holy Spirit the Church has identified the forty-six books of the Old Testament and the twenty-seven books of the New Testament to be the inspired word of God. We call this the canon of Scripture.

The Old Testament tells the exciting story of the Covenant that God entered into with humankind. The story of the Covenant begins at creation. It continues with the stories of Noah, Abraham, Moses, and the prophets.

In the Old Testament, we read that God promised to send a savior. The New Testament tells the story about the fulfillment of that promise. Jesus is God's Promised One. Jesus is the new and everlasting Covenant.

 What Scripture stories do you remember? Why?

Sharing God's Love

Look up your favorite passage in the Bible. First decide whether the passage is in the Old Testament or New Testament. For example, if you look up Mark 8:1–9: Mark = the Book of the Bible, 8 = the chapter, and 1–9 = the verses. Read the passage and write what the story tells about God's love. Share the message with a friend or member of your family.

_____

_____

_____

_____

Torah scroll

The Old Testament

The Old Testament has four different kinds of books, or writings. They are the Torah, the historical books, the wisdom books, and the prophetic books.

The Torah

The Torah, also known as the Pentateuch, contains the Ten Commandments and other laws and teachings that guide God's people to live the Covenant. The five books of the Old Testament that make up the Torah are Genesis, Exodus, Leviticus, Numbers, and Deuteronomy.

The Historical Books

The sixteen historical books are Joshua, Judges, Ruth, 1 and 2 Samuel, 1 and 2 Kings, 1 and 2 Chronicles, Ezra, Nehemiah, Tobit, Judith, and 1 Maccabees and 2 Maccabees. In these books of the Old Testament, we hear stories about how the Israelites lived the Covenant both successfully and unsuccessfully.

The historical books also reveal that God always remained faithful to his people. He always forgave his people and gave them another chance to live the Covenant faithfully.

The Wisdom Books

The seven wisdom books of the Old Testament are Job, Psalms, Proverbs, Ecclesiastes, Song of Songs, Wisdom, and Sirach (Ecclessiasticus). These writings teach us practical ways to live God's Law. They include short sayings and longer stories.

Scribe repairing old Torah scrolls in Jerusalem

The Prophetic Books

God chose certain members of his people to speak in his name. These people are called **prophets**. There are eighteen prophetic books in the Old Testament. These books contain the teachings of the prophets. The prophetic books in the Old Testament are Isaiah, Jeremiah, Lamentations, Baruch, Ezekiel, Daniel, Hosea, Joel, Amos, Obadiah, Jonah, Micah, Naham, Habakkuk, Zephaniah, Haggai, Zechariah, and Malachi.

When God's people, the Israelites, turned away from the Covenant, God called them back through the prophets. When hardship and exile discouraged his people, God sent prophets to help them live with faith and hope. Through the prophets, God gave his people hope that his promises to them would come true. Again and again, God spoke through his prophets and promised to send his people a savior.

 QUESTION *What is God telling us through the Old Testament writings?*

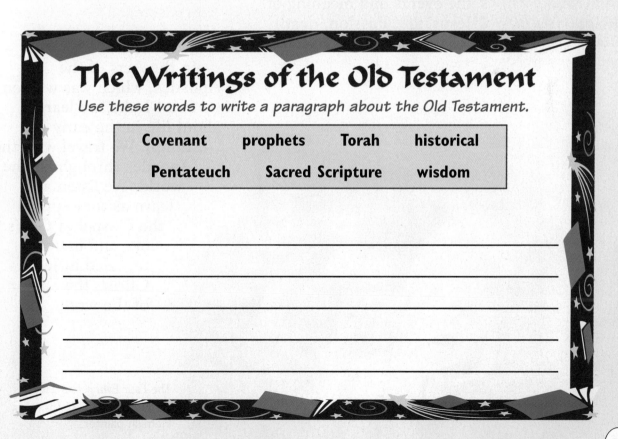

The Writings of the Old Testament

Use these words to write a paragraph about the Old Testament.

Covenant	prophets	Torah	historical
Pentateuch	Sacred Scripture		wisdom

_____

_____

_____

_____

_____

Faith Vocabulary

Gospels. The first four books of the New Testament that pass on the faith of the Apostles and the early Church about the life, death, Resurrection, Ascension, and teachings of Jesus Christ.

Gospel. The good news of God's love revealed in the life, death, Resurrection, and Ascension of Jesus Christ.

The New Testament

Jesus Christ is the new and everlasting Covenant. The New Testament reveals who Jesus is and the meaning of his work on earth. It includes the four **Gospels**, the Acts of the Apostles, the letters of Saint Paul the Apostle and other early Church writers, and the Book of Revelation.

The Four Gospels

The heart of the New Testament is the four **Gospels**. The word *gospel* means "good news." Each of the four accounts of the **Gospel** shares the events and meaning of Jesus' life, Passion, death, Resurrection, and Ascension.

Each of the four Gospels in its own way teaches that:

- Jesus fulfills all the promises of the Old Testament.
- Jesus calls people to discipleship.
- Jesus is the Savior of all people.
- Jesus enables us to live with God forever.

Saint John sums up why his and the other Gospels were written. We read:

But these are written that you may [come to] believe that Jesus is the Messiah, the Son of God, and that through this belief you may have life in his name. JOHN 20:31

Acts of the Apostles

In the Acts of the Apostles, which was written by Saint Luke, we learn about life in the early Church. We travel with the Apostles throughout the world. We listen and learn as they spread the Gospel of God's love and mercy revealed in Jesus Christ, the Savior of the world.

The Four Evangelists. Jacob Jordaens (1583–1678), Flemish painter.

The Epistles and Other Letters

The New Testament also contains the epistles, or letters, of Saint Paul the Apostle and other early Church writers. These twenty-one letters teach about Jesus and how Christians are to live. By reading and listening to these letters, we go back to the beginning of the Church. We learn who we are and how to live as disciples of Jesus.

Book of Revelation

The Book of Revelation is the last book of the Bible. It was written to encourage Christians who were suffering to remain faithful to Jesus Christ.

Jesus is the fullness of Divine Revelation. In Jesus, who is true God and true man, God most fully makes himself known. Jesus most fully reveals, more than anyone else did or will ever do, God and his love for us.

 What do the writings in the New Testament reveal?

Jesus Christ, Savior and Redeemer

Design an emblem with words and symbols for Jesus Christ.

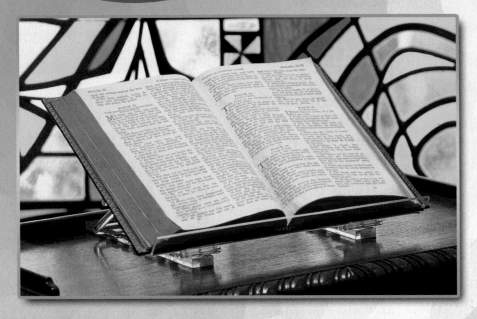

The Bible is the most widely read book in the world. Many Christian families have a family Bible. In it they write the key events of their family's faith story. They record Baptisms, marriages, and other important milestones in the faith history of their family.

Reverence for the Bible

The whole Christian life is strengthened by hearing and listening attentively and reverently to the word of God. Saint Jerome reminded us of the importance of the Bible in the life of Christians. He wrote, "Ignorance of the Scriptures is ignorance of Christ."

Before the printing press was invented in the sixteenth century, scribes copied the Bible by hand. Artists painted pages of the Bible with colors and decorated the edges of the pages with gold.

At every celebration of the Eucharist, we read the word of God aloud, or proclaim it. We carry the Book of the Gospels with dignity in procession and proclaim the word of God from a place of honor. That place is called the ambo. This shows the faith of the Church in God's presence in his word.

When we gather with other members of the Church or as a family to read and listen to the Bible, Jesus is there. We listen and ask, What is God saying to us right now? How can the living word of God come alive in our hearts today?

 When does your family and parish listen to the word of God?

Priest holding the Book of the Gospels

What Difference Does Faith Make in My Life?

As you listen to the Bible, the Holy Spirit helps you understand what God is saying to you. He gives you the knowledge and courage to put God's word into practice.

Take the time to become more familiar with the Old Testament and the New Testament. Select a passage, read it, and think about what God's word means for your life. Write your thoughts on these book pages.

God's Word Is Life-Giving

My Faith Choice

This week I will show that I believe it is important to listen to and live God's word. I will

_____

_____ .

Your Word, Lord, Is a Light for My Path

Praying with the Bible is an important form of prayer. It is a form of meditation. In a prayer of meditation, we spend quiet time with God, reading and listening to his word and trying to understand how to live it.

1. Sit quietly. Close your eyes. Breathe slowly.

2. In your mind, picture yourself someplace where you can talk and listen to God.

3. Open your Bible and read a favorite passage.

4. Take time to talk and listen to God. Say, "Your word, LORD, is a light for my path" (based on Psalm 119:105).

5. After a few quiet moments, ask the Holy Spirit, What is your word saying to me? Write down any key words or phrases that you remember.

6. Make a faith decision to put God's word into action.

7. Pray the following prayer together.

Leader: For revealing yourself to us in the Sacred Scriptures,

All: we thank you, LORD.

Leader: For showing us your love and calling us to be your people,

All: we thank you, LORD.

Leader: For sending us your Son, Jesus,

All: we thank you, LORD.

Leader: For sending us the Holy Spirit to help guide us,

All: we thank you, LORD.

What I Have Learned

Match each faith term in column A with the phrase in column B that best describes it.

Column A

_____ 1. Covenant

_____ 2. Sacred Scripture

_____ 3. Pentateuch

_____ 4. Gospels

_____ 5. wisdom books

Column B

a. books in the Old Testament that give advice on how to live

b. God's solemn agreement with his people

c. the writings of God's people inspired by the Holy Spirit

d. first four books of the New Testament

e. first five books of the Old Testament

Answer the following.

6. Explain the statement "The Holy Spirit inspired the writing of the Bible."

_____

_____

7. Describe the canon of Scripture.

_____

_____

8. Compare the Old Testament with the New Testament.

_____

_____

To Help You Remember

1. The Bible is the inspired written word of God.

2. The Old Testament tells the story of God's Covenant with his people.

3. The New Testament reveals that Jesus Christ, the Son of God, is the new and everlasting Covenant.

Growing in Faith

One important thing I learned this week is

_____

_____

_____.

This is important because

_____

_____

_____.

What will people see me doing as I live my faith choice this week?

_____

_____

_____

This Week . . .

In chapter 2, "The Word of God," your child deepened his or her understanding of the Bible, or Sacred Scripture. The Bible contains the holy writings that the Holy Spirit inspired God's people to write. This list of writings named by the Church is called the canon of Scripture. The Old Testament tells the first part of the story of the Covenant that God made with people and his promise to send a messiah and savior. The New Testament tells about the fulfillment of that promise in Jesus. Jesus is the new and everlasting Covenant that God made with all people.

For more on the teachings of the Catholic Church on Sacred Scripture, see *Catechism of the Catholic Church* paragraph numbers 50–133.

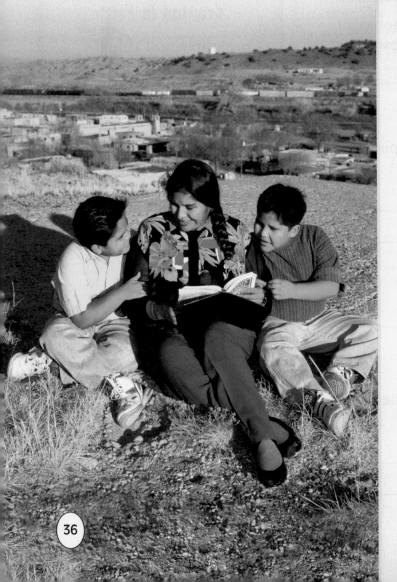

Sharing God's Word

Read together 1 Thessalonians 2:13. Emphasize that the Bible is God's word to us.

Praying

In this chapter your child prayed a prayer of meditation called lectio divina. Read and pray together this prayer on page 34.

Making a Difference

Choose one of the following activities to do as a family or design a similar activity of your own.

- Talk with each other about how the Bible can help guide you. Share practical ideas about how the Bible is a light for your family, guiding you to live as a follower of Jesus.

- Choose a Bible story that you are familiar with. Find it in the Bible and read it together. Talk about what it tells you about God.

- Invite each family member to name a favorite person in the Bible. Share with each other the stories about these people of faith.

For more ideas on ways your family can live your faith, visit the "Faith First for Families" page at **www.FaithFirst.com**. Click on "Bible Stories" and discuss the Bible story with your child this week.

ff

The Mystery of the Holy Trinity

We Pray

"Come," says my heart,
    "seek God's face";
your face, LORD,
    do I seek! PSALM 27:8

**Glory to the Father,
and to the Son,
and to the Holy Spirit.
        Amen.**

*What is something in life
that is a mystery to you?*

Life has many mysteries.
A mystery of faith is
something we could not
know unless God revealed
it to us.

*What do you already know
about the mystery of who
God is?*

Celtic cross. The unbroken
circle reminds us that God
created us to be happy
with him forever.

One God in Three Divine Persons

Faith Focus

Who is the Holy Trinity?

Faith Vocabulary

Holy Trinity. The central belief of the Christian faith; the mystery of one God in three divine Persons—God the Father, God the Son, and God the Holy Spirit.

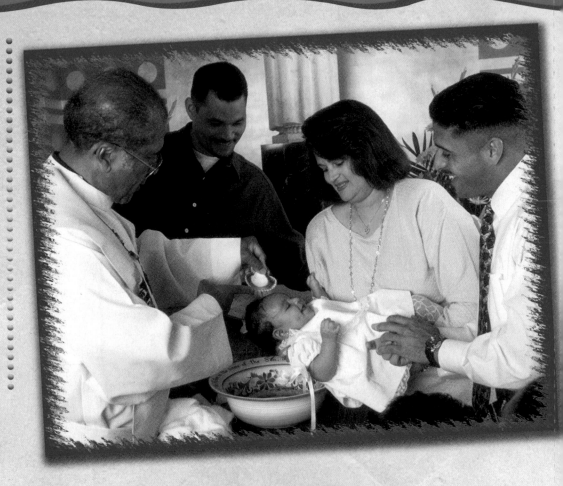

The Holy Trinity

The mystery of the **Holy Trinity** is the deepest and central belief of the Christian faith. The Holy Trinity is the mystery of one God in three divine Persons—God the Father, God the Son, and God the Holy Spirit. This is a truth about God we never could have known unless he revealed it.

Throughout his life on earth Jesus, the Son of God, taught about God the Father and God the Holy Spirit. Just before he ascended to his Father, the Risen Jesus met the eleven disciples on a mountain in Galilee. He said to them:

"Go, therefore, and make disciples of all nations, baptizing them in the name of the Father, and of the Son, and of the holy Spirit."

MATTHEW 28:19–20

Every time the Church baptizes a person, we name the mystery of who God is. We baptize the person in the name of the one God who is the Holy Trinity.

The Old Testament

In the Old Testament we read the beginning of the story of God's revelation of himself. This story is filled with people of faith.

God first revealed himself at creation to Adam and Eve. Then God made an everlasting Covenant with Noah and with all living things.

Years later God revealed himself to Abraham and Sarah. They lived in a land and at a time when people believed in many gods. God revealed to Abraham and Sarah that he alone is God. He invited Abraham and Sarah to put their faith and trust in him alone. God asked Abraham to leave his homeland. He said:

"Go forth from the land of your kinsfolk and from your father's house to a land that I will show you."

GENESIS 12:1

Abraham came to believe in God and trust in his plan for him. The descendants of Abraham were called Israelites. They kept faith in the one true God and shared that faith with others.

 QUESTION What is the mystery of the Holy Trinity?

I Believe in the Holy Trinity

Check (✔) the ways you express faith in the Holy Trinity.

☐ **Bless myself**

☐ **Pray the creeds of the Church**

☐ **Pray the Glory Prayer**

☐ _____

_____

_____

(another way)

What do the Gospels
tell us about who
God is?

Faith Vocabulary

Annunciation. The announcement to the Virgin Mary by the angel Gabriel that God had chosen her to be the Mother of Jesus, the Son of God, through the power of the Holy Spirit.

Mary, the Mother of Jesus

Many centuries after he revealed himself to Abraham, God invited the Virgin Mary to place her faith and trust in him. In the Gospel of Luke we read:

[T]he angel Gabriel was sent from God to a town of Galilee called Nazareth, to a virgin betrothed to a man named Joseph, of the house of David, and the virgin's name was Mary. . . . Then the angel said to her, "Do not be afraid, Mary, for you have found favor with God. Behold, you will conceive in your womb and bear a son, and you shall name him Jesus. He will be great and will be called Son of the Most High. . . . The holy Spirit will come upon you, and the power of the Most High will overshadow you. Therefore the child to be born will be called holy, the Son of God."

LUKE 1:26–27, 30–32, 35

This event is known as the **Annunciation**. It gives us a glimpse into the mystery of the Trinity.

The Annunciation, stained glass

God chose the Blessed Virgin Mary to be the Mother of Jesus, the Son of God and the Savior whom he promised to send. So special is the Virgin Mary's role in God's plan that she was free from all sin from the very first moment of her conception, or existence, and throughout her whole life. We call this Mary's Immaculate Conception.

Jesus Christ

Throughout his life on earth, Jesus, the Son of God, spoke clearly of the Father and the Holy Spirit. On one occasion Saint Philip the Apostle said to Jesus:

"Master, show us the Father, and that will be enough for us." JOHN 14:8

Listen carefully to Jesus' answer.

"Have I been with you for so long a time and you still do not know me, Philip? Whoever has seen me has seen the Father."
JOHN 14:9

Later in his conversation with Saint Philip and the other disciples, Jesus went on to say:

"I have told you this while I am with you. The Advocate, the holy Spirit that the Father will send in my name—he will teach you everything and remind you of all that [I] told you." JOHN 14:25–26

Jesus was speaking of one God, who is Father, Son, and Holy Spirit. Many years after the return of Jesus to his Father in heaven, the Church named this central mystery of faith the Holy Trinity.

 Why do we say that Abraham and Mary are models of faith for us?

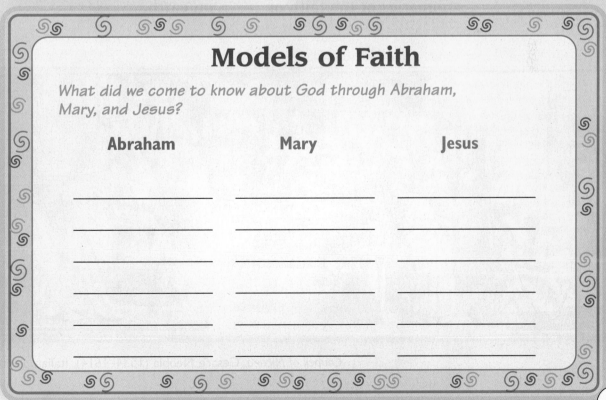

Models of Faith

What did we come to know about God through Abraham, Mary, and Jesus?

Abraham	Mary	Jesus
_____	_____	_____
_____	_____	_____
_____	_____	_____
_____	_____	_____
_____	_____	_____
_____	_____	_____

In what ways do we profess the Church's faith in the Holy Trinity?

Nicene Creed. A creed, or brief statement of the faith of the Church, written in the fourth century.

creeds. Statements of belief; professions of faith.

The Creeds of the Church

The Holy Spirit, as Jesus promised, has always helped the Church believe in and explain her faith in the mystery of one God, who is Father, Son, and Holy Spirit. Under the guidance of the Holy Spirit two early councils of the Church taught about the mystery of the Holy Trinity. These were the Council of Nicaea in A.D. 325 and the Council of Constantinople in A.D. 381.

The **Nicene Creed,** which we profess at Mass, comes from these two councils of the Church. The **creeds** of the Church are official statements and summaries of the faith of the Church. The two main creeds of the Church are the Apostles' Creed and the Nicene Creed. We profess faith in the Holy Trinity when we pray the Apostles' Creed or the Nicene Creed.

Praying the creeds of the Church connects us with all the other faithful Christians, past and present. With the Church we continue to hear God's invitation to believe in him who is one God—Father, Son, and Holy Spirit.

We can never fully understand the mystery of the Holy Trinity. But the Holy Spirit helps us grow in understanding this mystery of faith little by little throughout our life on earth.

Council of Nicaea. Cesare Nebbia (1534–1614), Italian painter.

When our life on earth is completed, we will live forever with God and all the saints in heaven. We will be drawn into the very life of God, who is Father, Son, and Holy Spirit. We will see God in a way we have never seen or known before. We call this the Beatific Vision. This is our great hope as Christians.

 What is the Nicene Creed?

Holy Water

The Church professes her faith in the Holy Trinity in many ways. Blessing ourselves with holy water as we say, "In the name of the Father, and of the Son, and of the Holy Spirit" is a sacramental of the Church. Each time we bless ourselves, we remember our Baptism and profess our faith in the Holy Trinity.

WE BELIEVE IN ONE GOD

Use each letter in the word TRINITY. Write a word or phrase that tells something about the Trinity or about how you profess your faith in the Trinity. Use the words or phrases to tell a friend or family member what the Catholic Church teaches about the Trinity.

T _____

R _____

I _____

N _____

I _____

T _____

Y _____

Legend of Saint Augustine

Many Christians have tried to understand the mystery of the Holy Trinity. You may remember reading about Saint Augustine in chapter 1. There is a famous legend about him and his efforts to learn more about God.

One day Augustine was walking on the beach. The vast ocean inspired him to think about God. As he was walking along, he met a young boy who was taking water from the sea with a small bucket. Augustine watched as the boy kept pouring the water, one bucket at a time, into a hole he had dug in the sand.

Augustine became very curious and asked, "Why do you keep pouring water into the hole?" The boy answered, "Isn't it plain to see? I'm putting this ocean in the hole."

Augustine began to laugh. "That's impossible," he told the boy. "The great sea is way too large for that small hole." With loving eyes, the boy looked up and said, "And God is too big for your little mind." Suddenly, the boy disappeared.

Little by little with the guidance of the Holy Spirit, we can come to know the mystery of God the Holy Trinity in whose image we have been created.

? What lesson did Saint Augustine learn? How can that lesson help you come to grow in your faith in God?

What Difference Does Faith Make in My Life?

There is one God in three Persons—God the Father, Son, and Holy Spirit. Little by little, the Holy Spirit helps you understand this wonderful mystery about God.

Many people have helped you grow in your knowledge and love of the Holy Trinity. In the space below write one way you show your love for God the Father, God the Son, and God the Holy Spirit.

I Show My Love

for God the Father by _____

_____ .

for Jesus, the Son of God, by _____

_____ .

for the Holy Spirit by _____

_____ .

My Faith Choice

This week I will profess my faith in the Holy Trinity. I will

_____

_____ .

45

Renewal of Faith

Leader: At Baptism we first profess the faith of the Church in the Trinity. Each year at Easter the baptized renew the faith they professed at Baptism. Let us join together and renew our baptismal profession of faith.

Do you believe in God, the Father almighty, creator of heaven and earth?

All: I do.

Leader: Do you believe in Jesus Christ,
his only Son, our Lord,
who was born of the Virgin Mary,
was crucified, died, and was buried,
rose from the dead,
and is now seated at the right
hand of the Father?

All: I do.

Leader: Do you believe in the Holy Spirit,
the holy catholic Church,
the communion of saints,
the forgiveness of sins,
the resurrection of the body,
and the life everlasting?

All: I do.

Leader: This is our faith. This is the faith of the Church. We are proud to profess it, in Christ Jesus our Lord.

All: Amen.

RITE OF BAPTISM

What I Have Learned

Circle whether each statement is true or false. Make false statements true.

1. The Holy Spirit is the mystery of one God in three divine Persons.

   True   **False**

2. The Gospel account of the Annunciation tells us about God the Father, God the Son, and God the Holy Spirit.

   True   **False**

3. Jesus never spoke to his disciples about the Holy Spirit.

   True   **False**

Answer the following.

4. Who does God reveal himself to be in the Old Testament?

   _____

   _____

5. Who does God reveal himself to be in the New Testament?

   _____

   _____

6. What does it mean to say that God is a mystery?

   _____

   _____

To Help You Remember

1. The Holy Trinity is the central belief of the faith of the Church.

2. The mystery of the Trinity was most fully revealed in Jesus Christ.

3. We profess our faith in the Holy Trinity when we pray the Nicene Creed at Mass.

Growing in Faith

One important thing I learned this week is

_____

_____

_____.

This is important because

_____

_____

_____.

What will people see me doing as I live my faith choice this week?

_____

_____

_____

This Week . . .

In chapter 3, "The Mystery of the Holy Trinity," your child learned more about the Holy Trinity. The Holy Trinity is the mystery of one God in three divine Persons—God the Father, God the Son, and God the Holy Spirit. The mystery of God the Holy Trinity is the central mystery of the Christian faith. It is a truth about God that we never could have known unless he revealed it. God revealed this mystery over a long period of time. We profess faith in the Holy Trinity at Baptism. Each time we pray the Nicene Creed at Mass, we renew and profess our faith in this great mystery.

For more on the teachings of the Catholic Church on the mystery of the Holy Trinity, see *Catechism of the Catholic Church* paragraph numbers 232–260.

Sharing God's Word

Read together Matthew 28:16–20, the Gospel account of Jesus commissioning his disciples. Emphasize that we profess our faith in the Holy Trinity and remember our Baptism when we pray the creeds of the Church.

Praying

In this chapter your child prayed a prayer renewing their baptismal profession of faith. Read and pray together this prayer on page 46.

Making a Difference

Choose one of the following activities to do as a family or design a similar activity of your own.

- When we pray the Nicene Creed, we profess our faith in the Holy Trinity. Make Nicene Creed puzzles to help you memorize this important creed of the Church. Write the Nicene Creed on a piece of paper. Cut the paper into small pieces. When you assemble the pieces, you will become more familiar with this creed.

- This week when your family takes part in Mass, be sure to bless yourself with holy water as you enter and leave the church. Pray the Sign of the Cross and remember that you were baptized with water "in the name of the Father, and of the Son, and of the Holy Spirit."

- Talk about how your family is an image of the Holy Trinity. Name ways that your actions and words are signs of your love for God and for one another.

For more ideas on ways your family can live your faith, visit the "Faith First for Families" page at **www.FaithFirst.com**. This week pay special attention to "Questions Kids Ask."

The Calming of the Sea
A Scripture Story

We Pray

Trust in the LORD and
do good
that you may dwell in
the land and live
secure.   PSALM 37:3

Father, send the Holy
Spirit to guide us and
strengthen our faith.
            Amen.

*What sign of God's love for
you have you seen today?*

Signs of God's love for us
are all around us. Jesus
was the greatest sign of
God's love and presence
among us. Jesus performed
many miracles to invite
people to believe in God.

*What are some of the Gospel
accounts you know that tell
about Jesus performing
miracles?*

*The Calming of the Storm
at Sea,* stained glass

49

Faith Focus

Why is Galilee an important location in the Gospels?

Faith Vocabulary

public ministry of Jesus. The work that God the Father sent Jesus, the Son of God, to do on earth with the help of the Holy Spirit.

disciples. People who learn from and follow the teachings of another person.

The Sea of Galilee, noted for its severe and sudden storms

Jesus' Public Ministry

All of Jesus' work on earth revealed God's love. All of Jesus' words and actions invited people to believe and trust in God.

The **public ministry of Jesus** was the work the Father sent him to do with the help of the Holy Spirit. Most of that ministry took place in Galilee. Galilee was a section, or province, of the land of Palestine in Jesus' time. It was there that Jesus began his preaching and first called people to be his **disciples**. A disciple is a person who learns from and follows the teachings of another person.

The Sea of Galilee is one of the most beautiful sights in Galilee. It is a large lake that is seven and one-half miles wide. Without warning, storms often rise up and rage over it. Cold air masses from the north sweep south and stir up the waters just as they are doing in the photo at the top of this page. Strong, biting winds and dark, towering waves often catch fishermen off guard.

Jesus' Work in Galilee

Jesus visited the Sea of Galilee and villages near it many times, and many Gospel stories take place near or on the sea.

Many of the first disciples of Jesus fished in the Sea of Galilee. The brothers Peter and Andrew often pulled nets full of fish from the lake. James and John and their father, Zebedee, also made their living by fishing.

Jesus used the experiences of his disciples to teach them. He spoke to his disciples of water and fish. He described the harvest of wheat the Galilean farmers brought into their barns. Turning toward the fields, he pointed out the lilies blooming in great splendor for all to see. He spoke of sheep and the courage of good shepherds.

Jesus used these examples from the daily lives of his followers to help them grow in faith and trust in God. This helped the disciples and others who listened to Jesus come to understand the meaning of his teaching.

QUESTION *Look at the map on this page. What do you know about the two towns in Galilee?*

GALILEE

SEA OF GALILEE

• Cana

• Nazareth

Jordan River

SAMARIA

Emmaus •
Jerusalem • • Bethany

Bethlehem •

DEAD SEA

JUDEA

Becoming Part of a Gospel Setting

Try to picture what Galilee was like in Jesus' time. This will help you understand the Gospels.

1. Using your imagination, place yourself at a lake or ocean.

2. Picture in your mind the details of the setting:
   Are the waters calm or rough?
   What are the different colors of the water?
   How does the water feel as you walk near the edge?
   What feelings are you experiencing?

3. Write a paragraph describing your setting.

_____

_____

_____

_____

Faith Focus

How does the story of Jesus calming the sea help us understand more about him?

Jesus Calms the Storm

Here is one story you may remember about Jesus and the Sea of Galilee. It takes place during the evening.

Jesus had spent the whole day teaching. In the early evening he told his disciples that he would like to cross the Sea of Galilee. Read to discover what happened:

Leaving the crowd, [the disciples] took [Jesus] with them in the boat just as he was. And other boats were with him. A violent squall came up and waves were breaking over the boat, so that it was already filling up. Jesus was in the stern, asleep on a cushion. They woke him and said to him, "Teacher, do you not care that we are perishing?" He woke up, rebuked the wind, and

said to the sea, "Quiet! Be still!" The wind ceased and there was great calm. Then he asked them, "Why are you terrified? Do you not yet have faith?" They were filled with great awe and said to one another, "Who then is this whom even wind and sea obey?" MARK 4:36–41

More and more, Jesus' disciples came to believe and trust in him. The more they watched and listened to him, the stronger their faith and trust in God became.

 When you feel afraid in a serious situation, how do you act?

News Flash!

Imagine that you interviewed the disciples after the boat landed. Write an account of what happened. Include what the disciples learned about Jesus.

_____

_____

_____

_____

_____

_____

_____

_____

Faith Focus

Why did Jesus calm the sea?

Faith Vocabulary

miracle. An occurrence that goes beyond the laws of nature and invites us to deepen our faith in God.

Stormy things sometimes happen in our lives. For example, a parent or friend becomes seriously ill. A parent loses a job. A parent gets a new job and we have to move away from our friends. Some of these things are out of our control and we feel powerless.

Faith and Trust

When the dark storm raged, the disciples felt powerless and turned to Jesus who was sleeping. When Jesus awoke, he asked his disciples, "Why are you terrified? Do you not yet have faith?" He then calmed the stormy sea and raging waves and quieted the wind.

The disciples were filled with great awe and said to one another, "Who then is this whom even wind and sea obey?" (Mark 4:41). The **miracles** of Jesus are also signs that he is the Son of God. They invite people to faith in Jesus.

The storm in this story symbolizes all the frightening storms in our lives. This Gospel story tells us we are not alone during those moments and in those situations. We are to trust in God above all else. God, who loves us and cares for us, is always with us. As the disciples did, we are to call on Jesus for help. We need only ask and trust.

Wonders and Signs

On that dark, stormy night, surrounded by violent and powerful waves, the disciples reached out to Jesus, addressing him as Teacher, saying, "Teacher, do you not care that we are perishing?" (Mark 4:38). This was really a plea for help. Jesus responded by calming the stormy sea and the raging waves crashing over the sides of the boat. "Quiet! Be still!" (Mark 4:39).

The Bible calls such actions "mighty deeds, wonders, and signs" (Acts of the Apostles 2:22). We also call what happened on the Sea of Galilee a **miracle**. A miracle is an action that goes beyond the laws of nature and invites us to deepen our faith in God. We cannot fully explain a miracle, for it goes beyond what any of us can do.

Miracles are important in the Bible because they remind us of God's mighty power and loving presence in our lives. When Jesus performed miracles, he was inviting his disciples, the people of his time, and the people of all times to believe and trust in God's everlasting, caring love for all people.

 What does the Gospel story teach us about being a disciple of Jesus?

Placing Our Faith and Trust in Jesus

Reading the Scriptures and reflecting on the word of God help us know and respond to God's invitation to place our faith and trust in him above all else.

1. Think about a time when you experienced something that could be compared to "a frightening storm" in your life.

2. Now think about Jesus calming the storm in the Scripture story you just read.

3. Compare the meaning of this Gospel story to your own "frightening storm" experience.

4. What did you learn from this reflection?

_____

_____

Catholic Relief Services distributing food at a mother/baby clinic in a village near Bembereke, Benin, West Africa

Catholic Relief Services

The Church is a sign of the loving presence of God in the world. In 1943 the bishops of the United States founded Catholic Relief Services to give witness to that presence.

The people of Catholic Relief Services preach the Gospel by their actions. With the help and guidance of the Holy Spirit, they live the Gospel among people who are suffering, and they announce the Gospel of God's love and justice proclaimed by Jesus.

When people are suffering from poverty, Catholic Relief Services is there assisting them and helping them find ways to better their lives. When people are suffering from natural disasters, such as earthquakes and floods, Catholic Relief Services is there. When people are suffering from man-made disasters, such as war, Catholic Relief Services is there helping people rebuild their communities.

Today the people of Catholic Relief Services are present in more than eighty countries. Like Jesus, they invite people by their words and actions to deepen their faith and trust in God.

QUESTION
What other ways do you see the Church living as a sign of God's caring love and presence in the world?

Young boy waiting to receive food in the Catholic Relief Services camp in Bujumbura, Burundi, Central Africa

What Difference Does Faith Make in My Life?

The Holy Spirit helps the Church live as a sign of God's love. Through your kindness to people, God invites others to believe and trust in him.

Symbol of Trust and Faith in Jesus Christ

Design a symbol that reminds you of Jesus and his great love for you. Use your symbol to remember to place your trust in Jesus.

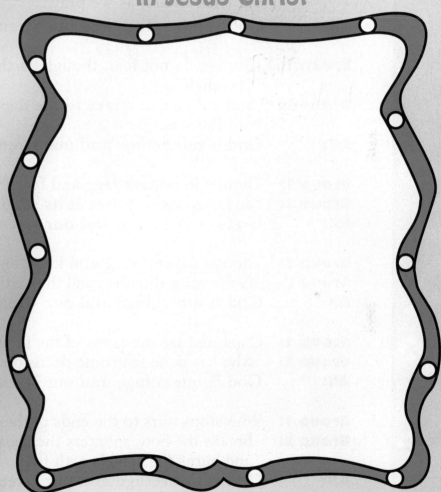

My Faith Choice

This week I will remember how much Jesus loves me and I will place my trust in him. I will do this by

_____

_____.

Lord, In You We Trust

Leader: The Book of Psalms is found in the Old Testament. When we pray the Psalms, the Holy Spirit inspires and teaches us to pray. Let us profess our faith in God and place our trust in him as we pray.

All: **God is our refuge and our strength.**

Group 1: Thus we do not fear, though earth
    be shaken

Group 2: and mountains quake to the depths
    of the sea.

All: **God is our refuge and our strength.**

Group 1: Though its waters rage and foam

Group 2: and mountains totter at its surging.

All: **God is our refuge and our strength.**

Group 1: Though nations rage and kingdoms totter,

Group 2: God's voice thunders and the earth trembles.

All: **God is our refuge and our strength.**

Group 1: Come and see the works of the LORD,

Group 2: who has done fearsome deeds on earth;

All: **God is our refuge and our strength.**

Group 1: Who stops wars to the ends of the earth,

Group 2: breaks the bow, splinters the spear,
    and burns the shields with fire;

All: **God is our refuge and our strength.**

PSALM 46:2–4, 7, 9–10

What I Have Learned

1. Circle the words hidden in the puzzle. Use each word in a sentence and share its meaning with a partner.

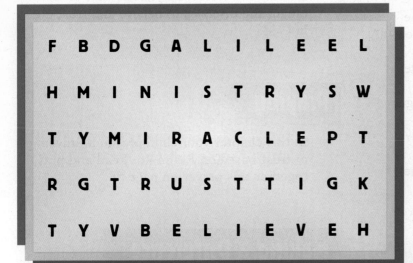

```
F B D G A L I L E E L
H M I N I S T R Y S W
T Y M I R A C L E P T
R G T R U S T T I G K
T Y V B E L I E V E H
```

Answer the following.

2. Describe the work God the Father sent Jesus to do.

_____

_____

_____

3. Explain the meaning of miracles in the ministry of Jesus.

_____

_____

_____

4. Summarize the message of the Gospel account of Jesus calming the sea.

_____

_____

_____

To Help You Remember

1. Most of the public ministry of Jesus took place in Galilee.

2. Jesus' calming the storm on the Sea of Galilee was one of the miracle stories in the Gospel that reveal that Jesus is the Son of God.

3. Jesus performed miracles to invite people to believe and trust in God.

Growing in Faith

One important thing I learned this week is

_____

_____

_____.

This is important because

_____

_____

_____.

What will people see me doing as I live my faith choice this week?

_____

_____

_____

This Week . . .

In chapter 4, "The Calming of the Sea: A Scripture Story," your child listened to and reflected on the miracle of Jesus calming the Sea of Galilee. Much of the ministry of Jesus that is recorded in the Gospels takes place in Galilee. This Gospel story is one of the many miracle stories that are part of Jesus' public ministry. The miracles of Jesus were signs and wonders pointing to the saving presence of God in the world. They were invitations to deepen one's faith and trust in God and to believe in Jesus, the Son of God, sent by the Father.

For more on the teachings of the Catholic Church on the public ministry of Jesus, see *Catechism of the Catholic Church* paragraph numbers 534–560.

Sharing God's Word

Read together Mark 4:35–41 about Jesus calming the storm. Emphasize that Jesus taught the disciples to believe and trust in God.

Praying

In this chapter your child prayed a prayer of trust based on Psalm 46. Read and pray together this prayer on page 58.

Making a Difference

Choose one of the following activities to do as a family or design a similar activity of your own.

- Imagine that you were one of the disciples in the boat with Jesus on the Sea of Galilee. Share what you would tell people when you reached the shore.

- Make an ichthus (see page 55). Display the symbol where it can serve as a reminder of your faith in Jesus Christ, the Son of God and Savior of the world.

- Identify ways that the members of your family show their trust in Jesus' love for you. Decide some ways that, as a family, you can invite others to believe and trust in Jesus.

For more ideas on ways your family can live your faith, visit the "Faith First for Families" page at **www.FaithFirst.com**. Take time to read an article from "Just for Parents" this week.

Great Is the Lord, Our God

5

We Pray

Sing to the LORD a
    new song;
  sing to the LORD,
    all the earth. PSALM 96:1

Blessed are you,
Lord, God of
all creation.   Amen.

*What is an image you
would use to describe
yourself?*

We use images to describe
the qualities of people.
For example, we might
say, "She's as fast as
lightning." Look at the
world. Creation helps us
come to know God.

*What image from God's
creation tells something
about his goodness?*

God the Father, the Creator

Faith Focus

What qualities named in the Bible help us understand who God is?

Faith Vocabulary

attributes of God. Qualities of God that help us understand the mystery of God.

YHWH. The four letters of the Hebrew alphabet for the name for God that God revealed to Moses.

The Hebrew word for *Adonai*, or Lord. Lord is a title of honor the Bible uses for God.

Attributes of God

God is infinite. He is a God of wonder and awe. He is a mystery whom we will never be able to come to fully know. No matter how much we come to know about God, there will always be more to know. To help us understand who God has revealed himself to be, the inspired writers of the Bible have used certain qualities to describe him. These qualities are called **attributes of God.**

Here are a few of the attributes God has revealed about himself. Learning about these attributes helps us come to know who God has revealed himself to be.

One

God is one. There is only one God. There is no one and nothing like him.

Hear, O Israel! The LORD is our God, the LORD alone! DEUTERONOMY 6:4

Lord

God revealed the divine name **YHWH** to describe himself. The writers of the Bible used the name *Adonai*, or Lord, in place of the divine and sacred name *YHWH*.

"But," said Moses to God, "when I go to the Israelites and say to them, 'The God of your fathers has sent me to you,' if they ask me, 'What is his name?' what am I to tell them?" God replied, "I am who I am." Then he added, "This is what you shall tell the Israelites: I AM sent me to you." EXODUS 3:13–14

Almighty

God is almighty. This means that he alone can do anything.

May God Almighty bless you . . . that you may become an assembly of peoples. GENESIS 28:3

Eternal

God is eternal. He always has been and always will be. He had no beginning and will have no end.

> The LORD is the eternal God. ISAIAH 40:28

Truth and Love

God is always abounding in love and faithfulness. His word is always true.

> For the LORD's word is true;
> all his works are trustworthy. PSALM 33:4

God is love. His very being is Truth and Love. God is love.

> 1 JOHN 4:16

Holy

God is holy. The word *holy* means "set apart." No one and no thing that he created is equal to him.

> "Holy, holy, holy is the LORD of hosts!"
> ISAIAH 6:3

 What is your favorite attribute of God? Why?

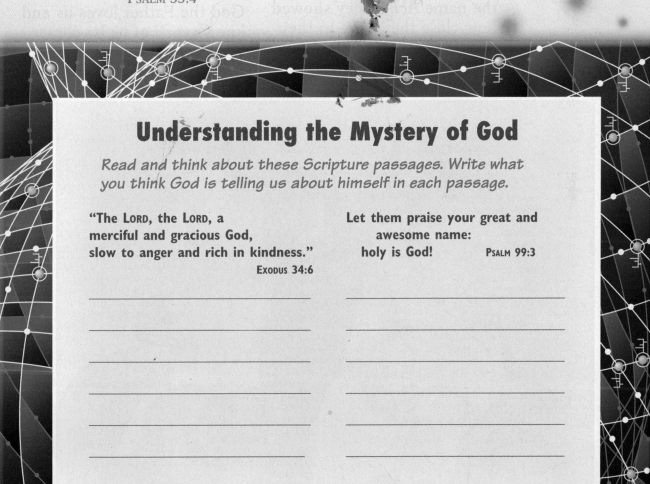

Understanding the Mystery of God

Read and think about these Scripture passages. Write what you think God is telling us about himself in each passage.

"The LORD, the LORD, a merciful and gracious God, slow to anger and rich in kindness." EXODUS 34:6

Let them praise your great and awesome name: holy is God! PSALM 99:3

_____

_____

_____

_____

_____

_____

_____

_____

_____

_____

Faith Focus

What does it mean to call God "Father"?

Faith Vocabulary

Abba. The name Jesus used for God the Father that reveals the love and trust that exist between Jesus, God the Son, and God the Father.

God the Father

We have already learned that God has revealed himself most fully in Jesus Christ. Everything Jesus said and did on earth taught us about God. Most of all he spoke about God the Father. Everything Jesus said and did was connected with his Father.

Jesus had a very special name for God the Father. He called God **Abba,** which means "dear Father" or even "Dad." When people used the name *Abba,* they showed how close they were to their father. They expressed how much they loved and trusted their father. When Jesus called his Father Abba, he revealed how much he loved and trusted his Father.

Jesus invited his disciples to trust God the Father as he did. When his disciples asked Jesus to teach them to pray, he answered:

"This is how you are to pray:
Our Father . . ."

MATTHEW 6:9

Jesus revealed that his Father is our Father too. God the Father loves us and knows each of us by name. We love and trust God the Father, God our Abba.

Children of God

When we call God our Father, we are really saying that we are all children of God. The Bible tells us:

See what love the Father has bestowed on us that we may be called the children of God.

1 JOHN 3:1

As his children we share God's love with all people everywhere. So close to us is God the Father that he knows and loves each one of us by name. The Bible tells us:

Can a mother forget her
    infant,
  be without tenderness
    for the child of her
    womb?
Even should she forget,
  I will never forget you.
See, upon the palms of
    my hands I have
    written your name.

ISAIAH 49:15–16

 Faith-Filled People

Thérèse of Lisieux

Saint Thérèse of Lisieux took great pride in being a child of God. Thérèse lived a simple life of trust in God. Thérèse loved nature and often used nature to explain how God's loving care is everywhere. The Church celebrates the feast day of Saint Thérèse of Lisieux on October 1.

God is our Father, our Abba. How happy we are that God has shared this truth about himself and about us.

QUESTION What does it mean that God has revealed himself to be our Father?

Abba

When you speak to God, what name do you use for him? Write and decorate that name in this space. Use that name today and often. Always remember that God knows and loves you by name.

God the Creator

In the Apostles' Creed, we profess:

I believe in God,
the Father almighty,
Creator of heaven
and earth.

Creation shows the great glory of God. He created the whole universe and all creatures, seen and unseen, out of nothing and without any help. Everyone and everything God created is good.

The Bible teaches that God created human beings by breathing his own life into them. He created all people in his image and likeness. The Book of Psalms helps us understand what this means. We read:

What are humans that
you are mindful
of them,
mere mortals that you
care for them?
Yet you have made them
little less than a god,
crowned them with
glory and honor.

PSALM 8:5–6

God created us with a body and a spiritual and immortal **soul**. This means our soul will never die.

The writers of the Bible gave the names Adam and Eve to the first humans. No matter the color of our skin, the life we live, or the language we speak, we all belong to one family—the family of God.

Original Sin

Sadly, Adam and Eve were not satisfied with God's plan of goodness and holiness for them. They preferred their own way to God's plan and disobeyed him. The Church calls this decision to live apart from God **original sin**. It is called original sin because it is the beginning of all evil and sin in the world.

Original sin wounded everyone and everything God created. Each person is born sharing in the effects of original sin. Because of original sin, there is evil in the world.

We feel the effects of original sin when we let jealousy and hatred and greed influence our actions. We see its effects in hunger and homelessness and in sickness and injustice and war.

Despite original sin, God still invites us and helps us share in his goodness and happiness. God the Father sent us Jesus Christ, his only Son, to redeem us and restore our friendship with him.

QUESTION Why is it important to know about original sin and how it has affected our world?

All Creation Is Good

We are called to respect all God's creation. Everyone and everything good has been created by God. Illustrate one way you can show your respect for creation.

Our Church Makes a Difference

Blessing of Animals

Blessing Prayers

Blessings are one of the ways the Church shows that we believe God the Creator is always with his creation. He is always blessing us with his love. Blessing prayers remind us of this important truth about God.

Catholics use many blessing prayers. We pray grace before and after meals. At the conclusion of Mass, we ask God to bless us.

We ask God's blessing on every newly married couple. Some people ask for a blessing when they move into a new home or before they go off to college. Catholics also bless religious objects, such as medals, rosaries, and crucifixes.

All our blessings remind us that God, who knows and loves each of us by name, is always with us. This is the greatest good and blessing we ever could have.

 Why is blessing a person, place, or object a sign of faith?

Blessing of meals

Blessing of Easter foods

Blessing of teens celebrating Quinceañera, their fifteenth birthday

What Difference Does Faith Make in My Life?

You show that you believe in and trust in God the Father, as Jesus did, in many ways. You pray. You treat others and the world with respect and kindness.

Imagine you are a movie director. You are directing a movie entitled All About God. In this space illustrate or write about a scene in that movie.

All About God

My Faith Choice

This week I will share my faith in God by making known one quality about him. I will

_____

_____.

Lord, You Alone Are God!

Leader: In a prayer of praise we address God with a title of his greatness. Praise God using this simple prayer.

God, you are Abba.
All: **Amen! You alone are God.**

Leader: God, you are most holy.
All: **Amen! You alone are God.**

Leader: God, you are love.
All: **Amen! You alone are God.**

Leader: God, you are one Lord, the Almighty One.
All: **Amen! You alone are God.**

Leader: God, you are eternal.
All: **Amen! You alone are God.**

Leader: God, you created the whole universe and all creatures.
All: **Amen! You alone are God.**

Leader: God, you created us in your image and likeness.
All: **Amen! You alone are God.**

Leader: God, our Father, you called us to be your children. You love us and hold us in the palm of your hand. Help us trust you every day of our life. We ask this through your Son, Jesus Christ, and the Holy Spirit.
All: **Amen.**

We Remember

What I Have Learned

Match the terms in column A with the descriptions in column B.

Column A

_____ 1. almighty

_____ 2. eternal

_____ 3. create

_____ 4. original sin

_____ 5. Abba

Column B

a. always living

b. having all power

c. trustworthy, loving Father

d. the first sin

e. to make something out of nothing

Answer the following.

6. What are the attributes of God?

_____

_____

_____

7. How do the attributes of God help us come to know and love God?

_____

_____

_____

8. What does the name *Abba* tell about God's love for us?

_____

_____

_____

Growing in Faith

One important thing I learned this week is

_____

_____

_____.

This is important because

_____

_____

_____.

What will people see me doing as I live my faith choice this week?

_____

_____

_____

This Week . . .

In chapter 5, "Great Is the Lord, Our God," your child discovered the meaning of several attributes, or qualities, that the inspired biblical writers used to describe God. In particular, your child listened once again to Jesus' love and trust for his Father, whom he addressed as Abba. Your child also deepened his or her understanding of what it means to call God the Creator by discussing what the biblical stories of creation and original sin mean for our lives.

For more on the teachings of the Catholic Church on the mystery of God, Father and Creator, see *Catechism of the Catholic Church* paragraph numbers 199–227, 268–274, and 279–412.

Sharing God's Word

Read together and quietly think about the Scripture verses on pages 62 and 63 one at a time. Emphasize that as amazing as God is, Jesus taught us to call God a simple and familiar name, Father.

Praying

In this chapter your child prayed a prayer of praise. Read and pray together this prayer on page 70.

Making a Difference

Choose one of the following activities to do as a family or design a similar activity of your own.

- Choose one of the Scripture verses on pages 62 and 63. Design a banner, using the verse. Display the banner where it can remind everyone in your family how wonderful God is.

- God created the entire universe. Choose one thing you can do to give God honor and glory by respecting his creation.

- This Sunday when you take part in Mass, take time to look at the religious statues or artwork in your church. Talk about how these works of art help you honor and worship God.

For more ideas on ways your family can live your faith, visit the "Faith First for Families" page at **www.FaithFirst.com**. You will find the "Contemporary Issues" page helpful this week.

Jesus Christ, Son of God

6

We Pray

O LORD, our Lord,
   how awesome is your
   name through all the
   earth!   PSALM 8:2

Lord, God our Father,
may we who honor
the holy name of Jesus,
your Son, enjoy his
friendship both in this
life and in his kingdom
forever.

                    Amen.

*Why are people's names
important to them?*

Your name is very
important. The angel told
Joseph to name Mary's
Son Jesus.

*What does the name
Jesus mean?*

Cristo Redentor
(Christ the Redeemer),
Corvocado Mountain,
Rio de Janeiro, Brazil

73

Faith Focus

How do the names and titles for Jesus found in the Scriptures help us understand who he is?

Faith Vocabulary

Lord. A title for Jesus that states that he is truly God.

Christ. A title for Jesus that states that he is the Messiah whom God promised to send to save his people.

The Name *Jesus*

Naming a baby is a special decision for a family. Parents take time making this important decision. They consider their hopes and dreams for the soon-to-be-born child. They think about the names of family members and of saints. They check books that list names and their meanings.

In the Bible people's names often describe the roles they played in God's plan of salvation. In Matthew's Gospel we are told that an angel appeared to Joseph. The angel told him that Mary would give birth to a son and that he was to name the child Jesus. The Hebrew name *Jesus* means "God saves." The very name of Jesus reveals that he is the Savior of the world.

Titles for Jesus

All of God's promises in the Bible come true in Jesus. Jesus is the center and heart of God's loving plan of creation and salvation. He is the Messiah, the **Lord** and Savior of the world. These titles express our faith in who Jesus is and the work the Father sent him to do.

Messiah

Throughout the Old Testament, God promised to send a messiah. The title *messiah* means "anointed one." The Messiah would save, or deliver, God's people from their enemies. Matthew's Gospel tells that Saint Peter the Apostle confessed his faith in Jesus to be the Messiah. Jesus asked the disciples:

"But who do you say that I am?" Simon Peter said in reply, "You are the Messiah, the Son of the living God."

MATTHEW 16:15–16

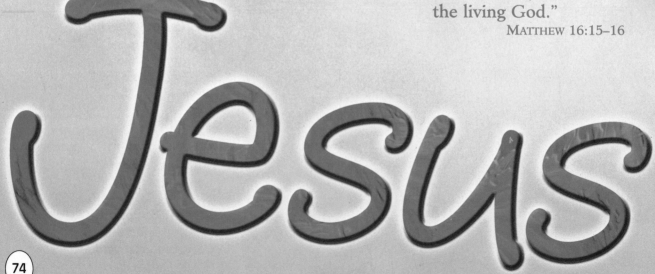

Christ

The English word *Christ* is used for the Hebrew word *messiah* and for the Greek word *kristos*. Jesus is the **Christ**—the Messiah, the Anointed One.

This title for Jesus is used over 160 times in the New Testament. In him we have been saved. We have been freed from sin and given new life. Saint Timothy, who often joined with Saint Paul the Apostle to preach the Gospel, wrote:

> This saying is trustworthy and deserves full acceptance: Christ Jesus came into the world to save sinners. 1 TIMOTHY 1:15

Lord

The Israelites used the word *Lord* for God in place of the divine name YHWH. When we call Jesus "Lord," we are professing our faith that Jesus Christ is truly God. He is the Son of God, the second divine Person of the Holy Trinity. Jesus Christ is true God and true man.

The Church has always proclaimed her faith in Jesus Christ as the Lord. Saint Paul the Apostle wrote:

> And no one can say, "Jesus is Lord," except by the holy Spirit.
> 1 CORINTHIANS 12:3

 How do all the above titles taken together help you come to know who Jesus is?

Titles for Jesus

Jesus is the Savior and Lord. He is the Christ, the Messiah promised by God. Solve this crossword puzzle to find out more about Jesus.

DOWN
1. ____ created us.
3. The Risen Jesus appeared to the ____.
4. Jesus is the ____, the Anointed One.
5. ____ is true God and true man.

ACROSS
2. ____ is a title that expresses our belief that Jesus is truly God.
4. Jesus is both God and ____.
6. To have faith is to ____.
7. Jesus is our ____ because he saves us from sin.

Faith Vocabulary

Incarnation. From the Latin word meaning "putting on flesh," to have a real body; the Son of God "putting on flesh," or becoming human, while keeping his divinity.

The Announcement of the Birth of Jesus

You have read and listened to the account of Jesus' birth many, many times. In chapter 3 we learned that the angel Gabriel announced to the Blessed Virgin Mary that God had chosen her to be the Mother of his Son. The angel told Mary that the Holy Spirit would come to her and that she would conceive a son and name him Jesus. We call this moment in the life of Mary the Annunciation.

After the birth of Jesus, Luke's Gospel tells us that an angel of God appeared to shepherds, announcing to them the birth of Jesus. Luke writes:

> The angel said to them, "Do not be afraid; for behold, I proclaim to you good news of great joy that will be for all people. For today in the city of David a savior has been born for you who is Messiah and Lord."
>
> LUKE 2:10–11

The Birth of Jesus

The Church names the mystery of the Son of God becoming man the **Incarnation.** The word *incarnation* means "putting on flesh." It is the word the Church has chosen to name the mystery of faith that the Son of God, the second divine Person of the Holy Trinity, became fully human without giving up his divinity. Jesus is true God and true man. Luke's Gospel tells us:

> Joseph too went up from Galilee from the town of Nazareth to Judea, to the city of David

Visit of the Shepherds, stained glass

that is called Bethlehem, . . . to be enrolled with Mary, his betrothed, who was with child. While they were there, the time came for her to have her child, and she gave birth to her firstborn son.   LUKE 2:4–7

Each year during the Christmas season, we remember and celebrate this great mystery of faith. Churches, homes, neighborhoods, towns, and cities are filled with the sights and sounds of Christmas joy. The story of the birth of the infant Jesus lying in the manger in Bethlehem is told over and over, year after year, throughout the whole world.

The Incarnation of the Son of God is the distinctive sign of our Christian faith. Jesus Christ is true God and true man. He is the Lord and Messiah, the Savior of the world.

 Why did the Son of God become one of us?

Faith-Filled People

Matthew and Luke

The account of the birth of Jesus is found only in the Gospels of Saint Matthew and Saint Luke. Saint Matthew was a tax collector and an Apostle. Saint Luke was a physician and a companion of Saint Paul the Apostle.

Jesus Christ Is Lord and Savior

Use words or pictures to describe what you can do to proclaim your faith in Jesus Christ.

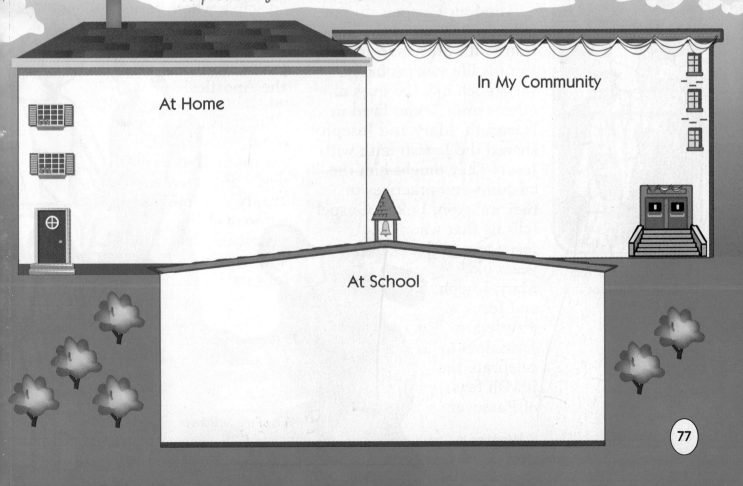

At Home

In My Community

At School

Faith Vocabulary

Mother of God. Mary, the Mother of Jesus who is true God and true man.

Holy Family

Mary and the Beloved Disciple at the foot of the Cross

Mary, the Mother of Jesus

The four Gospels do not tell us much about the life of Jesus with Mary and Joseph. But his life was probably very much like the lives of other families who lived in Nazareth. Mary and Joseph shared the Jewish faith with Jesus. They taught him the customs and practices of their religion. Luke's Gospel tells us that when Jesus was twelve years old, Mary, Joseph, and Jesus traveled to Jerusalem to celebrate the Jewish feast of Passover.

When Jesus was an adult, Mary sometimes traveled with him and the disciples. She listened to him as he preached and taught. John's Gospel tells us that at a wedding in Cana, Mary pointed out that there was very little wine left. Jesus responded by changing the water in six stone jars into wine. Each jar contained over twenty gallons of water.

Mary also stood by Jesus' side during the final days of his life on earth. When he was crucified, Mary, several other women disciples, and the "disciple whom Jesus loved" were there with him. Tradition tells us that the "disciple whom Jesus loved" was John, the youngest of the Apostles.

Wedding in Cana

Mary, the Mother of God

Mary is truly the **Mother of God.** She is the Mother of Jesus who is true God and true man. Each year on January 1, the Solemnity of Mary, the Mother of God, we remember and celebrate this truth about Mary. This honor with which God has blessed Mary is a mystery of faith.

Mary, Our Mother

Mary is our Blessed Mother. She is the Mother of the Church. In John's Gospel we read:

When Jesus saw his mother and the disciple there whom he loved, he said to his mother, "Woman, behold, your son." Then he said to the disciple, "Behold, your mother." And from that hour the disciple took her into his home.

JOHN 19:26–27

We take Mary, our mother, into our homes and into our hearts as the disciple John and the early Church did. We believe and trust that Mary cares for us, watches over us, and wants us to grow closer to her Son, Jesus.

 Why do we honor Mary as our Blessed Mother?

Holy Mary, Mother of God

How can you show Mary your love for her? Write your ideas in this space.

_____

_____

_____

_____

_____

_____

Madonna and Child

From the days of the early Church, the Church has expressed her devotion to Mary, the Mother of Jesus, through art. Christian artists have expressed their faith and the faith of the Church in Mary in many ways. They have used paintings and icons, mosaics and frescoes, sculptures and wood carvings, hymns and other forms of music. The Blessed Virgin Mary holding her Child Jesus is one of the favorite ways Christian artists have portrayed Mary.

These works of art, which have been created by Christian artists around the world, have come to be named "Virgin and Child" and "Madonna and Child." The word *Madonna*, which means "My Lady," manifests the love and devotion of the Church for Mary.

QUESTION What does the art of the Madonna and Child on this page tell you about the faith of the Church in Mary and her Child?

Marble sculpture

Mosaic

Wood carving

What Difference Does Faith Make in My Life?

Each year during Christmastime, you celebrate God's love for you, for your family, and for all people. The Holy Spirit invites you to celebrate and share that love with others each and every day.

Sharing the Good News

Create a banner. Use words, pictures, or symbols that tell others about Jesus Christ.

My Faith Choice

This week I will show others that I believe in Jesus Christ. I will

_____

_____.

Praise the Name of the Lord

Leader: God, our loving Father,
out of your love and mercy,
you sent us your only Son.
Send the Holy Spirit
to strengthen our faith in him.

Reader: A reading from the holy gospel according
to Luke.

All: **Glory to you, O Lord.**

Reader: Now there were shepherds in that region living
in the fields and keeping the night watch over
their flock. The angel of the Lord appeared to
them and the glory of the Lord shone around
them, and they were struck with great fear.
The angel said to them, "Do not be afraid; for
behold, I proclaim to you good news of great joy
that will be for all the people. For today in the
city of David a savior has been born for you
who is Messiah and Lord. And this will be a
sign for you: you will find an infant wrapped in
swaddling clothes and lying in a manger." And
suddenly there was a multitude of the heavenly
host with the angel, praising God and saying:
"Glory to God in the highest
and on earth peace to those on
whom his favor rests." LUKE 2: 8–14
The gospel of the Lord.

All: **Praise to you, Lord Jesus Christ.**

Leader: Let us ask Jesus to help us know and love him better.
Jesus, Son of the living God,

All: **have mercy on us.**

Leader: Jesus, Son of the Virgin Mary,
All: **have mercy on us.**

Leader: Jesus, the Good Shepherd,
All: **have mercy on us.**

We Remember

What I Have Learned

Match each title of Jesus in the word box with its meaning. Write the title next to its meaning.

Messiah   Christ   Lord   Jesus

Meaning	Title
1. God saves	_____
2. Anointed One	_____
3. Truly God	_____
4. Messiah	_____

Answer the following.

5. Describe how the name *Jesus* reveals the work that his Father sent him to do.

_____

_____

6. Explain the term *Incarnation*.

_____

_____

7. Describe what the Gospels tell us about Mary.

_____

_____

8. Explain what the Church celebrates each year on January 1.

_____

_____

To Help You Remember

1. Jesus Christ is the Son of God who became one of us to save us from our sins.

2. Jesus Christ is Lord. He is true God, the second Person of the Holy Trinity, who became true man without giving up being God.

3. The Blessed Virgin Mary is the Mother of Jesus, the Son of God.

Growing in Faith

One important thing I learned this week is

_____

_____

_____.

This is important because

_____

_____

_____.

What will people see me doing as I live my faith choice this week?

_____

_____

_____

This Week . . .

In chapter 6, "Jesus Christ, Son of God," your child learned more about Jesus and the mystery of the Incarnation. The name *Jesus* means "God saves." It reveals to us that Jesus is truly the Savior of the world. Other names, or titles, for Jesus, such as Christ, Lord, and Messiah, help us understand who Jesus is and the work God the Father sent him to do. The mystery of the Son of God taking on flesh and becoming fully human without giving up being God is called the Incarnation. We believe that Jesus Christ is true God and true man. Mary, the Mother of Jesus, is truly the Mother of God because Jesus is true God and true man.

For more on the teachings of the Catholic Church on the mystery of the Incarnation, see *Catechism of the Catholic Church* paragraph numbers 422–451, 456–478, and 484–507.

Sharing God's Word

Read together Luke 2:1–20. Emphasize what this Gospel account of Jesus' birth tells about who he is and the work he was sent to do.

Praying

In this chapter your child prayed a prayer of praise. Read and pray together the praise prayer on page 82.

Making a Difference

Choose one of the following activities to do as a family or design a similar activity of your own.

- The angel Gabriel told Mary to name her child Jesus. Talk about how each family member's name was chosen.

- Jesus showed his love for his Mother. Discuss why it is very important to show our love for family members. Choose to do special things this week to show your love for one another.

- Saint Nicholas is the patron saint of children. Find out more about this generous saint. Look in your local library, parish library, or on the Internet by visiting *The Catholic Encyclopedia* Web site.

For more ideas on ways your family can live your faith, visit the "Faith First for Families" page at **www.FaithFirst.com**. This week share some of the ideas with one another on the "Gospel Reflections" page.

The Death, Resurrection, and Ascension of Jesus

7

We Pray

This is the day the LORD
 has made;
 let us rejoice in it
 and be glad.
PSALM 118:24

God our Father,
you raised Christ
your Son from the dead.
Raise us to new life
in Christ by the Holy
Spirit who is within us.
Amen.

*What are some of the key
events in the life of your
family?*

Every person's life has
key events. Each time we
celebrate the Eucharist,
we remember the Paschal
Mystery of the Passion,
death, Resurrection, and
glorious Ascension of
Jesus Christ.

*What do you know about
the Passion, death,
Resurrection, and Ascension
of Jesus?*

Jesus (oil on wood). Daniel
Nevins, contemporary
American painter.

Faith Focus

What is the meaning of the Jewish celebration of Passover?

Faith Vocabulary

Passover. The Jewish feast celebrating the sparing of the Hebrew children from death and the passage of God's people from slavery in Egypt to freedom in the land God promised them.

Egypt and Israel, NASA.

God's People in Egypt

One of the most important events in the history of God's people was his freeing them from slavery in Egypt. After calling Abraham to leave his homeland, God entered the Covenant with him, blessing and choosing him to be the father of God's people.

The LORD said to Abram: "Go forth from the land of your kinsfolk and from your father's house to a land that I will show you.
"I will make you a great nation, and I will bless you. . . . All the communities of the earth shall find blessing in you." GENESIS 12:1–3

The descendants of Abraham became known by several names. They were known as Israelites, Hebrews, or Jews. Years later when they were suffering from a great famine, Abraham's descendants traveled to Egypt in search of food. Joseph, Abraham's great-grandson, was already living there and had become a highly respected leader in Egypt. Joseph, recognizing his family, fed them and invited them to stay.

Over a period of time, the number of Hebrews in Egypt became so large that Pharaoh, the Egyptian king, and the Egyptians began to fear them. To protect themselves and their land, the Egyptians made the Hebrews their slaves.

The Great Sea

Moab

Edom

Goshen

Red Sea

Egypt

Sinai

Possible route the Hebrews traveled

Passover

As slaves, the Hebrews suffered greatly. They prayed, asking God to deliver, or free, them from slavery. God listened and answered their cries. He chose and sent Moses to lead the Hebrews to freedom. Moses, accompanied by his brother Aaron, bravely faced Pharaoh. Over and over he tried to persuade Pharaoh to let the Hebrews leave Egypt.

Again and again, Pharaoh refused despite the many signs that God sent. Then something happened. Many young Egyptians were dying in their homes, but the Hebrews and their children were spared. Death "passed over" the homes of the Hebrews.

Finally, Pharaoh let God's people go. The Hebrews, or Israelites, passed over from slavery in Egypt to freedom in a land promised to them by God. From that time in the history of God's people, the Jewish people have gathered each year to remember and celebrate what happened. They call the celebration **Passover**.

 How can faith in God help a person deal with suffering?

Celebrating Freedom and a New Life

Find and circle the words in the puzzle. Use the words you found to explain the meaning of Passover to your family.

famine
Egypt
Covenant
Passover
Pharaoh
Hebrews
slaves
life
freedom

```
W N C O V E N A N T Z
Y G Q L W R J Y B F H
E D L I C A Q H E A S
G Y P F R E E D O M T
Y U A E B G K Q B I O
P A S S O V E R K N H
T K C J P S L A V E S
F P H A R A O H B T X
N E A K E C I N P D J
A R G V H E B R E W S
```

Faith Focus

What is the Paschal Mystery of Jesus?

Faith Vocabulary

Paschal Mystery. The "passing over" of Jesus from life through death into new and glorious life; the Passion, death, Resurrection, and glorious Ascension of Jesus.

Jewish family celebrating Passover meal

The Paschal Mystery

Passover is celebrated today by Jewish people each spring as it was in Jesus' time. During Passover the Jewish people share a special meal to remember and celebrate God's freeing them from Egypt and leading them to a new life in the land he promised them. During the week in which Jesus died, he went to Jerusalem and celebrated Passover with his disciples for the last time.

The Passion, death, Resurrection, and glorious Ascension of Jesus is called the **Paschal Mystery**. It is the passing over of Jesus from life through his Passion and death into a new and glorious life. It is the most important event in Jesus' life and the central theme of the Gospel.

The Passion Narrative

The part of the Gospel that tells about Jesus' suffering and death is called the Passion narrative.

Last Supper

Christians have named the last Passover meal Jesus celebrated with his disciples the Last Supper. We read:

When the day of the feast of Unleavened Bread arrived, the day for sacrificing the Passover lamb, [Jesus] sent out Peter and John, instructing them, "Go and make preparations for us to eat the Passover." LUKE 22:7–8

It was at that Passover meal that Jesus gave the Church the Eucharist.

Betrayal and Arrest

After the Last Supper, Judas Iscariot led a group of Jesus' enemies to the Garden of Gethsemane where Jesus was praying. It was there Judas betrayed Jesus and handed him over to be arrested.

Trial and Sentencing

Falsely accusing Jesus of blasphemy, his enemies handed him over to Pontius Pilate to be tried. Fearing the Roman emperor and the crowd, Pilate handed Jesus over to be crucified.

Suffering, Death, and Burial

Jesus carried his cross to Calvary, a hill outside Jerusalem where criminals were crucified. It was there that Jesus died. After Jesus died, Joseph of Arimathea and other disciples of Jesus placed his body in a new tomb.

 What does the Passion narrative tell us?

Faith-Filled People

Veronica

The Church passes on to us the tradition that as Jesus was carrying his cross he was met by Veronica, one of his disciples. Veronica reached out and wiped the blood and sweat off Jesus' face with her veil. This act of faith and compassion is remembered in the Sixth Station of the Way of the Cross. The Church celebrates the feast day of Saint Veronica on July 9.

Witnessing the Passion and Death of Jesus

Imagine you are with the disciples at Jesus' Passion and death. On this journal page describe your thoughts and feelings.

Faith Vocabulary

Resurrection. The event of Jesus being raised from the dead to a new and glorious life.

Ascension. A word meaning "a going up"; the return of the Risen Christ in glory to his Father.

The Resurrection

All four Gospels proclaim that three days after Jesus died and was buried, he was raised to new life. We call this mighty deed of God the **Resurrection** of Jesus. It is the heart of our Christian faith.

It is difficult to imagine the amazement and wonder that Mary Magdalene and the other disciples felt when they first saw that the tomb in which Jesus was buried was empty. We read:

> But at daybreak on the first day of the week they took the spices they had prepared and went to the tomb. They found the stone rolled away from the tomb; but when they entered, they did not find the body of the Lord Jesus. While they were puzzling over this, behold, two men in dazzling garments appeared to them. . . . They said to them, "Why do you seek the living one among the dead? He is not here, but he has been raised.
>
> LUKE 24:1–4, 5–6

When we say that Jesus was raised from the dead, we do not mean that he simply came back to life. We

The Risen Lord Blessing the Disciples Before the Ascension, stained glass

mean much more than that. While the Risen Christ appeared to his disciples in the body they knew, they did not recognize him at first. His body was gloriously changed by the Holy Spirit. God raised Jesus into a new and glorious life.

The Ascension

For forty days after his Resurrection, the Risen Jesus met with his disciples and continued to teach them. During one final meeting on Mount Olivet, which is near Jerusalem, he ascended to his Father. We call this the **Ascension** of Jesus.

When we say Jesus ascended to his Father, we mean several things:

- Jesus has returned in glory and majesty to his Father.
- Jesus has gone to prepare a place for us. Where Christ has ascended, we hope one day to follow.
- We are responsible for continuing the mission of Jesus on earth.

Through his Paschal Mystery, Jesus frees us from sin. Raised to new life by the power of the Holy Spirit, Christ shares with us the fullness of life with God. With Christ we can "pass over" from sin and death to new life with him, his Father, and the Holy Spirit. God's plan of salvation is fulfilled in Jesus Christ.

 What is the Paschal Mystery of Jesus?

Rejoice in the Lord!

At Mass we proclaim "We proclaim your Death, O Lord, and profess your Resurrection until you come again." Draw a sign or symbol that illustrates the Paschal Mystery.

Our Church Makes a Difference

Interior of Church of the Holy Sepulchre, Jerusalem, site of the Tenth Station through the Fourteenth Station

Stations of the Cross

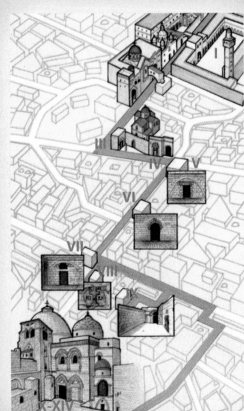

Location of Stations of the Cross, Jerusalem

Since the early centuries of Christianity, people have made pilgrimages to the Holy Land to visit the places associated with the life, death, and Resurrection of Jesus Christ. Because not everyone could visit the Holy Land, shrines to commemorate the Passion and death of Christ were placed in churches throughout the world. These shrines became known as the Stations, or Way, of the Cross.

When we make our pilgrimage and pray the Stations of the Cross, we profess our faith in the Paschal Mystery and announce that God's plan of salvation is fulfilled in Jesus Christ. By his death and Resurrection Jesus has conquered death and won life everlasting for all people.

QUESTION As you pray the Stations of the Cross what might you say to Jesus to express your love for him?

What Difference Does Faith Make in My Life?

Through Baptism you were made a sharer in the death and Resurrection of Christ. You received the gift of the Holy Spirit and the promise and hope of eternal life.

In this space create a symbol or design a banner that announces the good news of Jesus' Resurrection.

My Faith Choice

This week I will share my faith in the Risen Christ with others. I will

_____

_____.

Rejoice! Rejoice!

Leader: The Easter Vigil is the Church's great celebration of the Resurrection. At the Easter Vigil the Exsultet is sung. The Exsultet is a joyful proclamation announcing the Resurrection of Jesus and the gift of hope to the world.

Let us pray together the beginning of the Exsultet.

Group 1: Exult, let them exult, the hosts of heaven, exult, let Angel ministers of God exult,

Group 2: let the trumpet of salvation sound aloud our mighty King's triumph!

All: ALLELUIA! SOUND ALOUD THE TRUMPET OF SALVATION!

Group 1: Be glad, let earth be glad as glory floods her, ablaze with light from her eternal King,

Group 2: let all corners of the earth be glad, knowing an end to gloom and darkness.

All: ALLELUIA! SOUND ALOUD THE TRUMPET OF SALVATION!

Group 1: Rejoice, let Mother Church also rejoice, arrayed with the lightning of his glory,

Group 2: let this holy building shake with joy, filled with the mighty voices of the peoples.

All: ALLELUIA! SOUND ALOUD THE TRUMPET OF SALVATION!

Roman Missal

What I Have Learned

Use the clues to discover the events and meaning of the Paschal Mystery.

DOWN

1. Forty days after Easter we celebrate the ___.

2. Jesus was crucified on a hill called ___.

ACROSS

3. The ___ Supper is the Passover meal Jesus celebrated with his disciples.

4. We call Jesus being raised from the dead the ___.

Answer the following.

5. Describe the Paschal Mystery of Jesus as his "Passover."

6. Compare the Last Supper to the Eucharist.

7. Describe the meaning of the Resurrection.

8. Describe the Church's teaching about the Ascension.

To Help You Remember

1. The Passover is the feast the Jewish people celebrate to remember God's freeing them from slavery in Egypt and leading them to a new life in the land he had promised them.

2. The Paschal Mystery of Jesus is his Passion, death, Resurrection, and glorious Ascension.

3. By his Paschal Mystery Christ freed people from death and sin and gained for all the promise and hope of eternal life.

Growing in Faith

One important thing I learned this week is

_____

_____

_____.

This is important because

_____

_____

_____.

What will people see me doing as I live my faith choice this week?

_____

_____

_____

This Week . . .

In chapter 7, "The Death, Resurrection, and Ascension of Jesus," your child deepened his or her faith in the Passion, death, Resurrection, and glorious Ascension of Jesus Christ. During the week in which he died, Jesus celebrated a Passover meal with his disciples. Passover is the Jewish feast that celebrates the passage of God's people from slavery in Egypt to freedom. The Paschal Mystery of Jesus is his Passion, death, Resurrection, and glorious Ascension—his passover from suffering and death into new and glorious life.

For more on the teachings of the Catholic Church on the Paschal Mystery of Christ, see *Catechism of the Catholic Church* paragraph numbers 571–664.

Sharing God's Word

Invite each person to share what they know about the Gospel accounts of Jesus' Passion, death, Resurrection, and Ascension. Emphasize that each time we celebrate the Eucharist, we are made sharers in the Paschal Mystery.

Praying

In this chapter your child prayed the Exultet. Read and pray together this prayer on page 94.

Making a Difference

Choose one of the following activities to do as a family or design a similar activity of your own.

• At Mass we celebrate the Paschal Mystery. When you take part in Mass this week, look for the crucifix and the Easter, or Paschal, candle. Talk about how these remind you of the Paschal Mystery.

• Imagine that you were present with the disciples when Jesus was arrested and put on trial. Talk about how you would have felt or what you would have thought.

• This week when you take part in Mass, spend time afterward walking the Stations of the Cross. Stop at each station and talk about what each station tells about Jesus' Passion and death.

For more ideas on ways your family can live your faith, visit the "Faith First for Families" page at **www.FaithFirst.com**. Click on "Family Prayer" to find a special prayer to pray together this week.

The Promise of a Helper
A Scripture Story

8

We Pray

I wait for you,
   O LORD. . . .
In you I trust.   PSALM 25:1, 2

Father,
we turn to you
in all our troubles.
We give you thanks
in all our joys.   Amen.

What kinds of promises do people make to each other?

Promises are important. The Bible passes on to us story after story of God keeping his promises to people.

What are some of God's promises?

Descent of Holy Spirit upon the Disciples, stained glass

97

Faith Vocabulary

Evangelists. The writers of the four Gospels in the New Testament—Matthew, Mark, Luke, and John.

The New Testament

Many important people have lived and died in the past one hundred years. We read their biographies. We watch and listen as their stories unfold before our eyes on TV or the movie screen. Passing on the values and meaning of the lives of such people helps us learn not only about them but also about ourselves.

The New Testament shares with us who Jesus is and what his life and work among us means. It passes on to us the story of God's love for us revealed in Jesus Christ, the Son of God.

After Jesus' Ascension the Apostles and other disciples first preached about Jesus and the importance of his life, suffering and death, Resurrection, and Ascension. Inspired by the Holy Spirit, the **Evangelists**—Matthew, Mark, Luke, and John— wrote the four Gospels, which are the heart and center of the New Testament.

The word *evangelist* means "one who announces good news." The Gospels according to Matthew, Mark, Luke, and John pass on to us the faith of the early Church in Jesus Christ. They announce and share the good news of God's great love for us that was revealed in Jesus Christ.

The Gospel According to John

John's Gospel is the fourth Gospel in the New Testament. It was written toward the end of the first century. These were difficult times for the early Church. Many believers suffered and were being persecuted. Some were martyred, put to death because of their faith in Jesus Christ.

John's Gospel reminded the early Church that before Jesus died he had promised he would always be with them. After commissioning the disciples to "make disciples of all nations," he promised:

> "And behold, I am with you always, until the end of the age."
> MATTHEW 28:20

Hearing this promise over and over again strengthened their faith in Jesus Christ. It also strengthened their trust in the Holy Spirit, whom Jesus had promised the Father would send to them in his name.

 How is your faith in Jesus a source of strength for you?

Sharing the Good News

Create a Web page of pictures and phrases that tell about Jesus.

Faith Focus

Why does Jesus send the Holy Spirit?

Faith Vocabulary

Holy Spirit. The third Person of the Holy Trinity, sent to us by the Father in the name of his Son, Jesus Christ.

Jesus' Promise

The Gospel of John tells more about the Last Supper than do the Gospels of Matthew, Mark, and Luke. Chapters 13 through 17 of John's Gospel include the Last Supper discourse, or lengthy conversation, of Jesus with his disciples. As we listen to the words of Jesus, it is as though he is speaking directly to us.

In this discourse Jesus spoke to his disciples about many things. He told them he would soon be leaving them and returning to his Father. He taught them to love one another as he had loved them. He warned his disciples about the difficulties they would face living as his followers. He also made this important promise:

"But now I am going to the one who sent me, and not one of you asks me, 'Where are you

Last Supper Discourse, stained glass

going?' But because
I told you this, grief has
filled your hearts. But
I tell you the truth, it is
better for you that I go.
For if I do not go, the
Advocate will not come
to you. But if I go, I will
send him to you."

JOHN 16:5–7

Jesus promised the
disciples that the Advocate,
the **Holy Spirit**, would
come to them. The Holy
Spirit would keep Jesus'
memory alive in their minds
and hearts. They would not
be left alone.

 *When do you pray
to the Holy Spirit?*

The Gift of the Holy Spirit

*Unlock the code to discover how the Holy Spirit will help
the Apostles.*

A .-	F ..-.	K -.-	O ---	S ...	W .--
B -...	G --.	L .-..	P .--.	T -	X -..-
C -.-.	H	M --	Q --.-	U ..-	Y -.--
D -..	I ..	N -.	R .-.	V ...-	Z --..
E .	J .---				

_ _ _ _   _ _ _ _ _ _ _ _ _
- .... --.. .... --- .--. .. . -

_ _ _ _ _   _ _ _ _ _ _ _
... .   - . .. .-.. ....

_ _ _ _ _   _ _ _ _ _ _   _ _ _ _ _ .
- ....-.. -- .-. -   .... -. ... .

BASED ON JOHN 14:25

101

Faith Focus

What does it mean to believe that we have received the gift of the Holy Spirit?

Faith Vocabulary

Advocate. Title or name for the Holy Spirit, which means "one who is at our side," or "one who speaks for us."

The Advocate

Jesus promised the disciples that his Father would send them the **Advocate**, the Holy Spirit, in his name. An advocate is someone who stands by our side and speaks for us.

The disciples listened to Jesus at the Last Supper, but they did not fully understand what he was saying. They did not know who the Holy Spirit was or how he would come. They only knew that although they were frightened, they trusted Jesus. They did not know what they would do once he returned to his Father.

Saint Luke in his Acts of the Apostles tells us that the Holy Spirit came upon the disciples as Jesus promised. The Holy Spirit is always with us. He gives us strength for all the hard times in our lives. He gives us the grace to live our faith in Jesus with courage and confidence. The Holy Spirit never leaves us alone.

St. Vincent de Paul Society, high school volunteers

The Spirit of Truth

The Holy Spirit is always at work in the Church. He is the Spirit of Truth, the Teacher who helps us understand and live what Jesus taught.

The Holy Spirit is the Advocate and Teacher who always gives the Church the charisms, or gifts, necessary to do her work on earth. He makes us ready and eager to prepare the way for the coming of the Kingdom of God by living Jesus' command to love one another as Jesus did.

As Christians we pray for the grace to open our hearts and minds to the Holy Spirit. We pray to the Holy Spirit to fill our hearts with the fire of his love. Praying to the Holy Spirit and responding to his grace make all the difference in the way we live each day.

 Why is the Holy Spirit called the Advocate?

COME, HOLY SPIRIT

Complete this prayer and make it your own personal prayer. Keep a copy of your prayer in your Bible or some other place. Pray it each day.

COME, HOLY SPIRIT, INTO MY LIFE

_____

_____

_____

_____

_____

_____

Hymns

From the days of the early Church, Christians have lifted up their hearts and minds in prayer to God in song. Hymns are one form of song that has long been a part of the prayer tradition of the Church.

Some hymns are found in the New Testament. Other hymns have been composed recently. Many of the hymns we sing as a faith community are found in your parish hymnal. The words of the hymns express the Church's faith. There are hymns about God the Father and Creator. Other hymns profess our faith in Jesus and the saving events of his life.

This hymn to the Holy Spirit was written in the ninth century:

Come, Holy Spirit,
Creator blest,

And in our hearts
take up thy rest;

Come with thy grace
and heavenly aid

To fill the hearts
which thou hast made.

There are other hymns about Mary and the other saints. There are hymns that help us celebrate the liturgical seasons. Singing hymns is one way we profess the faith of the Church and proclaim it to others.

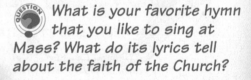

QUESTION *What is your favorite hymn that you like to sing at Mass? What do its lyrics tell about the faith of the Church?*

What Difference Does Faith Make in My Life?

The Holy Spirit is always by your side. He is the Advocate and Teacher, guiding you to be a person of faith and hope and love.

Choose one of these two situations. Write what the Holy Spirit can help you do or say in that situation.

Come, Holy Spirit

1. The city or town where you live does not want a homeless shelter for people who are poor. What can you say or do?

   _____

   _____

   _____

   _____

2. A group you belong to will allow only certain kinds of people to join the group. You feel all people should be allowed to be members. What can you say or do?

   _____

   _____

   _____

   _____

My Faith Choice

 I will remember that the Holy Spirit is always with me. When I am faced with a difficult choice to live my faith, I will

_____

_____.

Prayer to the Holy Spirit

Leader: On Pentecost the Church prays aloud or sings the prayer, "Veni, Sancte Spiritus," or "Come, Holy Spirit." Pray this prayer, using prayer gestures as you pray.

Come, Holy Spirit,
fill the hearts of your faithful.

All: **And kindle in them
the fire of your love.**

Leader: Send forth your Spirit
and they shall be created.

All: **And you will renew the face of the earth.**

**Holy Spirit, Lord Divine,
Come, from heights of heav'n and shine,
     Come with blessed radiance bright!
Come, O Father of the poor,
Come, whose treasured Gifts endure,
     Come, our heart's unfailing light!
Amen.**

What I Have Learned

1. *Create an acrostic using the letters of the word ADVOCATE. Tell what you learned about the Holy Spirit. The letters can appear in any place in the words and phrases you use.*

A _____

D _____

V _____

O _____

C _____

A _____

T _____

E _____

Answer the following.

2. **What is the importance of the Last Supper discourse in John's Gospel?**

_____

_____

3. **What does naming the Holy Spirit the Advocate tell us about the work of the Holy Spirit?**

_____

_____

_____

4. **How does the Holy Spirit help the Church do her work in the world?**

_____

_____

_____

To Help You Remember

1. Jesus promised that he would not leave his disciples alone after he returned to his Father.

2. Jesus promised that the Advocate would come to the disciples.

3. The Holy Spirit is the Advocate who Jesus promised would always be with the disciples and the Church.

Growing in Faith

One important thing I learned this week is

_____

_____

_____.

This is important because

_____

_____

_____.

What will people see me doing as I live my faith choice this week?

_____

_____

_____

This Week . . .

In chapter 8, "The Promise of a Helper: A Scripture Story," your child deepened their understanding of the Gospel, the announcement of the good news of salvation in Jesus Christ. The four writers of the Gospel—Matthew, Mark, Luke, and John—are called the Evangelists. The Gospel according to John, also known as the Fourth Gospel, records that at the Last Supper, Jesus promised that the Holy Spirit would always be with the Church as her advocate and teacher.

For more on the teachings of the Catholic Church on the mystery of the Holy Spirit, see *Catechism of the Catholic Church* paragraph numbers 683–741.

Sharing God's Word

Read together John 16:5–7. Emphasize that the disciples listened to Jesus and trusted that the Advocate, the Holy Spirit, would come to them.

Praying

In this chapter your child prayed part of a traditional prayer of the Church to the Holy Spirit that is prayed on Pentecost. Read and pray together this prayer on page 106.

Making a Difference

Choose one of the following activities to do as a family or design a similar activity of your own.

- Pray the Prayer to the Holy Spirit on page 106 as your family prayer this week. Remember that the Holy Spirit is always with you as your advocate and teacher.

- When you take part in Mass this week, find the ambry. The ambry is a special place where the sacred oils that are used in the celebration of the liturgy are kept. Recall that all the baptized are anointed with the sacred oil of chrism at Confirmation as the words "Be sealed with the Gift of the Holy Spirit" are prayed.

- Read together John 14:15–21. Talk about how the Holy Spirit helps your family.

For more ideas on ways your family can live your faith, visit the "Faith First for Families" page at **www.FaithFirst.com**. The "Make a Difference" page goes especially well with this chapter.

Different Gifts, the Same Spirit

We Pray

When you send forth
   your breath, they
   are created,
   and you renew the
   face of the earth.
                    PSALM 104:30

Come, Holy Spirit,
fill our hearts with
light and lead us to
all truth.   Amen.

*What does it mean to say
that a person or group has
"spirit"?*

Having spirit is an
important quality of a
person. God has given the
Church the gift of the
Holy Spirit.

*What does it mean to the
Church to have the gift of
the Holy Spirit?*

The Work of the Holy Spirit

What images did the writers of the Old Testament use to describe the work of the Holy Spirit?

Images of the Holy Spirit

Christians are people of the Holy Spirit. Not only do we have spirit, zeal, and enthusiasm to live the Gospel, but, much more importantly, the Holy Spirit lives within each of us and within the Church. The writers of the Bible use many images to help us understand the work of the Holy Spirit. "Mighty wind" and "breath of God" are two of those images.

Mighty Wind

When Jesus promised that the Father would send the Holy Spirit to them, the disciples were not hearing a new word. When listening to the Bible story of creation, they heard about the work of a "mighty wind," a *ruah*—the Hebrew word for "spirit."

In the beginning, when God created the heavens and the earth, the earth was a formless wasteland, and darkness covered the abyss, while a mighty wind swept over the waters.

GENESIS 1:1–2

Breath of God

This "mighty wind" is also the "breath," or "spirit," of God that the disciples sang about in the Psalms:

When you send forth your breath, they are created,
and you renew the face of the earth.

PSALM 104:30

The Spirit Promised by the Prophets

Later in the history of the Israelites, the prophets often spoke of the Spirit of God at work in the world among God's people. Isaiah the Prophet proclaimed:

The spirit of the Lord GOD is upon me, because the LORD has anointed me.

ISAIAH 61:1

God's promise to send the Spirit upon all people was also a key message of Ezekiel the Prophet. Ezekiel proclaimed:

I will give you a new heart and place a new spirit within you, taking from your bodies your stony hearts and giving you natural hearts. I will put my spirit within you and make you live by my statutes, careful to observe my decrees.

EZEKIEL 36:26–27

The Church has come to understand that the Spirit spoken about in the Old Testament is the Holy Spirit, the third Person of the Holy Trinity.

QUESTION *How does the word* ruah *help us understand the work of the Holy Spirit in the life of Christians?*

New Heart, New Spirit

Give an example of a "stony heart," for example, lying to avoid being embarrassed. Then describe the "new heart" that replaces it, for example, telling the truth.

Faith Focus

What does the New Testament reveal about the work of the Holy Spirit both in the life of Jesus and in the early Church?

Faith Vocabulary

charisms. Graces, or gifts, given by the Holy Spirit to build up the Church on earth for the good of all people and the needs of the world.

Jesus in the Synagogue, James Tissot (1836–1902), French painter

The Holy Spirit in the Work of Jesus

The Holy Spirit was active in Jesus' life on earth, from its beginning to its end. At the very beginning of his public ministry, Jesus announced and described his work. Luke's Gospel tells us:

> He came to Nazareth. . . .
> He stood up to read
> and was handed a scroll
> of the prophet Isaiah.
> He unrolled the scroll
> and found the passage
> where it was written:
> "The Spirit of the Lord
>   is upon me,
>   because he has
>   anointed me to
>   bring glad tidings
>   to the poor.
> He has sent me to
>   proclaim liberty
>   to captives
> and recovery of
>   sight to the blind,
>   to let the oppressed
>   go free,
> and to proclaim a year
>   acceptable to the
>   Lord."   LUKE 4:16–19

Nazareth, the "Church-Synagogue," traditional site of where Jesus preached on the Sabbath

112

The Holy Spirit in the Church

After receiving the Holy Spirit on Pentecost, Saint Peter courageously preached about Jesus. Moved by the Holy Spirit, more than three thousand people asked to be baptized that day.

The Church is the Temple of the Holy Spirit. The Holy Spirit blesses each of us with **charisms,** or special graces, that we are to use to help build up the Church on earth. Saint Paul wrote:

There are different kinds of spiritual gifts but the same Spirit; there are different forms of service but the same Lord; there are different workings but the same God who produces all of them in everyone.

1 CORINTHIANS 12:4–6

What does Saint Paul's teaching tell us about the work of the Holy Spirit in the Church?

Descent of Holy Spirit, stained glass

Different Gifts, the Same Spirit

Choose one of your talents, or charisms. Describe one way you can use that charism to help others.

_____

_____

_____

_____

_____

_____

113

Faith Vocabulary

Sacred Tradition. The passing on of the teachings of Christ by the Church through the power and guidance of the Holy Spirit.

Bishop Oscar Solis, first Filipino-American bishop in the United States

The Holy Spirit Today

The Holy Spirit lives and is active in the Church today. The Holy Spirit is our teacher and sanctifier.

Teacher

The Holy Spirit guides the Church in understanding and teaching what God has revealed in Jesus Christ. The Holy Spirit guides the pope and the bishops to teach clearly and authentically what God has revealed through Sacred Scripture and **Sacred Tradition**. Sacred Tradition is the passing on of the teachings of Christ by the Church through the power and guidance of the Holy Spirit.

Sanctifier

The Holy Spirit is also our sanctifier. He is the One who makes us holy. Through him we receive sanctifying grace. This is the gift of holiness that makes us sharers in the very life and love of God. We also receive the gift of actual graces. This is the help the Holy Spirit gives us to live holy lives as Jesus taught.

Volunteers preparing Christmas dinner, Camillus House for the homeless, Miami, Florida

Witnesses to the Spirit

The lives that holy women and men have given, and continue to give, witness to the presence and the activity of the Holy Spirit within the Church. He strengthened Saints Agnes, Charles Lwanga, and other martyrs who died for their faith. The Holy Spirit gave comfort to the sick and dying through Saint Martin de Porres and Blessed Mother Teresa of Calcutta.

The Holy Spirit announced and worked for justice through Saint Peter Claver and Saint Katharine Drexel. The Holy Spirit helped people understand what Jesus taught and did through teachers like Saints Elizabeth Ann Seton and John Neumann.

The Holy Spirit makes us one with Christ and one another. The Holy Spirit is, and will continue to be, at work in the Church to help her prepare for the coming of the Kingdom of God. At that time Christ will come again in glory, and his work on earth will be finished.

QUESTION *How do the saints and other holy people help us recognize the work of the Holy Spirit?*

Continuing the Work of Christ

Create a saying for this banner that shows the Holy Spirit is helping the Church continue the work of Christ in the world today.

Our Church Makes a Difference

Saint Katharine Drexel

The Holy Spirit is always at work in the world. He is the same Holy Spirit who was at work in the life of Jesus during his time on earth. From the time of the Apostles, the Holy Spirit has helped the Church continue the work, or mission, Jesus gave to his disciples.

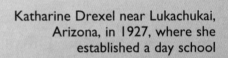

Katharine Drexel near Lukachukai, Arizona, in 1927, where she established a day school

Some Christians leave their homes and families and travel great distances to preach and live the Gospel. Many leave their own country and work with people living in other lands. We call these people missionaries.

Katharine Drexel was a missionary who lived and worked in the United States. She left her home and family to live the Gospel. She used her family inheritance to work with Native Americans and African-Americans in the United States. Today, members of the religious community founded by Saint Katharine Drexel continue the missionary work she began.

 How can you be a missionary?

What Difference Does Faith Make in My Life?

The Holy Spirit gives you gifts, or charisms, to continue the work of Jesus wherever you are.

A magazine has decided to write an article about you. They have learned what you are doing to make your neighborhood a better place. Write the opening paragraph of the article. Include the role the Holy Spirit has played in your helping others.

Local Fifth Grader Is Making a Difference

 My Faith Choice

This week I will use one of the gifts the Holy Spirit has given me to make the world a better place. I will use the gift of

_____

to _____.

Prayer for the Spread of the Gospel

Leader: At Baptism we are joined to Christ. We receive the gift of the Holy Spirit and become members of the Church. All the baptized receive the grace and call to spread the Gospel.

Reader: A reading from the holy Gospel according to Matthew.

All: **Glory to you, O Lord.**

Reader: The eleven disciples went to Galilee, to the mountain to which Jesus had ordered them. When they saw him, they worshiped, but they doubted. Then Jesus approached and said to them, "All power in heaven and on earth has been given to me. Go, therefore, and make disciples of all nations, baptizing them in the name of the Father, and of the Son, and of the holy Spirit, teaching them to observe all that I have commanded you. And behold, I am with you always, until the end of the age." MATTHEW 28:16–20

The Gospel of the Lord.

All: **Praise to you, Lord Jesus Christ.**

Leader: Let us join together and pray that we cooperate with the Holy Spirit and share the Gospel with everyone.

All: **Father, you will your Church to be the sacrament of salvation for all people. Send the Holy Spirit to inspire the hearts of all the baptized to continue the saving work of Christ everywhere. We ask this in the name of your Son, Jesus Christ. Amen.**

We Remember

What I Have Learned

Use words from this chapter to complete the sentences.

1. _____ and _____ are two images for the Holy Spirit.

2. The Holy Spirit blesses us with _____ to continue the work of Christ.

3. The Holy Spirit dwells in the _____ today.

4. The Holy Spirit is the _____, or the One who makes us holy.

5. The Holy Spirit helps the _____ and the _____ to authentically teach what Jesus taught.

Answer the following.

6. Describe the teachings of Isaiah the Prophet and Ezekiel the Prophet about the Holy Spirit.

   _____

   _____

7. Compare the work of the Holy Spirit in the life of Jesus and in the life of the Church.

   _____

   _____

8. Explain how the Holy Spirit helps the Church renew the face of the earth.

   _____

   _____

To Help You Remember

1. The writers of the Old Testament used the images of "mighty wind" and "breath of God" to describe the work of the Holy Spirit.

2. The Holy Spirit was active in Jesus' life on earth and guided the early Church to pass on the teachings of Christ.

3. The Holy Spirit guides the Church in understanding and teaching what God revealed in Jesus and sanctifies the Church, or makes the Church holy.

Growing in Faith

One important thing I learned this week is

_____

_____

_____.

This is important because

_____

_____

_____.

What will people see me doing as I live my faith choice this week?

_____

_____

_____

This Week . . .

In chapter 9, "Different Gifts, the Same Spirit," your child deepened their understanding of and faith in the Holy Spirit. They learned that the images of wind and breath help us understand the work of the Holy Spirit in the Church, which is the Temple of the Holy Spirit. The Holy Spirit was active in the life of Jesus and has been active in the Church since her very beginning. The Holy Spirit is our teacher and guide. He is our sanctifier, the One who makes us holy and gives us the grace to live holy lives.

For more on the teachings of the Catholic Church on the mystery of the Holy Spirit, see *Catechism of the Catholic Church* paragraph numbers 691–693, 797–801, and 1091–1109.

Sharing God's Word

Read together 1 Corinthians 12:4–7. Emphasize that the Holy Spirit gives each of the baptized special graces, or charisms, to help them continue the work of Christ.

Praying

In this chapter your child prayed a prayer for the spread of the Gospel. Read and pray together this prayer on page 118.

Making a Difference

Choose one of the following activities to do as a family or design a similar activity of your own.

• Take turns telling one another what special talents, or gifts, you see in one another. Encourage one another to use your gifts to spread the Gospel.

• Talk about how the Holy Spirit can help us make good decisions and choices. Choose to do one thing this week to live your faith by helping others.

• Find out more about Saint Katharine Drexel or another saint. Talk about how this saint used their gifts to continue the work of Jesus Christ. Look for information about saints in your parish library or visit the *Catholic Encyclopedia* Web site on the Internet.

For more ideas on ways your family can live your faith, visit the "Faith First for Families" page at **www.FaithFirst.com**. Click on "Games" and make learning fun for your child.

Thy Kingdom Come!

We Pray

Happy are those who
   dwell in your house!
   They never cease to
   praise you.   PSALM 84:5

**Our Father,
who art in heaven.
Thy kingdom come.**

                    Amen.

*Why is it so much easier to
do a project when people
work together?*

We all like to work with
other people. The Church
is the People of God. We
work together to continue
the work of Jesus Christ
until the end of time.

*How would you describe the
work that the Church does?*

One Faith, One Lord

Faith Focus

What do we mean when we say the Church is the Body of Christ?

Faith Vocabulary

Church. The Body of Christ; the new People of God called together in Christ by the power of the Holy Spirit.

The Body of Christ

We all need and like to belong to groups. Our family is the most important group to which we belong. The Holy Spirit has invited us to belong to another larger group, the **Church**. The Church is the Body of Christ. It is the new People of God who God the Father has called together through Jesus Christ by the power of the Holy Spirit.

Saint Paul the Apostle used the image of a human body to help us understand what it means to belong to the Church. He wrote:

> As a body is one though it has many parts, and all the parts of the body, though many, are one body, so also Christ. For in one Spirit we were all baptized into one body . . . and we were all given to drink of one Spirit. . . .
>
> Now you are Christ's body, and individually parts of it.
>
> 1 CORINTHIANS 12:12–13, 27

Christ is the Head of his Body, the Church. All the faithful are its members. Each of us has a different role or responsibility in the Church. Let us look at some of the different roles and responsibilities of members of the Body of Christ.

122

Laity, or Lay Faithful

Almost all of the baptized are members of the laity. We all have the responsibility to work together to serve the world as Jesus did.

Ordained Ministers

The Holy Spirit calls some members of the Body of Christ to serve the whole Church as bishops, priests, and deacons. They form the clergy. The pope is the bishop of Rome. He is the pastor of the whole Church on earth.

Religious Communities

Some of the laity and ordained consecrate their lives to God in a special way. They live as members of religious communities. They support one another in living their Baptism and serve the Church in many ways.

 How does the image of the Body of Christ help you understand the Church?

Working Together as the Body of Christ

Interview a member of the laity, a member of a religious community, a priest, or a deacon. Ask the person What does it mean to be a member of the Church? Write a summary of his or her response in this space.

Faith Focus

How do the Marks of the Church help us understand the Church?

Faith Vocabulary

Marks of the Church. One, holy, catholic, apostolic; the four signs, or essential qualities, of the Church founded by Jesus.

The Marks of the Church

The Church, the Body of Christ, has four essential characteristics that identify her as the Church founded by Jesus. We call these the **Marks of the Church.** We profess and name these characteristics in the Nicene Creed. They are one, holy, catholic, and apostolic.

One

The Church is one. We believe in one faith and one Lord. The New Testament teaches:

> [There is] one Spirit . . . one Lord, one faith, one baptism; one God and Father of all, who is over all. EPHESIANS 4:4–6

Holy

Our sharing in the life of the Holy Trinity is the source of the Church's holiness. Saint Timothy, who was a companion of Saint Paul's, wrote "[God] saved us and called us to a holy life" (2 Timothy 1:9).

Catholic

The Risen Christ gave the Apostles the work to "make disciples of all nations" (Matthew 28:19). The word *catholic* means "universal." The Church invites all people to be baptized and to follow and live by the teachings of Jesus Christ.

Pope Benedict XVI, greeting crowd on day of his election as 265th pope

Apostolic

The Church traces her faith back to the Apostles. In the New Testament we read:

[You are the] holy ones and members of the household of God, built upon the foundation of the apostles and prophets, with Christ Jesus himself as the capstone. EPHESIANS 2:19–20

The pope, the bishop of Rome, is the successor of Saint Peter, and the other bishops are the successors of the other Apostles. They share in the responsibilities Jesus gave to the Apostles to teach in his name and make disciples of all nations.

True members of the Church share the faith of the Church and believe what she teaches. They pray together and celebrate the sacraments together with Christ and the Holy Spirit. They serve others by sharing Jesus' healing, forgiveness, and hope with all people.

 What do the Marks of the Church tell us about the Church?

Belonging to the Church

Design a bookmark that illustrates and describes one of the Marks of the Church.

125

Faith Vocabulary

Kingdom of God. All people and creation living in communion with God at the end of time when the work of Christ will be completed, and he will come again in glory.

Communion of Saints. All the faithful followers of Jesus, both the living and the dead, those on earth, in purgatory, and in heaven.

Eternal Life

Kingdom of God

Jesus began his public ministry by announcing:

> "This is the time of fulfillment. The kingdom of God is at hand. Repent, and believe in the gospel."   MARK 1:15

As members of the Body of Christ, we are called to proclaim the Gospel and serve others in the world as Jesus did. We are called to continue the work of Christ and prepare the way for the coming of the **Kingdom of God.**

Jesus taught that the Kingdom of God, or Kingdom of Heaven, is a place of eternal happiness. It will fully come about at the end of time, and there will be "new heavens and a new earth" (2 Peter 3:13).

Jesus has promised that all who love God and follow his commandments will live forever in the Kingdom of Heaven. God wants our happiness—today and always. This is God's desire for all people. God does not want anyone separated from his love.

Life After Death

At the moment of death, our lives will be individually judged by God. Life after death includes heaven, purgatory, and hell.

Heaven. All those who have been faithful to God will live with God the Father, Jesus, and the Holy Spirit in happiness forever.

Purgatory. Some people are not ready to receive the gift of eternal happiness at the moment of their death. God will give them the opportunity to grow in their love for him to prepare them for heaven. This opportunity is called purgatory.

Hell. When people sin seriously and do not ask God for forgiveness, they choose to stay separated from him now and forever. We call this separation from God hell.

At the end of time at the Last Judgment, all who have been faithful to God will be called forth to live in heaven. All the faithful believers in Christ, both the living and the dead, form the **Communion of Saints**. The Communion of Saints includes all those who are faithful to God—those in heaven, those in purgatory, and those living on earth.

 What is the difference between heaven, purgatory, and hell?

Thy Kingdom Come

Write or draw an example of one way we can help prepare the way for the coming of the Kingdom of God.

Our Church Makes a Difference

Devotion to Mary

Christians have always honored the saints. Mary is the greatest saint. We honor Mary, the mother of Jesus, above all the other saints. God has brought Mary, with her body and soul, to heaven, where she lives in the glory of her Son. We call this the Assumption of Mary.

Mary, whom we honor as Queen of Heaven, reminds us that at the end of time we too shall live forever with a new body, a resurrected body. The original plan of God for us to live in happiness with him will be restored.

Catholics in the United States honor Mary as the patroness of the United States of America. We honor her under the title of the Immaculate Conception. This professes our faith that Mary was free from original and all personal sin from the very first moment of her conception and that she remained free from all sin throughout her entire life.

Other countries in the Americas also honor Mary, using other titles. In Puerto Rico Mary is honored as Our Lady of Providence; in Costa Rica, as Our Lady of the Angels; in the Dominican Republic, as Our Lady of Altagracia; and in Cuba, as Our Lady of Caridad del Cobre. Mary, Our Lady of Guadalupe, is the patroness of all the Americas.

 How do you and your family honor Mary? How do you show your love for her?

The Basilica of the National Shrine of the Immaculate Conception, Washington, D.C. The patronal church of the United States.

128

What Difference Does Faith Make in My Life?

You are a member of the Church, the Body of Christ. The Holy Spirit helps you use your gifts, as Mary and the saints did, to prepare for the coming of the Kingdom of God.

Think about your talents, or gifts. Then list three of your gifts. Describe how you can use those gifts to work together with other members of the Church to prepare the way for the coming of the Kingdom of God.

Thy Kingdom Come

Gifts _____

_____

_____

How I can use them _____

_____

_____

_____

_____

My Faith Choice

This week I will try to use my gifts to continue the work of Christ. I will

_____

_____.

Thy Kingdom Come

Leader: The Our Father, or Lord's Prayer, is a summary of the Gospel. In the Our Father we pray, "Thy kingdom come." Listen to this Gospel reading about the Kingdom of Heaven and pray the Our Father together.

Reader: A reading from the holy gospel according to Matthew.

All: **Glory to you, O Lord.**

Reader: [Jesus said], "Do not think that I have come to abolish the law or the prophets. I have come not to abolish but to fulfill. Amen, I say to you, until heaven and earth pass away, not the smallest letter or the smallest part of a letter will pass from the law, until all things have taken place. Therefore, whoever breaks one of the least of these commandments and teaches others to do so will be called least in the kingdom of heaven. But whoever obeys and teaches these commandments will be called greatest in the kingdom of heaven." MATTHEW 5: 17–19

The gospel of the Lord.

All: **Praise to you, Lord Jesus Christ.**

Group 1: Our Father, who art in heaven,
Group 2: hallowed be thy name;

Group 1: thy kingdom come;
Group 2: thy will be done on earth as it is in heaven.

Group 1: Give us this day our daily bread;
Group 2: and forgive us our trespasses
as we forgive those who trespass against us;

Group 1: and lead us not into temptation,
Group 2: but deliver us from evil.

All: **For the kingdom, the power and the glory are yours, now and for ever. Amen.**

We Remember

What I Have Learned

1–4. Design four symbols to describe each of the four Marks of the Church.

Answer the following.

5. Describe the Church as the Body of Christ.

_____

_____

6. Compare the work of the lay faithful, the ordained ministry, and the members of religious communities within the Church.

_____

7. Compare heaven, purgatory, and hell.

_____

8. Describe the Communion of Saints.

_____

_____

To Help You Remember

1. The Church, the Body of Christ, is made up of the lay faithful, the ordained, and members of religious communities.

2. The Church that Jesus founded has four essential characteristics, or Marks. They are one, holy, catholic, and apostolic.

3. Jesus promised that all who love God and follow his commandments will live forever in the Kingdom of Heaven.

Growing in Faith

One important thing I learned this week is

_____

_____

_____.

This is important because

_____

_____

_____.

What will people see me doing as I live my faith choice this week?

_____

_____

_____

With My Family

This Week . . .

In chapter 10, "Thy Kingdom Come!" your child learned that all the members of the Church, the one Body of Christ, have different roles and responsibilities to continue the work of Christ. The Holy Spirit is guiding the Church to continue that work until the end of time. At the end of time, there will be "new heavens and a new earth." The Kingdom of God will be established in its fullness, and God's original plan of happiness will be restored in Christ.

For more on the teachings of the Catholic Church on the mystery of the Church, the Communion of Saints, and life everlasting, see *Catechism of the Catholic Church* paragraph numbers 668–679, 787–795, and 811–972.

Sharing God's Word

Read together Saint Paul's teaching on the Church as the Body of Christ in 1 Corinthians 12:12–31. Emphasize that Christ is the Head of his Body, the Church. All of the baptized are its members.

Praying

In this chapter your child prayed the Our Father. Pray the Our Father as a family.

Making a Difference

Choose one of the following activities to do as a family or design a similar activity of your own.

- Pray the Our Father at mealtimes this week. Praise God and ask him for grace to strengthen you to prepare the way for the coming of the kingdom.

- Talk about all the ways your parish continues the work of Christ. If you need ideas, look in the parish bulletin. Decide one way you can work as a family with other members of your parish to continue the work of Christ.

- The Church reaches out to all people. Do something this week to reach out to others.

For more ideas on ways your family can live your faith, visit the "Faith First for Families" page at **www.FaithFirst.com**. Click on "Make a Difference" to discover how your family can continue the work of Christ.

Reduce and Conserve

This reservoir is the main source of water for the nearby town. A severe drought over the past five years has reduced the water level in the reservoir to dangerously low levels.

The situation is even more serious because no water conservation plan has been put into effect. Businesses and homes which rely on the water continue to use the same amounts of water that they used when the reservoir was full.

The drought has affected the ecosystem of the area as well, particularly the fish and animals who live downstream. The community must act responsibly and find ways to reduce water consumption.

We Care for God's Creation

God has given us this world and, with it, the responsibility to preserve its beauty and resources. Sometimes we can take the natural resources around us for granted. When we do, nature is harmed.

Making Connections . . .

It is easy to take for granted God's natural gifts, such as water. Humans and all of creation rely on water to live. Conserving water is one way we can take care of God's creation.

with Language Arts

Look at the pictures on the previous page. Imagine you are the water and write a paragraph describing what you see. In your paragraph give human attributes to the water. This is called personification. Let the water use all five senses when describing what is happening. For example, include descriptions of how water feels and what the water thinks about what is happening to it.

with Creative Arts

Imagine that your family's water supply comes from a well, but the well is not functioning. Make a list of the things that you are unable to do for one day as a result of having no water. Create a rap song that describes ways to conserve water at home. Use the phrase "Drip, Drip, Drip."

with Math and Science

Use "Our Average Daily Water Use" chart and "If We Conserve Water" chart to calculate your average daily water use. Interview household members to estimate gallons used for each activity. Then calculate how much water in gallons you would save per day if you implemented water-conserving strategies. Then help the community in the story on page 133 understand how much water they can save.

⮑ **Faith Action** What is one thing you can do at home to conserve water? How will this help preserve God's creation?

Name _____

A. Best Response

Read each statement and circle the best answer.

1. In whom does God reveal himself most fully?
   a. the prophets
   b. the baptized
   c. Jesus Christ
   d. the Church

2. Where in the Bible do you read about the life, death, and Resurrection of Jesus?
   a. Psalms
   b. Gospels
   c. Proverbs
   d. Torah

3. What is the central belief of the Christian faith?
   a. Annunciation
   b. Our Father
   c. Holy Trinity
   d. Ascension

4. Which one of the following is not an attribute of God?
   a. holy
   b. powerless
   c. truth
   d. almighty

5. What mystery of faith tells us Jesus is true God and true man?
   a. Annunciation
   b. Creation
   c. Holy Trinity
   d. Incarnation

6. What are the most important events of Jesus' life?
   a. the Paschal Mystery
   b. the Last Supper
   c. the Annunciation
   d. Pentecost

7. Which of the following is an image of the Holy Spirit?
   a. cross
   b. Body of Christ
   c. mighty wind
   d. water

8. Who are not ordained ministers of the Church?
   a. bishops
   b. deacons
   c. priests
   d. lectors

9. What are the four Marks of the Church?
   a. one, holy, joyful, catholic
   b. holy, faithful, catholic, apostolic
   c. one, holy, catholic, apostolic
   d. one, holy, diverse, catholic

10. What is Mary's relationship to the Church?
    a. Mother of God
    b. Mother of the Church
    c. Mother of Jesus
    d. all of the above

B. Matching Words and Phrases

1. Use the terms in the word bank to finish these sentences from the Nicene Creed.

> **Father   Son   Holy Spirit   Lord   creator**

   a. I believe in one God, the _____ almighty, maker of heaven and earth, of all things visible and invisible.

   b. I believe in one _____ Jesus Christ, the Only Begotten _____ of God.

   c. I believe in the _____, the Lord, the giver of life.

2. Match the faith terms in column A with their descriptions in column B.

Column A

_____ 1. miracles

_____ 2. Evangelists

_____ 3. Sacred Tradition

_____ 4. Church

_____ 5. charisms

Column B

a. teachings of Christ passed on by the Church

b. graces given by the Holy Spirit to build up the Church on earth

c. the new People of God, the Body of Christ

d. actions that go beyond the laws of nature

e. the writers of the four Gospels

C. What I Have Learned

1. Write three things you learned in this unit. Share them with the group.

   _____

   _____

   _____

2. Look at the list of faith terms in "Words to Know" on page 12. Circle the terms you know now.

D. From a Scripture Story

The story of Jesus calming the storm at sea invites us to believe and trust in him. Write two more ideas that you learned from this Gospel story.

   _____

   _____

Unit 2 • We Worship

What works of the Church do these pictures show?

What I Have Learned

What is something you already know about these three faith terms?

Eucharist

_____

_____

Sacraments of Healing

_____

_____

Christian vocation

_____

_____

Words to Know

Put an X next to the faith terms you know. Put a ? next to the faith terms you need to know more about.

Faith Vocabulary

_____ liturgy

_____ Baptism

_____ Confirmation

_____ Pentecost

_____ Eucharist

_____ sacrifice

_____ breaking of bread

_____ epistle

_____ Reconciliation

_____ Anointing of the Sick

Questions I Have

What questions would you like to ask about the Eucharist?

_____

_____

_____

_____

A Scripture Story

Christians reading a letter
from Saint Paul the Apostle

Why did Saint Paul write letters to the Christians to whom he had preached the Gospel?

Celebrating the Liturgy

11

We Pray

We thank you, God,
  we give thanks;
  we call upon your name,
  declare your
    wonderful deeds.

PSALM 75:2

Father,
all-powerful and
ever-living God, we
give you thanks always
and everywhere
through Jesus Christ,
our Lord.   Amen.

How do you show your thanks to people?

Gracias. Asante. Cám ón. All these words mean "thank you." The Church, the People of God, gathers at Mass to thank God.

What are some of the ways you thank God at Mass?

We Worship God

Faith Vocabulary

liturgy. The work of the Church, the People of God, of worshiping him through which Christ continues the work of Redemption in, with, and through his Church.

The Liturgy

God is the source of all our blessings. The Church gathers to worship God. The work of the Church, the new People of God, is to worship God. We gather to pray, honor, thank, and give glory to God for all he has done and continues to do for us.

When the Church comes together to worship God, we celebrate the **liturgy**. The word *liturgy* means "work of the people." The liturgy of the Church includes the celebration of the seven sacraments and the Liturgy of the Hours. The center of the liturgy of the Church is the Eucharist.

The sacraments are the seven main liturgical signs of the Church that have been given to us by Christ. They make Christ's saving work present and make us sharers in the life of God, the Holy Trinity. The Liturgy of the Hours is the official daily prayer of the Church.

140

The Work of the Whole Church

The liturgy of the Church is the work of the whole Church. It is the work of Christ, the Head of the Church, and of all the members of the Body of Christ.

When the Church celebrates the liturgy, we join with Jesus Christ, and through the power of the Holy Spirit we remember and share in the Paschal Mystery. Each time we celebrate the liturgy, we are made sharers in Christ's Passion, death, Resurrection, and Ascension. We share more fully in the new life that Jesus gained for us.

- We are changed.
- We become more like Jesus.
- We find strength to live as Jesus wants us to live.
- We bring Jesus' life and love to the world.

The Holy Trinity is present with the Church when we celebrate the liturgy. We worship one God in three divine Persons. We pray to the Father, through the Son, and in the Holy Spirit.

 What do we celebrate in the liturgy?

Signs of Jesus' Life and Love

Illustrate with words or pictures one way you try to bring Jesus' life and love to the world.

Faith Vocabulary

liturgical year. The Church's yearly cycle of seasons and feasts that celebrate the mysteries of Jesus' birth, life, death, and Resurrection.

The Liturgical Year

Throughout the ages people have set aside time to worship God. They have set aside time to remember all that God has done for them. They set aside time to praise, honor, and thank God. The Church does the same.

The Church celebrates the liturgy every day and all year long. This yearly cycle of the Church's celebration of the liturgy is called the **liturgical year**. The liturgical year of the Church is the cycle of seasons and feasts that make up the Church's year of worship. All year long, each and every day, we hear and take part in God's great plan of saving love for us.

The liturgical year is a "year of the Lord's grace." It is the celebration of the mysteries of the birth, life, suffering and death, Resurrection, and Ascension of Jesus Christ. It includes the weekly celebration of Sunday (the Lord's Day), the yearly cycle of the seasons of the Church's year, and the feasts of the Lord and of Mary and the other saints.

QUESTION Why is the liturgical year a year of grace?

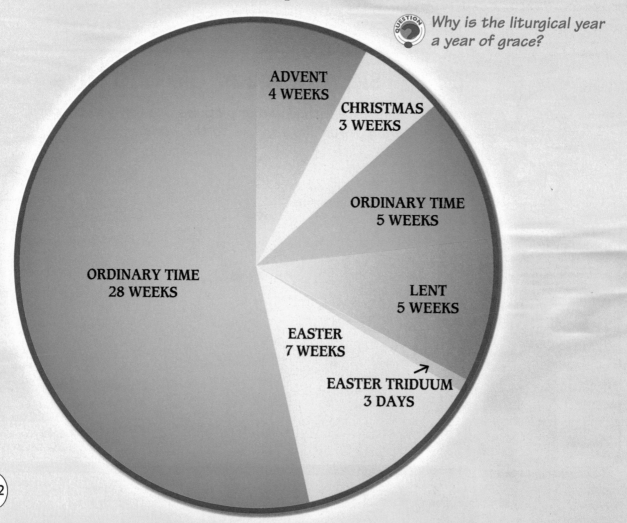

ADVENT
4 WEEKS

CHRISTMAS
3 WEEKS

ORDINARY TIME
5 WEEKS

ORDINARY TIME
28 WEEKS

LENT
5 WEEKS

EASTER
7 WEEKS

EASTER TRIDUUM
3 DAYS

The Year of the Lord's Grace

Advent. During Advent the Church celebrates God's coming among us. We get ready to remember Jesus' birth on Christmas Day. We remember Jesus' promise to come again in glory at the end of time.

Christmas. We remember and celebrate that the Son of God, Jesus the Savior, came and lived among us.

Lent. With the help of the Holy Spirit we strive to grow in our life in Christ. We support those preparing to be baptized at Easter. We prepare to renew our own baptismal promises.

Triduum. This three-day celebration of Holy Thursday, Good Friday, and Easter Vigil/Easter Sunday is the heart and center of the liturgical year.

Easter. For fifty days we joyfully reflect on the Resurrection and our new life in Christ. On the fiftieth day of the celebration, we celebrate the solemnity of Pentecost.

Ordinary Time. The other weeks of the year are called Ordinary Time. We listen to what Jesus said and did and learn ways to live our lives as his followers.

Celebrating the Liturgical Year

Write ways you can take an active part in your parish's celebration of the seasons of the Church's liturgical year.

_____

_____

_____

_____

_____

Faith Vocabulary

sacraments. The
seven main liturgical
signs of the Church,
given to the Church
by Jesus Christ,
that make his saving
work present and
make us sharers in
the life of God, the
Holy Trinity.

The Seven Sacraments

Throughout the liturgical year we continually hear and are made sharers in God's love. We do this in a unique way when we celebrate the seven **sacraments**.

Before Jesus returned to his Father, he promised:

"I am with you always, until the end of the age."
MATTHEW 28:20

Jesus is especially present with his Church when we celebrate the sacraments. The seven sacraments are Baptism, Confirmation, Eucharist, Reconciliation (Penance), Anointing of the Sick, Holy Orders, and Matrimony.

Jesus gave the Church the sacraments. The sacraments are signs of God's work among us. They put us in contact with the saving work of Jesus Christ. He touches our lives through the sacraments, and we are changed.

The sacraments are the seven main celebrations of the liturgy. They are grouped together into the Sacraments of Christian Initiation, Sacraments of Healing, and Sacraments at the Service of Communion.

Baptism

Confirmation

Eucharist

Holy Orders

Anointing of the Sick

Penance and Reconciliation

Matrimony

Sacraments of Christian Initiation

Baptism, Confirmation, and Eucharist are the Sacraments of Christian Initiation. Through these three sacraments we are joined to Christ and become full members of the Church. We are made sharers in God's life and receive his grace to live as children of God.

Sacraments of Healing

Penance and Reconciliation, or Reconciliation, and Anointing of the Sick are the Sacraments of Healing. Through these sacraments we celebrate and share in God's healing love.

Sacraments at the Service of Communion

Holy Orders and Matrimony are the Sacraments at the Service of Communion. Through these sacraments some members of the Church are consecrated to serve the whole Body of Christ, the Church. The word *consecrated* means "set aside for a holy purpose."

All the sacraments build up the Body of Christ. They make us sharers in God's life and love. They give us the grace to live as children of God. We are changed more completely into the image of Christ. Our life with the Holy Trinity is strengthened.

 What is a sacrament?

Our Catholic Identity

Liturgical Colors

The Church uses different colors to celebrate the liturgical year. Purple or violet is used for Advent and Lent. White is used for Holy Thursday and for the Christmas and Easter seasons. Red is used on Palm Sunday of the Lord's Passion, Good Friday, and Pentecost. Green is used during Ordinary Time.

Understanding the Sacraments

For each letter in the word SACRAMENT write a word or phrase that has that letter in it. Choose words that tell about the sacraments. Share your words and phrases with a partner and your family.

S _____
A _____
C _____
R _____
A _____
M _____
E _____
N _____
T _____

Feasts of the Lord

The Church proclaims the wonderful works of God among us when we celebrate the liturgy. In addition to the cycle of the seasons of the Church's year and the feasts of the Lord connected with those seasons, the Church celebrates other feasts of the Lord. The feast of the Sacred Heart of Jesus and the feast of the Triumph of the Cross are two of those feasts. The Sacred Heart of Jesus and the cross are both symbols of the love of Jesus.

Jesus commanded that his followers are to love and serve one another as he serves and loves us. The celebration of the liturgy is always a proclamation to the world of the saving love and work of Christ and a call to a life of loving service. Celebrating these feasts deepens our faith in the mystery of Christ's sacrificial love for us. It strengthens us to live out that love in our service of God and others.

 How do you see the people of your parish living as signs of God's love?

Sacred Heart of Jesus, stained glass

What Difference Does Faith Make in My Life?

You join with Christ and other members of the Church throughout the year to celebrate the liturgy. Each season of the Church's liturgical year helps you grow in and live your faith.

Choose a liturgical season. Create and design this banner to help you celebrate it. Include a message about living the season. Be sure to use the liturgical color for that season.

Celebrating Our Faith

My Faith Choice

This week I will worship God in all I do and say. I will

_____

_____.

Lift Up Your Heart

Leader: The liturgy is the Church's work of worshiping God. As the Body of Christ, the Church, we give thanks, praise, honor, and glory to God.

Let us join together and and pray this prayer of blessing and adoration.

All: **Hosanna in the highest.**

Group 1: Holy, Holy, Holy Lord God of hosts.

Group 2: Heaven and earth are full of your glory.

All: **Hosanna in the highest.**

Group 1: Blessed is he who comes in the name of the Lord.

Group 2: Blessed is he who comes in the name of the Lord.

All: **Hosanna in the highest.**

BASED ON PREFACE ACCLAMATION

We Remember

What I Have Learned

Match the faith terms in column A with the descriptions in column B.

Column A

___ 1. sacraments

___ 2. Paschal Mystery

___ 3. Easter

___ 4. liturgical year

___ 5. liturgy

Column B

a. Jesus' Passion, death, Resurrection, and glorious Ascension

b. the cycle of seasons and feasts that celebrates God's great plan of saving love

c. work of the People of God

d. seven liturgical celebrations of the Church given to us by Christ

e. a season of the Church during which we rejoice in Christ's Resurrection

Answer the following.

6. Describe the Church's year of grace.

_____

_____

7. Describe the liturgy as the work of the whole Church.

_____

_____

8. Name and describe the three categories into which the sacraments are grouped.

_____

_____

To Help You Remember

1. The liturgy is the Church's work of worshiping God.

2. The liturgical year is the Church's cycle of worship that celebrates God's great plan of saving love for us.

3. The sacraments make the saving work of Jesus Christ present to us and make us sharers in the life of God, the Holy Trinity.

Growing in Faith

One important thing I learned this week is

_____

_____

_____.

This is important because

_____

_____

_____.

What will people see me doing as I live my faith choice this week?

_____

_____

_____

This Week . . .

In chapter 11, "Celebrating the Liturgy," your child learned about the liturgy, the Church's work of worshiping God. The liturgy includes the celebration of the seven sacraments. The sacraments are the signs of God's work among us that Jesus gave us. Jesus touches our lives through the sacraments, and we are changed. Like the calendar year, the Church's liturgical year of worship is made up of a cycle of seasons and feast days. The seasons of the Church's year are Advent, Christmas, Lent, Easter, and Ordinary Time. The Easter Triduum, or three days, of Holy Thursday, Good Friday, and the Easter Vigil/Easter Sunday is the heart of the liturgical year.

For more on the teachings of the Catholic Church on the liturgy and the sacraments in general, see *Catechism of the Catholic Church* paragraph numbers 1135–1186.

Sharing God's Word

Read together Psalm 75:2. Emphasize that our whole life should give honor, glory, and praise to God.

Praying

In this chapter your child learned a prayer of praise and honor to God. Read and pray together this prayer on page 148.

Making a Difference

Choose one of the following activities to do as a family or design a similar activity of your own.

• Invite each family member to name the liturgical seasons they like best. Talk about how this season helps them give honor, glory, and praise to God.

• Decorate your home according to the current liturgical season. Allow the decorations to help you remember that God is always with you.

• When your family takes part in the celebration of Mass this week, pay close attention to the liturgical colors and decorations. Talk about how the liturgical season that the Church is celebrating helps you remember and share in God's great plan of saving love for the world.

For more ideas on ways your family can live your faith, visit the "Faith First for Families" page at **www.FaithFirst.com**. Click on "Games" to review the seven sacraments with your child.

Baptism and Confirmation

12

We Pray

O God our savior, . . .
You visit the earth and
water it,
make it abundantly
fertile.   PSALM 65:6, 10

**Father, in Baptism
we use your gift of
water, and you give us
the grace of new life
in Christ.   Amen.**

*What would your life be
like without water?*

Water is essential for life.
Imagine a day without
water. The Church uses
water to celebrate Baptism,
the sacrament of new life
in Christ.

*Why is water the best symbol
for Baptism?*

Becoming Followers of Christ

Faith Vocabulary

Baptism. The Sacrament of Christian Initiation in which we are first joined to Jesus Christ, become members of the Church, are reborn as God's adopted children, receive the gift of the Holy Spirit, and original sin and our personal sins are forgiven.

chrism. One of the three oils blessed by the Church to use in the celebration of the liturgy.

The Sacrament of Baptism

Imagine a day without water. Imagine planet Earth without water. Without water life as we know it—plants and flowers, animals and fish, and people—would die! Water is so vital to life that the Church uses water to celebrate the Sacrament of **Baptism**.

Baptism is one of the three Sacraments of Christian Initiation, which are Baptism, Confirmation, and Eucharist. Jesus told Nicodemus:

"Amen, amen, I say to you, no one can see the kingdom of God without being born from above."

JOHN 3:3

Through Baptism we are reborn of water and the Holy Spirit. Baptism is the first sacrament we receive.

Celebrating Baptism

Each part of the rite of Baptism shows that the people who are being baptized are receiving the gift of new life from God. The words, actions, and objects used in the celebration of Baptism and the other sacraments point to what is happening. All the parts of the rite of Baptism point to the deeper meaning of what we are seeing and hearing.

Here is a summary of the rite of Baptism.

The Rite of Baptism

Blessing of the water. After the celebration of the Liturgy of the Word, the celebrant of Baptism, who is usually a priest or deacon, greets everyone at the baptismal font or baptismal pool. He says, "My dear brothers and sisters, God uses the sacrament of water to give his divine life to those who believe in him." Blessing the water, he retells the story of salvation.

Renunciation of sin and profession of faith. All present join with those to be baptized and reject sin. All promise to live as God's children. All profess faith in God, the Holy Trinity.

Baptism in water. The person to be baptized now enters, or is immersed in, the water or has water poured on his or her head three times, as the celebrant says the words, "(Name), I baptize you in the name of the Father, and of the Son, and of the Holy Spirit."

Anointing with chrism. The celebrant anoints the top of the head of each of the newly baptized with the holy oil of **chrism**. This shows that the Holy Spirit is with the baptized to strengthen them to live as members of the Body of Christ, the Church.

White garment and lighted candle. The newly baptized receive a white garment and a candle lighted from the Easter candle. Clothed in Christ, the baptized are to keep the flame of faith alive in their heart.

 QUESTION

What do the parts of the rite of Baptism tell us about Baptism?

The Flame of Faith

Decorate this candle with a message about Baptism.

Faith Vocabulary

sanctifying grace. The gift of God's life and love that makes us holy and helps us live holy lives.

Effects of Baptism

Many of us were baptized when we were infants. Our parents brought us to the Church. They wanted us to receive the gift of new life promised by Jesus. They wanted us to share the faith of the Catholic Church and become members of the Body of Christ.

We call what happens in the celebration of the sacraments the effects, or sacramental graces, of the sacrament. Baptism, like each of the other sacraments, has special graces. These are the effects of the Sacrament of Baptism.

Children of the Father

In the Gospel of John, Jesus tells Nicodemus that he needs to be reborn of water and the Spirit. We are reborn to new life in Baptism. Through Baptism we receive new life in Jesus Christ, the Son of God. Joined to Christ forever in Baptism, we are reborn as adopted children of God the Father. Saint John reminds us:

> See what love the Father has bestowed on us that we may be called the children of God. Yet so we are.   1 JOHN 3:1

Members of the Church, the Body of Christ

Through Baptism we become members of the Body of Christ. We become members of the new People of God of the New Covenant. We become part of a larger family of faith, the Church. Saint Paul the Apostle reminds us:

> [I]n one Spirit we were all baptized into one body.
> 1 CORINTHIANS 12:13

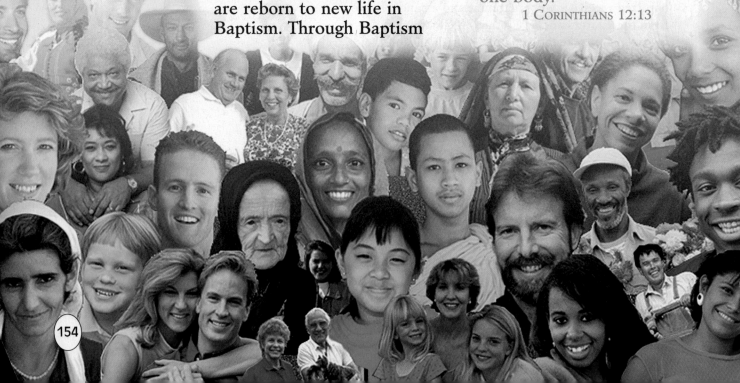

154

Temples of the Holy Spirit

Through Baptism we first receive the gift of the Holy Spirit. The Holy Spirit lives within the Church and within each of us. Listen to the words of Saint Paul the Apostle:

Do you not know that you are the temple of God, and that the Spirit of God dwells in you?

1 CORINTHIANS 3:16

We are temples of the Holy Spirit. Throughout our life he invites and helps us live as children of God and followers of Jesus Christ.

Forgiveness of Sin

Baptism frees us from original sin and all the personal sins that we may have committed. Everything that separates us from God is washed away. We receive the gift of **sanctifying grace**. We are made sharers in the life of God, the Holy Trinity. Sanctifying grace is the gift of God's life and love that makes us holy and helps us live holy lives.

 What happens to a person at Baptism?

LIVING MY BAPTISM

Write one thing you might do to live your Baptism.

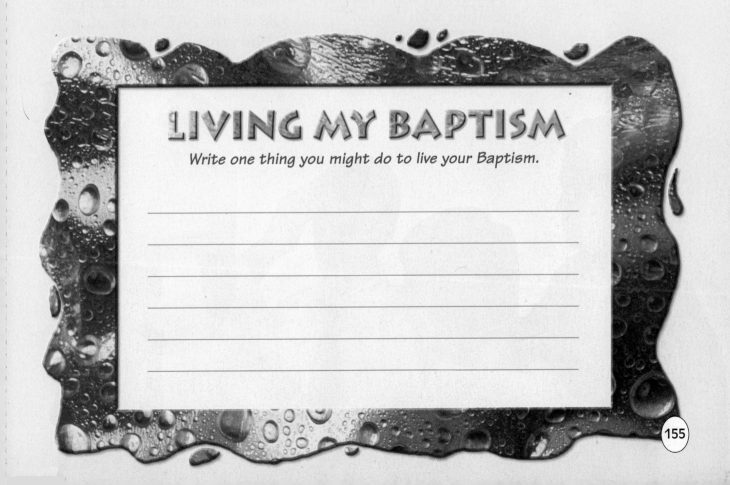

Faith Vocabulary

Confirmation. The
Sacrament of
Christian Initiation
that strengthens
the graces of
Baptism and in which
our new life in Christ
is sealed by the gift
of the Holy Spirit.

The Sacrament of Confirmation

We also celebrate the Sacrament of **Confirmation** as part of our being joined with Christ and becoming a member of the Church. Confirmation seals, or completes, our Baptism. It is the Sacrament of Christian Initiation that strengthens the graces of Baptism. In Confirmation our new life in Christ is sealed by the gift of the Holy Spirit.

The Sacrament of Confirmation is also called *chrismation*, a word meaning "anointing with chrism." Jesus is the Anointed One of God, who was "filled with the holy Spirit" (Luke 4:1).

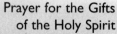

Prayer for the Gifts
of the Holy Spirit

Celebrating Confirmation

The bishop is the usual minister of Confirmation. Sometimes the bishop names a priest to celebrate Confirmation. This usually happens when people are confirmed at the Easter Vigil in their parish church. Each part of the rite of Confirmation shows that the Holy Spirit strengthens our Baptism.

Anointing
with chrism

Here is a summary of the rite of Confirmation.

The Rite of Confirmation

Laying on of hands. The bishop holds out his hands and extends them over the candidates for Confirmation. He prays, asking God, the Father of our Lord Jesus Christ, to pour out the Holy Spirit upon the candidates to be their Helper and Guide.

Anointing with chrism. One by one the candidates go with their sponsors to the bishop. The sponsor places his or her right hand on the shoulder of the candidate and presents the candidate by name to the bishop. The bishop places his right hand on top of the head of the candidate and makes a sign of the cross on the candidate's forehead with chrism. As he does this, he prays, "(Name), be sealed with the Gift of the Holy Spirit." Anointing is a sign that God is calling the confirmed and giving them the grace to serve his people.

The newly confirmed says he or she believes what is happening by responding, "Amen." The bishop then says, "Peace be with you." The newly confirmed responds, "And with your spirit."

 What is the connection between Baptism and Confirmation?

Our Catholic Identity

Sacramental Character

Baptism and Confirmation can be received only one time. Each of these sacraments marks us in a specific way as belonging to Christ forever. This spiritual mark is indelible and permanent.

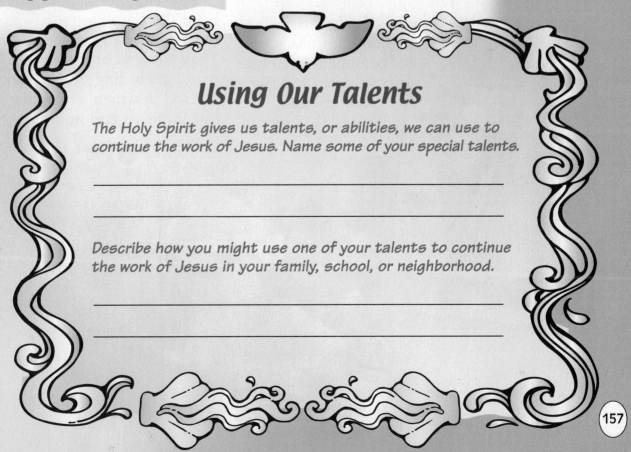

Using Our Talents

The Holy Spirit gives us talents, or abilities, we can use to continue the work of Jesus. Name some of your special talents.

_____

_____

Describe how you might use one of your talents to continue the work of Jesus in your family, school, or neighborhood.

_____

_____

Our Church Makes a Difference

Lights of Faith

Some Christians are called to live their Baptism and Confirmation as members of a religious order or religious congregation. These communities are groups of men or women who consecrate their lives to the service of the Gospel of Jesus Christ. They are lights of faith in the world.

Religious communities commit themselves to prayer and the Corporal and Spiritual Works of Mercy. They strive to live the gifts of the Holy Spirit. Some religious communities, such as the Trappists and Poor Clares, devote themselves to a life of prayer. Other communities, such as the Dominicans and Jesuits, combine their life of prayer with a life of serving others. Other religious communities serve people who are poor, sick, or homeless.

Some work with people in prisons and with those suffering from injustice. Others help with the Church's work of education. Other religious communities serve God and people as missionaries.

All religious communities keep the flame of faith burning brightly in the world. They work to bring about a world according to the plan of God in which all people live in peace and justice.

QUESTION *How do members of religious communities live as lights of faith for the world?*

What Difference Does Faith Make in My Life?

The Holy Spirit lives within you and gives you the grace to live the Gospel and be a light of faith in the world.

Illustrate a scene that shows what fifth graders might do to live the Gospel.

My Faith Choice

This week I will try to live my Baptism. I will be a light of faith in the world by

_____

_____.

Prayer for the Gifts of the Holy Spirit

Leader: We have been anointed and sealed with the gift of the Holy Spirit. The Holy Spirit lives within the Church and within each member of the Church. He is always teaching us and strengthening us to live the Gospel.

Let us listen to a reading from the book of the prophet Isaiah.

Reader: A reading from the book of Isaiah:
The spirit of the LORD shall rest upon him:
  a spirit of wisdom and of understanding,
A spirit of counsel and of strength,
  a spirit of knowledge and of fear of the LORD,
  and his delight shall be fear of the LORD.

ISAIAH 11:2

The word of the Lord.

All: **Thanks be to God.**

Leader: Let us pray to the Holy Spirit to guide us
to live as faithful followers of Jesus Christ.
God, Father of our Lord Jesus Christ,
send us the gift of the Holy Spirit.
Send us the spirit of wisdom and understanding.

All: **May your Holy Spirit continue to work
in the world through all who believe.**

Leader: Send us the spirit of right judgment and counsel.

All: **May your Holy Spirit continue to work
in the world through all who believe.**

Leader: Send us the spirit of knowledge and reverence.

All: **May your Holy Spirit continue to work
in the world through all who believe.**

Leader: Send us the spirit of wonder and awe.

All: **May your Holy Spirit continue to work
in the world through all who believe.**

What I Have Learned

1. Circle the sacrament words hidden in the puzzle. Describe what each word tells about becoming a follower of Jesus Christ.

```
E R T Y Y A N O I N T I N G H K E
W M Q F B B A P T I S M Q E R V I
X N C O N F I R M A T I O N Q L S
N H J O P S K A W A T E R D F S Z
```

Answer the following.

2. Describe what the use of water in Baptism tells us about what happens in Baptism.

_____

_____

3. Describe what the actions of laying on of hands and anointing tell us about what happens in Confirmation.

_____

_____

4. What does it mean to be reborn of water and the Holy Spirit?

_____

_____

To Help You Remember

1. In Baptism we are reborn of water and the Holy Spirit.

2. In Baptism we are joined to Christ, and original sin and our personal sins are forgiven. We are reborn as God's children. We receive the gift of the Holy Spirit and become members of the Church.

3. In Confirmation we are sealed with the gift of the Holy Spirit, and the graces of Baptism are strengthened.

Growing in Faith

One important thing I learned this week is

_____

_____

_____.

This is important because

_____

_____

_____.

What will people see me doing as I live my faith choice this week?

_____

_____

This Week . . .

In chapter 12, "Baptism and Confirmation," your child learned more about the celebration and effects of Baptism and Confirmation. Baptism brings us into new life in Christ and makes us members of the Body of Christ, the Church. Through Baptism we receive the gift of the Holy Spirit. By God's gift, through water and the Holy Spirit, original sin and everything that separates us from God is washed away. Confirmation confirms, or seals, our Baptism. The Holy Spirit strengthens us with his sevenfold gifts to live the Gospel and proclaim Jesus Christ to others.

For more on the teachings of the Catholic Church on the Sacraments of Baptism and Confirmation, see *Catechism of the Catholic Church* paragraph numbers 1210–1274 and 1285–1314.

Sharing God's Word

Read together Luke 4:16–22. Emphasize that through Baptism we first receive the gift of the Holy Spirit and in Confirmation we are sealed with the gift of the Holy Spirit.

Praying

In this chapter your child prayed for the Gifts of the Holy Spirit. Read and pray together this prayer on page 160.

Making a Difference

Choose one of the following activities to do as a family or design a similar activity of your own.

- When your family participates in Mass this week, go to the ambry after Mass. The ambry is the place where the chrism and other sacred oils used in the celebration of the liturgy are kept. Recall that we are anointed with chrism at Baptism and Confirmation.

- Look at your family photo albums and find Baptism pictures. Share stories about each person's Baptism. Talk about who was there and why Baptism is an important event in the life of your family.

- Talk about all the ways your family lives Baptism.

For more ideas on ways your family can live your faith, visit the "Faith First for Families" page at **www.FaithFirst.com**. Click on "Contemporary Issues" this week to find an article on an especially interesting topic.

Pentecost
A Scripture Story

13

We Pray

Give thanks to the LORD,
  invoke his name;
  make known among
  the peoples his
  deeds!   PSALM 105:1

God our Father,
may the work of the
Holy Spirit continue
through all who
believe in Jesus Christ,
your only Son.   Amen.

*Why is it important for
countries or groups to
celebrate their beginnings?*

On the Fourth of July, you
can feel the spirit of the
United States as the birth
of the nation is celebrated.
Each year on Pentecost
Sunday, the Church
celebrates the beginning
of her work.

*What does the Church
remember on Pentecost?*

Pentecost, stained glass   163

Bible Background

Faith Focus

What did the Jewish people of Jesus' time celebrate on Pentecost?

Faith Vocabulary

Pentecost. The feast and holy day on which the Church celebrates the coming of the Holy Spirit on the disciples.

The Festival of Weeks

People of every religion celebrate holy days. They remember and celebrate the important days of their history. The Jewish people of Jesus' time celebrated holy days too. One of these celebrations was the Festival of Weeks. For seven weeks, or forty-nine days, from the time of Passover, the Jewish people prepared for the celebration of the Festival of Weeks.

This festival is also known as the Festival of the First Fruits and **Pentecost**. The word *pentecost* means fiftieth." It was called Pentecost because on the fiftieth day after Passover, the festivity and celebration began.

Raising of Torah Scrolls during Shavout prayers

Festival of Weeks (Shavout) Prayer, Mount Gerizim, Samaria

During the festival, barley, wheat, and other crops filled the marketplace. Farmers carrying their grain joyfully walked together in procession into Jerusalem to the Temple. Jewish people traveled from all over the Middle East to Jerusalem for one purpose. They came to remember and to thank God for the grain harvest.

After the destruction of the Temple in Jerusalem in A.D. 70, the festival also celebrated God's freeing the Israelites from Egypt and his giving them the Law at Sinai. That is why this festival also came to be known as the Festival of the Giving of Law, and the solemn reading of the Ten Commandments became part of the celebration.

QUESTION

How do you thank God for the blessings he has given you?

Celebrating Festivals

Think about the ways people celebrate state fairs. Compare and contrast those festivals to the Festival of Weeks.

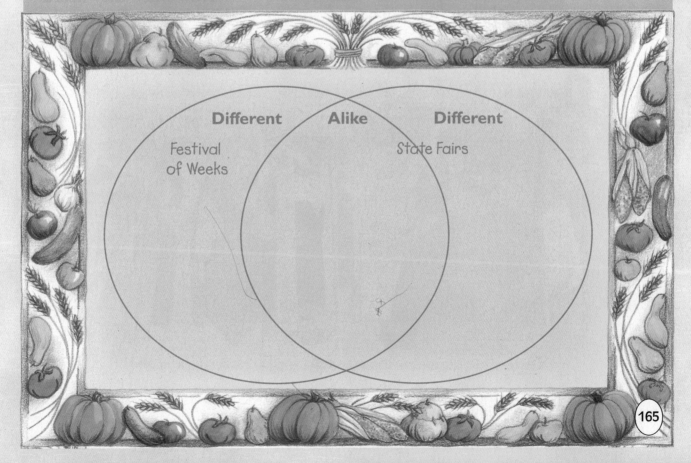

Different — Festival of Weeks

Alike

Different — State Fairs

Reading the Word of God

Faith Focus

What do Christians remember and celebrate on Pentecost?

Faith Vocabulary

Apostles. The first shepherds of the Church, the disciples to whom Jesus gave the responsibility and authority to baptize and to teach in his name.

Pentecost

During the preparation for Pentecost the disciples gathered with Mary, the Mother of Jesus. They met in an upper room of a home in Jerusalem. On that Pentecost the Holy Spirit promised by Jesus came upon Saint Peter the **Apostle** and the other disciples.

At nine o'clock in the morning, Saint Peter and the other disciples, filled with the Holy Spirit, left the room. Entering the streets, Saint Peter spoke to the crowds who had come from "every nation under heaven [and were] staying in Jerusalem." Everyone, we are told, understood Peter in their own language.

Saint Peter reminded the people of what God had promised them through David and the prophets. Then he recalled how Jesus had died, and how he himself was a witness to the fact that Jesus was raised to new life:

"Exalted at the right hand of God, he received the promise of the holy Spirit from the Father and poured it forth, as you [both] see and hear. . . . Therefore let the whole house of Israel know for certain that God has made him both Lord and Messiah, this Jesus whom you crucified."

Now when they heard this, they were cut to the heart, and they asked

Peter and the other apostles, "What are we to do, my brothers?" Peter [said] to them, "Repent and be baptized, every one of you, in the name of Jesus Christ for the forgiveness of your sins; and you will receive the gift of the holy Spirit. For the promise is made to you and to your children and to all those far off, whomever the Lord our God will call." He testified with many other arguments, . . ." Those who accepted his message were baptized, and about three thousand persons were added that day.

ACTS OF THE APOSTLES
2:33, 36–41

Filled with the Holy Spirit, Saint Peter preached the Good News of Jesus that day. The Apostles began the work Jesus gave them to do.

 What did Saint Peter tell the Jewish pilgrims gathered in Jerusalem?

Proclaiming Jesus

Imagine you are one of the Jewish pilgrims in Jerusalem on that first Pentecost. As Saint Peter speaks, what do you hear him saying that makes you want to become a follower of Jesus?

_____

_____

_____

_____

_____

_____

Understanding the Word of God

Faith Focus

How does the Church continue the work Saint Peter and the other disciples began?

Faith Vocabulary

evangelization. The Church's responsibility to care for and share the Gospel with all people "so that it may enter the hearts of all men and renew the human race."

Saint Peter's Message

In Saint Luke's account of the event of that Pentecost in Jerusalem, Saint Peter enthusiastically proclaimed Jesus. Saint Peter told the Jewish pilgrims that the "mighty deeds, wonders, and signs" of Jesus were a sign that Jesus was Lord and Messiah. Jesus was the Anointed One whom they were waiting for God to send to them.

Saint Peter courageously spoke of how Jesus was put to death and was raised from the dead. He affirmed that all God's promises were fulfilled in Jesus. We are told that Peter's listeners were "cut to the heart." The Holy Spirit had opened their hearts and they eagerly asked him, "What are we to do?"

Saint Peter responded very simply and very clearly, "Repent and be baptized." He told them that they needed to change their hearts and believe in what God had done for them through Jesus.

The Church's Message

Jesus began his public ministry, proclaiming, "Repent, and believe in the Gospel" (Mark 1:15). The Acts of the Apostles describes Saint Peter beginning the work of the Church with a similar proclamation.

The Church today continues the same work Saint Peter began on that Pentecost in Jerusalem. The work of proclaiming the Gospel and inviting people to become followers of Jesus is the main work of the Church. It is the work of **evangelization**. It is the work of proclaiming the Gospel.

Through the words and actions of the Church, the Holy Spirit invites people to change their hearts, to believe in what God has done for them in Jesus Christ. He invites people to be baptized and to become disciples of Jesus Christ.

 QUESTION How is the work Saint Peter did and the work of the Church today the same?

Qualities of an Evangelizer

On each line write a character trait that you think helped Saint Peter proclaim the Gospel. Share with a partner how the traits can help you tell others about Jesus.

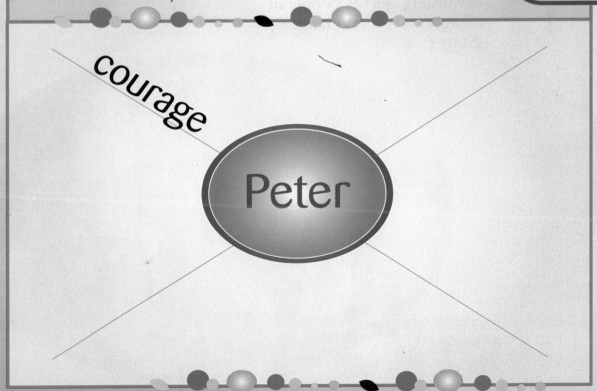

courage

Peter

Our Church Makes a Difference

Glenmary priest reading Bible stories to Vacation Bible School students in Arkansas

Glenmary Home Missioners

The Glenmary Home Missioners bring the Gospel of Jesus Christ to rural areas of Appalachia, the South, and the Southwest United States. This community of Catholic priests and brothers, joined by the Glenmary Home Mission Sisters and lay coworkers, serves people of all ages, races, and language groups.

The Glenmary Home Missioners work to build up the Catholic Church in parts of America where less than one in every one hundred people is Catholic. They work for social justice among the poorest families in America.

One summer the O'Connor family decided to make their family summer vacation different. They left their home in the city and spent two weeks working with the Glenmary Home Missioners. They were eyewitnesses of all the good that happens when we live the Gospel.

 How can a family join with the Church in telling others about Jesus?

Glenmary priest celebrating Mass in migrant camp in South Georgia

What Difference Does Faith Make in My Life?

On Pentecost "tongues as of fire" came to rest on Saint Peter and the other disciples. They were filled with the Holy Spirit. You received the gift of the Holy Spirit at Baptism.

In the two flames write ways you can share the Good News of Jesus with others.

"Go, Tell All Nations!"

_____

_____

_____

_____

_____

_____

_____

My Faith Choice

This week I will cooperate with the Holy Spirit and join with other members of the Church to tell others about Jesus. I will

_____

_____ .

Prayer for Vocations

Leader: God calls all the baptized to share our faith in Jesus Christ with others. Let us ask God to help us know how he wishes us to do this important work.

God the Father gives us the gift of the Holy Spirit to continue the work of his Son, Jesus. Let us listen to the word of God.

Reader: A reading from the holy gospel according to Matthew.

All: **Glory to you, O Lord.**

Reader: Jesus went around to all the towns and villages, teaching in their synagogues, proclaiming the gospel of the kingdom, and curing every disease and illness. At the sight of the crowds, his heart was moved with pity for them because they were troubled and abandoned, like sheep without a shepherd. Then he said to his disciples, "The harvest is abundant but the laborers are few; so ask the master of the harvest to send out laborers for his harvest."

Matthew 9:35–38

Reader: The gospel of the Lord.

All: **Praise to you, Lord Jesus Christ.**

Leader: Let us take a moment to think about the work God is calling us to do. *(Pause.)* Lord God our Father, teach us to know and follow the vocation to which you are calling us. Send us the Holy Spirit to help us serve your people as Jesus, your only Son, did.

All: **Amen.**

We Remember

What I Have Learned

1. *Imagine you were with Saint Peter in Jerusalem on Pentecost. What will you share with your family when you return home?*

_____

_____

_____

_____

_____

Answer the following.

2. **Explain the importance of Pentecost for the Church.**

_____

_____

3. **Compare the work of Saint Peter with the work of the Church today.**

_____

_____

_____

4. **Describe the importance of the Church celebrating Pentecost each year.**

_____

_____

_____

To Help You Remember

1. The Jewish people were celebrating Pentecost when the Holy Spirit came upon the disciples as Jesus promised.

2. On Pentecost Saint Peter preached to the crowds and began the work that Jesus gave to the Church.

3. The work of proclaiming Jesus to all people is the main work of the Church.

Growing in Faith

One important thing I learned this week is

_____

_____

_____.

This is important because

_____

_____

_____.

What will people see me doing as I live my faith choice this week?

_____

_____

_____

This Week . . .

In chapter 13, "Pentecost: A Scripture Story," your child learned more about the origin and meaning of the feast of Pentecost. Saint Peter and the other disciples were filled with the Holy Spirit. They left the upper room of the home where they were staying and went into the marketplace, where Jews from many nations had gathered for the celebration of the Festival of Weeks. It was the fiftieth day of the celebration, or Pentecost. Saint Peter preached to the people that in Jesus, all the promises God had made to the Israelites were fulfilled. On that day the work of the Church began. The Church today continues to invite people to repent, believe in Jesus, be baptized, and become disciples of Christ.

For more on the teachings of the Catholic Church on the Pentecost event and on the missionary mandate of the Church, see *Catechism of the Catholic Church* paragraph numbers 696, 731–732, 767, and 849–852.

Sharing God's Word

Read together Acts of the Apostles 2:36–41, the New Testament account of Saint Peter proclaiming Jesus to be the Lord and Messiah. Emphasize that the people believed in Jesus Christ and were baptized.

Praying

In this chapter your child prayed a prayer for vocations. Read and pray together this prayer on page 172.

Making a Difference

Choose one of the following activities to do as a family or design a similar activity of your own.

- On Pentecost the Holy Spirit came to the Apostles. Invite each family member to talk about how they can cooperate with the Holy Spirit and use their gifts and talents to tell others about Jesus.

- Make a mural of Pentecost. Hang your mural where it will remind the family that the Holy Spirit is always with you.

- Name the ways the Holy Spirit helps your family. Talk about how the Holy Spirit helps you believe in Jesus and how he helps you share the Good News of Jesus with others.

For more ideas on ways your family can live your faith, visit the "Faith First for Families" page at **www.FaithFirst.com**. Click on "Gospel Reflections" and talk with your family about Sunday's Gospel reading.

One Bread, One Cup

14

We Pray

I will offer a sacrifice
   of thanksgiving
   and call on the name
   of the LORD.
                    PSALM 116:17

Lord, we are renewed
by the breaking
of one bread.
Help us live the new
life we received in
Baptism.   Amen.

*Imagine you are a health
expert. What foods
would you include in a
healthful meal?*

Besides food for our body,
we need food for our
spirit. At the Last Supper,
Jesus gave us his Body
and Blood to nourish our
spirit.

*Why can we call the Mass
a holy meal?*

Do This in Memory of Me

Faith Focus

Why do we celebrate the Eucharist?

Faith Vocabulary

Eucharist. The Sacrament of Christian Initiation in which we share in the Paschal Mystery of Christ, receive the Body and Blood of Christ, and are joined most fully to Christ and to the Church, the Body of Christ.

sacrifice. Freely giving up something of value out of love for God.

The Bread of Life

Jesus is the Bread of life. After he had fed the crowd with five loaves and two fish, he crossed back over the Sea of Tiberias, which is also called the Sea of Galilee. The crowd, realizing that Jesus had left, followed him by land. When they caught up with Jesus and the disciples, he said to them:

"Amen, amen, I say to you, you are looking for me not because you saw signs but because you ate the loaves and were filled. Do not work for food that perishes but for the food that endures for eternal life, which the Son of Man will give you." . . .

So they said to him, "Sir, give us this bread always." Jesus said to them, "I am the bread of life; whoever comes to me will never hunger, and whoever believes in me will never thirst. . . .

"I am the living bread that came down from heaven; whoever eats this bread will live forever; and the bread that I will give is my flesh for the life of the world."

JOHN 6:26–27, 34–35, 51

At the Last Supper Jesus gave us the gift of his Body and Blood. He gave us the Sacrament of the **Eucharist.** Each time we celebrate the Eucharist, we do what Jesus did at the Last Supper. We do what he told us to do. After giving his disciples the gift of his Body and Blood, Jesus said to them:

"Do this in memory of me." LUKE 22:19

Last Supper, mosaic

176

The Sacrifice of the Cross

The next day Jesus gave up his life on the cross to save us from sin. He offered himself, or sacrificed his life, to his Father. Through the Eucharist we join in Jesus' **sacrifice** of his life for us. Saint Paul reminds us:

> For as often as you eat this bread and drink the cup, you proclaim the death of the Lord until he comes.
>
> 1 CORINTHIANS 11:26

When we celebrate the Eucharist, we remember and share in the one sacrifice of Christ. We offer ourselves with Jesus through the power of the Holy Spirit to God the Father.

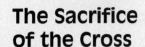 **Why does the Church call the Eucharist the sacrament of the Body and Blood of Christ?**

Living as a Disciple of Jesus

Look up Matthew 16:24. Imagine Jesus is speaking to you and read his words. Write about or draw yourself making a sacrifice out of your love for God and family.

Faith Focus

What other names does the Church use for the Eucharist to help us understand the mystery of the Eucharist?

Faith Vocabulary

Mass. The main sacramental celebration of the Church at which we gather to listen to God's word and share in the Eucharist.

The Mystery of the Eucharist

The Eucharist is a great mystery of our faith. The Church uses many names for the Eucharist. These help us understand the meaning of this mystery of God's love.

The Lord's Supper

The Eucharist is called the Lord's Supper. We join with the Lord, the Head of the Church. We give thanks and praise to the Father as Jesus did with his disciples at the Last Supper.

Breaking of Bread

The Eucharist is the sacred meal and banquet that Jesus gave to the Church. Through the words of the priest and the power of the Holy Spirit, the unleavened bread and wine made from grapes are changed into the Body and Blood of Christ. In Holy Communion we receive the Bread of Life. The consecrated bread and wine are truly Jesus.

The Holy Sacrifice

In the Eucharist the one sacrifice of Jesus Christ is made present again. Joined to Christ we offer ourselves through the power of the Holy Spirit to God the Father.

Entrance procession at Mass

The Mass

The word *mass* comes from the Latin word *missio*, which means "mission" or "sending." At the conclusion of **Mass** we are sent forth on a mission. We are to "go and announce the Gospel of the Lord."

By sharing in the Eucharist we share in the fullness of life in Jesus. We are more fully joined to Jesus and to one another. We are made sharers in the Paschal Mystery of the Passion, sacrificial death, Resurrection, and glorious Ascension of Jesus Christ. We share more fully in the life of the Holy Trinity. We look forward in hope to living forever with God, Mary, and all the saints in heaven.

 What happens when we share in the Eucharist? How are we changed?

"Go and announce the Gospel of the Lord."

"Go and announce the Gospel of the Lord."

"Go and announce the Gospel of the Lord."

We Are Sent Forth

At the end of Mass we are sent forth with these or similar words, "Go and announce the Gospel of the Lord." Write a paragraph about one way you can live those words this week.

_____

_____

_____

_____

_____

_____

"Go and announce the Gospel of the Lord."

Faith Focus

How do we celebrate the Mass?

Faith Vocabulary

assembly. The Church gathered to celebrate the sacraments and the liturgy.

The Celebration of Mass

The Eucharist is the center of the Christian life. The Church celebrates the Eucharist at Mass. The Mass is the central gathering of the Church. We worship God. We listen to the word of God. We join with Jesus in the power of the Holy Spirit to give thanks and praise to God the Father. Every member of the worshiping **assembly** has an active part in the celebration of Mass. Here is a description of the rites, or parts, of the Mass.

Introductory Rites

We remember and celebrate that God has called us together to be his people. We gather and form a worshiping community.

Liturgy of the Word

The Sunday celebration of Mass includes three Scripture readings. We listen and respond to God's word. The Gospel reading, which is the third reading, is the center of the Liturgy of the Word. After the proclamation of the Gospel, the deacon or priest preaches a homily. This helps us understand and live the word of God. We then pray the Profession of Faith, or Creed, and the Prayer of the Faithful.

Liturgy of the Eucharist

The Liturgy of the Eucharist begins with the Preparation of the Gifts. In the Eucharistic Prayer, which follows, we join with Christ and give thanks and praise to God the Father. By the power of the Holy Spirit and the words of the priest, the bread and wine become the Body and Blood of Christ.

Blessed Sacrament

The Blessed Sacrament is another name for the Eucharist. The consecrated bread, which is the Body of Christ, is called the Blessed Sacrament. We reserve the Blessed Sacrament in the tabernacle for those who are sick and for the devotion of the people.

The whole assembly prays aloud or sings the Our Father and shares a sign of peace as we prepare for Holy Communion. We profess our faith in Jesus Christ, the Lamb of God who takes away the sins of the world. We walk in procession to receive the Body and Blood of Christ.

Concluding Rites

The priest asks God's blessing on the assembly. We are sent forth to carry on the work, or mission, of Jesus Christ.

 What happens in each part of the Mass?

The Source of the Church's Life

Write why the Eucharist is the center of your life as a Catholic.

_____

_____

_____

_____

Tapestry of Mother Teresa displayed at her Beatification ceremony

Beatification ceremony of Mother Teresa at the Vatican, Sunday, October 19, 2003

Blessed Teresa of Calcutta, the Saint of the Gutter

Blessed Mother Teresa of Calcutta wrote, "I see God in every human being. When I wash the leper's wounds, I feel that I am nursing the Lord himself."

The Eucharist was the center of Mother Teresa's life. Every day she took part in the Mass and shared the Eucharist. At the conclusion of the celebration of Mass, she too heard the words, "Go in peace to love and serve the Lord." Mother Teresa became known as the Saint of the Gutter because of her work with people who were left to die on the streets.

Mother Teresa received the Nobel Peace Prize in 1979. In 1985 she was awarded the Medal of Freedom by the president of the United States. On the night she died, the president of France said, "This evening, there is less love, less compassion, less light in the world." These and other honors recognized the difference Blessed Mother Teresa's life made for the world.

On October 19, 2003, just six years after she died, Pope John Paul II named Mother Teresa a Blessed of the Church. This honor recognizes that Mother Teresa faithfully lived the Gospel and is a model for all of us to follow.

 How does the Eucharist help you show your love for God and for others?

What Difference Does Faith Make in My Life?

The Eucharist is the center of the Christian life. Receiving the Eucharist strengthens you "to glorify the Lord by your life."

Describe how you can love and glorify the Lord in each of these places.

Glorifying the Lord

Home _____

_____

_____.

School _____

_____

_____.

Neighborhood _____

_____

_____.

My Faith Choice

This week through my acts and words, I will love and serve the Lord by

_____

_____.

Sacrament Most Holy

Each year on the second Sunday after Pentecost, we celebrate the Solemnity of the Most Holy Body and Blood of Christ. After the second reading we may pray aloud or sing the hymn Lauda Sion. We praise God for the gift of the Eucharist.

Leader: The Eucharist is the source and summit of the Church's life. Let us give thanks and praise to God for the gift of the Eucharist.

Group 1: The cup of blessing that we bless is the blood of Christ.

All: **Bring God all the praise you know.**

Group 2: The bread we break is the Body of Christ.

All: **Bring God all the praise you know.**

Group 3: Whoever eats the bread and drinks from the cup will live forever.

All: **Bring God all the praise you know.**

BASED ON 1 CORINTHIANS 10:16–17
JOHN 6:51, AND LAUDA SION

Leader: Lord Jesus Christ,
we worship you living among us
in the Sacrament of your Body and Blood.
May we offer to our Father in heaven
a solemn pledge of undivided love.
May we offer to our brothers and sisters
a life poured out in loving service of
that Kingdom
where you live with the Father and the
Holy Spirit,
one God, forever and ever.

PRAYER FROM "A HOLY HOUR OF PRAYER FOR LIFE,"
CATHOLIC HOUSEHOLD BLESSINGS AND PRAYERS

All: **Amen.**

We Remember

What I Have Learned

Complete this crossword puzzle. Each clue for the puzzle points to the mystery of the Eucharist.

DOWN

1. The _____ is the central celebration of the Church.
3. By sharing in the _____ we share in the fullness of life in Jesus.
4. The parts of the Mass are called _____.
5. In Holy Communion we receive _____.

ACROSS

2. The _____ bread, which is the Body of Christ, is called the Blessed Sacrament.
6. When we celebrate the Eucharist, we join in Jesus' _____ of his life for us.

Answer the following.

7. Explain why the Church celebrates the Eucharist.

_____

_____

_____

8. Explain how the term *Holy Sacrifice* helps us understand the mystery of the Eucharist.

_____

_____

_____

_____

To Help You Remember

1. The Eucharist is the center of the Christian life. Jesus gave us the Eucharist at the Last Supper.

2. The Eucharist is also called the Lord's Supper, Breaking of Bread, Holy Sacrifice, Mass, and Blessed Sacrament.

3. At Mass we listen to the word of God and celebrate the Eucharist. The bread and wine become the Body and Blood of Christ.

Growing in Faith

One important thing I learned this week is

_____

_____

_____.

This is important because

_____

_____

_____.

What will people see me doing as I live my faith choice this week?

_____

_____

_____

This Week . . .

In chapter 14, "One Bread, One Cup," your child learned more about the Sacrament of the Eucharist. The Eucharist is at the center of the Christian life. It is the sacrament of the Body and Blood of the Lord Jesus Christ. At the Eucharist the bread and wine truly become the Body and Blood of Christ through the power of the Holy Spirit and the words of the priest. When we celebrate the Eucharist, the one sacrifice of Jesus Christ is made present. We are made sharers in the Paschal Mystery of the Passion, death, Resurrection, and glorious Ascension of Christ and receive the promise of eternal life.

For more on the teachings of the Catholic Church on the Sacrament of the Eucharist, see *Catechism of the Catholic Church* paragraph numbers 1322–1405.

Sharing God's Word

Read together 1 Corinthians 11:23–26, Saint Paul's account of the institution of the Eucharist. Emphasize that on the day after the Last Supper Jesus offered his life on the cross.

Praying

In this chapter your child prayed a prayer praising God for the gift of the Eucharist. Read and pray together this prayer on page 184.

Making a Difference

Choose one of the following activities to do as a family or design a similar activity of your own.

* The word *sacrifice* means "to give up something out of love." Talk about the sacrifices your family makes for one another.

* When your family takes part in the celebration of Mass this week, spend some time after Mass at the tabernacle. You will notice a candle burning next to the tabernacle. This candle is called a sanctuary lamp.

* At the end of Mass the assembly is sent forth with these or similar words, "Go in peace, glorify the Lord by your life." All respond, "Amen." Choose one thing you can do this week to love and serve the Lord.

For more ideas on ways your family can live your faith, visit the "Faith First for Families" page at www.FaithFirst.com. Click on "Make a Difference" for ideas of ways your family can share God's love with others this week.

The Corinthians A Scripture Story

The Eucharist, stained glass

We Pray

LORD, you are the
  strength of your
  people. . . .
Save your people, bless
  your inheritance;
  feed and sustain them
  forever!   PSALM 28:8–9

Lord God, Father
of all, may sharing
in the Body and Blood
of Christ, your Son,
join all your people
in love.   Amen.

*What is one thing you know
about your family's history?*

Learning our family history
helps us understand who
we are. One thing we
learn about the history of
our Church is that we
have always gathered to
celebrate the Eucharist.

*Why do we celebrate the
Eucharist?*

Bible Background

Faith Focus

Why did Saint Paul write letters or epistles?

Faith Vocabulary

breaking of bread. A name used for the celebration of the Eucharist.

epistle. A type of formal letter found in the New Testament.

The Early Church

The first followers of Jesus were Jewish people who were baptized. They remained faithful to many of the prayers and religious customs of the Jewish people. They continued to take part in the life of the synagogue and worship in the Temple in Jerusalem. They listened to the Scriptures, learned about the Law, and joined with others in prayer.

After the Passion and death, Resurrection, and Ascension of Jesus, the Jewish people who had become followers of Jesus would return to their homes for the **breaking of bread** after participating in the synagogue or Temple. The term *breaking of bread* was used by the early Church for the Eucharist.

As the early Church grew, many non-Jews, or Gentiles, were baptized and became followers of Christ. They lived in towns and cities all around the Mediterranean Sea. Many of the letters in the New Testament were written to the particular churches founded in those places, which included Rome, Corinth, Galatia, Ephesus, Philippi, Colossae, and Thessalonica.

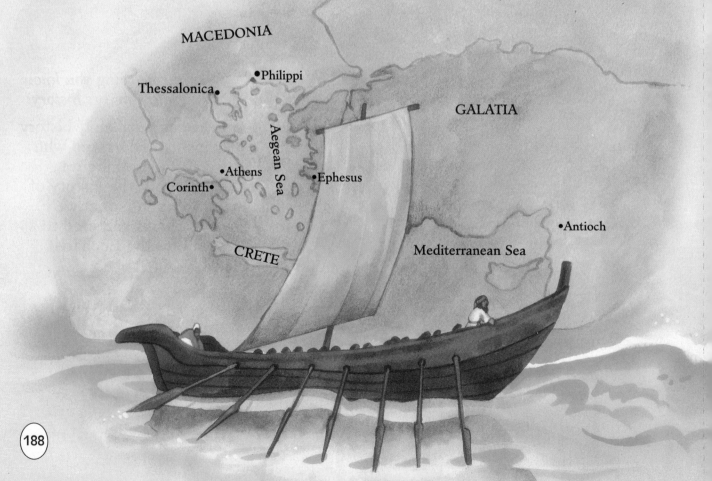

MACEDONIA

Philippi

Thessalonica

GALATIA

Aegean Sea

Athens

Ephesus

Corinth

Antioch

CRETE

Mediterranean Sea

Corinth

Corinth was a city in ancient Greece. It was a seaport city on the route connecting Europe and Asia. Saint Paul the Apostle preached the Gospel to the people of Corinth. He first came to Corinth in A.D. 51, about twenty years after the death, Resurrection, and Ascension of Jesus. He stayed there about eighteen months.

After Saint Paul preached in Corinth, he traveled by land and sea to other cities. Because he could not always travel back to the places that he had already visited, Paul sometimes wrote letters or dictated letters to a scribe who wrote them for him. One type of letter written by Saint Paul is called an **epistle**, which is a formal type of letter. Writing letters enabled Paul to remind the people of what he had taught them and to correct any false interpretations or misunderstandings of his teachings.

 Who were the Corinthians?

Teaching about Jesus

Write a letter to a friend. Share with your friend an important teaching of the Catholic Church about the Eucharist.

_____

_____

_____

_____

_____

_____

_____

_____

_____

_____

Reading the Word of God

Faith Focus

What did Saint Paul tell the Corinthians about the Eucharist?

The Lord's Supper

When Saint Paul was in the city of Ephesus, he learned that the Corinthians did not understand the true meaning of the celebration of the Lord's Supper. Addressing their lack of reverence and respect for the Eucharist, he wrote:

> I hear that when you meet as a church there are divisions among you. . . . When you meet in one place, then, it is not to eat the Lord's supper, for in eating, each one goes ahead with his own supper, and one goes hungry while another gets drunk.
>
> 1 CORINTHIANS 11:17–18, 20–21

Then Paul reminded the Corinthians of the true meaning of the Eucharist.

He reminded them that they were doing what Jesus did at the Last Supper. They were sharing in the Body and Blood of Christ. He continued:

> Therefore, whoever eats the bread or drinks the cup of the Lord unworthily will have to answer for the body and blood of the Lord. A person should examine himself, and so eat the bread and drink the cup.
>
> 1 CORINTHIANS 11:27–28

Saint Paul reminded the Corinthians that when they came together for the breaking of bread, they were sharing the Body and Blood of the Lord.

 Why did Saint Paul write to the Corinthians?

Participating in the Eucharist

Create a home page for your parish Web site. Include ways members of your parish may participate in the celebration of the Eucharist.

Understanding the Word of God

Faith Focus

How does our behavior at Mass express our belief in the Eucharist?

Faith Vocabulary

reverence. The attitude of awe, profound respect, and love.

Saint Paul's Teaching

Saint Paul reprimanded the Corinthians for their lack of **reverence** during the celebration of the Eucharist. Their words and actions did not show they understood what they were celebrating. They were arguing and quarreling. The people were divided into hostile groups.

They were eating as if they were sharing a regular meal. Some were even getting drunk.

Saint Paul admonished the Corinthians that when they shared the Eucharist, their behavior—their words and actions—needed to show that they understood what they were doing. They were remembering that Jesus died for them. They were recalling and making present the loving sacrifice of Jesus' life. They were not eating bread and drinking wine. They were sharing the Body and Blood of Christ, shed for the sins of the world.

The Eucharist Today

The way we celebrate the Eucharist is similar to the way the early Church did. We gather together to form a community of faith. We listen to the teachings of Jesus and the Apostles in the readings from Scripture. We do what Jesus did at the Last Supper. We break and share the bread, which has become the Body of Christ. We share and drink from the cup of wine, which has become the Blood of Christ.

We too need to listen to Saint Paul's words. When we celebrate the Eucharist, we must prepare ourselves. Our words and actions before Mass, during Mass, and after Mass must express what we believe. At Eucharist we share in the Body and Blood of Christ.

 Why do we show reverence for the Eucharist?

Showing Reverence

Write how you might prepare to take part properly in the Eucharist.

_____

_____

_____

_____

_____

_____

_____

_____

Our Church Makes a Difference

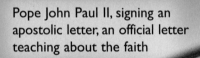

Pope John Paul II, signing an apostolic letter, an official letter teaching about the faith

Church Letters

The Church is our teacher. The pope and other bishops share in the responsibility Jesus gave the Apostles to teach in his name. The pope and the bishops, as Saint Paul did, sometimes teach us by writing letters. One type of letter the pope writes is called an apostolic letter. On Pentecost 1998, Pope John Paul II sent the apostolic letter *The Day of the Lord* to all the bishops to share with the people they serve.

In his letter Pope John Paul II taught that celebrating the Eucharist together as the Church is the heart of Sunday. Sunday is the Lord's Day. Resting from our work and other chores on Sunday helps us show our reverence for God the Creator and devote time to our families and to ourselves. When we keep Sunday holy, we build up not only the Church, but also our families and communities.

 What are some ways the Church helps people make the Lord's Day special?

194

What Difference Does Faith Make in My Life?

Every Sunday you go to church and take part in the Eucharist. There are many things you do and say that show reverence for the Eucharist.

Pretend you have been invited to help a first grader act reverently at Mass. In the space below write what you would tell the first grader.

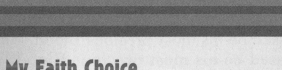

My Faith Choice

This week I will think about what is really happening when I take part in the Eucharist. To celebrate reverently I will

_____

_____.

The Divine Praises

Leader: At the celebration of Benediction of the Blessed Sacrament, the Church sometimes prays the Divine Praises. The Divine Praises is a prayer of blessing and adoration. We bless, or give honor and glory, to God.

Let us listen to the word of God and respond by blessing God for the gift of Jesus, the Bread of Life.

Reader: A reading from the holy Gospel according to Luke.
All: **Glory to you, O Lord.**

Reader: [Jesus] took the bread, said the blessing, broke it, and gave it to them, saying, "This is my body, which will be given for you; do this in memory of me." And likewise the cup after they had eaten, saying, "This cup is the new covenant in my blood, which will be shed for you." LUKE 22:19–20
The Gospel of the Lord.
All: **Praise to you, Lord Jesus Christ.**

Leader: Let us bless and praise God the Father for the gift of Jesus present with us as the Blessed Sacrament.
Blessed be Jesus Christ, true God and true man.
All: **Blessed be Jesus Christ, true God and true man.**

Leader: Blessed be the name of Jesus.
All: **Blessed be the name of Jesus.**

Leader: Blessed be his most Sacred Heart.
All: **Blessed be his most Sacred Heart.**

Leader: Blessed be his most precious Blood.
All: **Blessed be his most precious Blood.**

Leader: Blessed be Jesus in the most holy Sacrament of the altar.
All: **Blessed be Jesus in the most holy Sacrament of the altar.**

We Remember

What I Have Learned

Write a sentence describing these words and phrases.

1. breaking of bread _____
   _____

2. epistle _____
   _____

3. Lord's Supper _____
   _____

4. reverence _____
   _____

Answer the following.

5. Describe the role reverence plays in our taking part in the Eucharist.

   _____
   _____
   _____
   _____
   _____
   _____
   _____
   _____
   _____

To Help You Remember

1. Saint Paul admonished the early Church in Corinth to celebrate the Eucharist reverently.

2. Saint Paul wrote to the Corinthians reminding them that when they celebrated the Eucharist, they were sharing in the Lord's Supper.

3. When we celebrate the Eucharist, we are to celebrate it in a way that shows we truly believe that we are sharing the Body and Blood of the Lord.

Growing in Faith

One important thing I learned this week is

_____
_____
_____.

This is important because

_____
_____
_____.

What will people see me doing as I live my faith choice this week?

_____
_____
_____

This Week . . .

In chapter 15, "The Corinthians: A Scripture Story," your child learned about the Eucharist. Saint Paul the Apostle established the Church in many places on his missionary journeys. Among those communities was the Christian community in the seaport town of Corinth in ancient Greece. After Saint Paul left Corinth, he wrote to the early Church in Corinth from Ephesus to remind them that their words and actions must show their belief in the Eucharist. Our words and actions at the Eucharist must express our faith that Jesus is with us in the Eucharist.

For more on the teachings of the Catholic Church on the Eucharist as the Lord's Supper and the breaking of bread, see *Catechism of the Catholic Church* paragraph numbers 1328–1329.

Sharing God's Word

Read together 1 Corinthians 11:18–28. Emphasize that Saint Paul reminded the Corinthians that the Eucharist is the Body and Blood of Christ.

Praying

In this chapter your child prayed the Divine Praises. Read and pray together this prayer on page 196.

Making a Difference

Choose one of the following activities to do as a family or design a similar activity of your own.

- Invite each family member to share what they can remember about their First Communion day. Talk about how old they were, who was present, how they felt, and so on.

- Write a letter in your own words about the Eucharist. Include the importance of sharing in the Body and Blood of Christ regularly.

- Talk about how your words and actions show that the Eucharist, the Body and Blood, is Jesus.

For more ideas on ways your family can live your faith, visit the "Faith First for Families" page at **www.FaithFirst.com**. Check out "Bible Stories." Read and discuss the Bible story as a family this week.

Jesus' Work of Healing

We Pray

Bless the LORD, my soul;
 do not forget all the
 gifts of God,
Who pardons all
 your sins,
 heals all your ills.
 PSALM 103:2–3

Lord God,
share your mercy and
love with all who call
on you. Amen.

*Why is it important to
forgive and be forgiven?
Why is it important to help
people who are sick?*

Forgiveness and healing
are a part of our daily
lives. Jesus continues
his work of forgiveness
and healing through the
Sacraments of Healing.

*What are the Sacraments
of Healing?*

Faith Focus

Why do we celebrate the sacrament of Penance and Reconciliation?

Faith Vocabulary

Penance and Reconciliation. The Sacrament of Healing through which we receive God's forgiveness through the ministry of the priest for the sins we commit after Baptism.

sin. Freely choosing to do what we know is against God's will or freely choosing not to do something we know God wants us to do.

Our Need for God's Forgiveness

Everyone needs forgiveness. Everyone needs to forgive. God is always ready to forgive us when we **sin**. Sin is freely choosing to do or say what we know is against God's will. Sin is also freely choosing to not do or say what we know is God's will. Sin shows disrespect for God. There is no greater evil than sin.

When we sin, we offend God and harm other people and the community of the Church. When we sin, we harm, or hurt, the person God created us to be. We wound our human dignity.

Holy Spirit, stained glass

The Holy Spirit invites us to ask for and accept God's forgiveness for the sins we have committed. The Holy Spirit also helps us change our ways and live more like children of God. We need God's help, or grace, not to sin again.

The Sacrament of Penance and Reconciliation

After his Resurrection, Jesus appeared to his disciples and gave them the authority to forgive sins. He said:

"Peace be with you. As the Father has sent me, so I send you." And when he had said this, he breathed on them and said to them, "Receive the holy Spirit. Whose sins you forgive are forgiven them, and whose sins you retain are retained." JOHN 20:21–23

Lord, make me an instrument of your peace.

Jesus gave us the Sacrament of **Penance and Reconciliation**, or Reconciliation. Through this sacrament we receive both God's forgiveness for the sins we commit after Baptism and his grace to overcome temptation and not to sin.

 What do we celebrate in the sacrament of Penance and Reconciliation?

Thanking God for His Forgiveness

Write a prayer thanking God for his gift of forgiveness. Keep your prayer at home. Include it in the prayers you pray each day.

_____

_____

_____

_____

_____

_____

_____

Faith Focus

What are the parts of the Sacrament of Penance and Reconciliation?

Faith Vocabulary

absolution. The forgiveness of sins given by God through the ministry of the priest in the Sacrament of Penance and Reconciliation.

Celebrating the Sacrament of Penance and Reconciliation

In the Sacrament of Penance and Reconciliation, bishops and priests speak in the name of Jesus. Through the words of the bishop or priest and the power of the Holy Spirit, our sins are forgiven. We are reconciled, or made friends again, with God and the Church. We can celebrate this sacrament alone with the priest or we can gather as a community and celebrate this sacrament.

Absolution

Here is a summary of the rite of Reconciliation.

The Rite of Reconciliation

Confession of sins

We meet individually with a priest and confess, or tell, our sins to him. We always confess all mortal sins.

Contrition for sins

We pray an act of contrition. In this prayer we admit we have sinned. We express our sorrow for having offended God. Being truly sorry for our sins means we do not want to sin again. We really want to cooperate with the Holy Spirit to change the way we live.

Penance

The priest gives us a penance. He may ask us to say a prayer or do an act of kindness. Accepting and doing our penance shows that we are truly sorry for our sins and that we want to make up for the harm caused by our sins.

Absolution

Absolution is the forgiveness that the priest speaks in the name of God. When the priest says, "I absolve you," God speaks through him. *I absolve you* means "I forgive you. You are freed from your sins."

Forgiving Others

As God forgives us, we too are to forgive all those who sin against us. We need to learn ways to ask for forgiveness and to forgive others. When we are forgiven, we receive the gift of healing. When we forgive, we bring healing to others.

Jesus taught us that we must forgive others as generously as God forgives us. In one parable Jesus described a servant whose large debt was forgiven by a king. The same servant refused to forgive the debt another servant owed him.

This is what Jesus said about the unforgiving servant:

"You wicked servant! I forgave you your entire debt because you begged me to. Should you not have had pity on your fellow servant, as I had pity on you?"

MATTHEW 18:32–33

It is not enough just to say we are forgiven; we must forgive other people too. We must treat others the same way we ask God to treat us.

What are the four main parts of the celebration of the Sacrament of Reconciliation?

Faith-Filled People

Maria Goretti

Saint Maria Goretti was attacked by her neighbor when she was eleven years old. For twenty hours doctors tried to save Maria's life, but they could not. During that time Maria prayed for and forgave her attacker. Saint Maria Goretti is the patron saint of youth. The Church celebrates her feast day on July 6.

Living as Peacemakers

Write one way you might ask for forgiveness or give forgiveness to someone else.

Ask for Forgiveness

_____

_____

_____

_____

_____

Give Forgiveness

_____

_____

_____

_____

_____

Faith Vocabulary

Anointing of the Sick.
The Sacrament of Healing that strengthens our faith, hope, and love for God when we are seriously ill, weakened by old age, or dying.

The Sacrament of Anointing of the Sick

In Mark's Gospel we read about a time when Jesus healed a man who was paralyzed. Four friends of the paralyzed man were bringing him to Jesus. Unable to get near Jesus because of the crowd outside and inside the house, they climbed up onto the roof of the house, broke a hole into the roof, and let down the mat on which they were carrying the man. Seeing their faith, Jesus said to the paralyzed man, "[Y]our sins are forgiven."

Some of the people in the crowd objected to what Jesus was saying because they believed that only God could forgive sins. Knowing what they were thinking, Jesus said to them:

"But that you may know that the Son of Man has authority to forgive sins on earth"—he said to the paralytic, "I say to you, rise, pick up your mat, and go home."

MARK 2:10–11

When Jesus healed people who were sick, he not only healed their bodies. He also healed them spiritually. He helped them grow in faith, hope, and love for God.

Christ gave the Church the Sacrament of **Anointing of the Sick.** Through this sacrament, Christ continues his healing work among the sick. Christ's sufferings give new meaning to our suffering. Through union with Jesus, the sick find strength, peace, and courage.

Healing of Paralyzed Man, stained glass

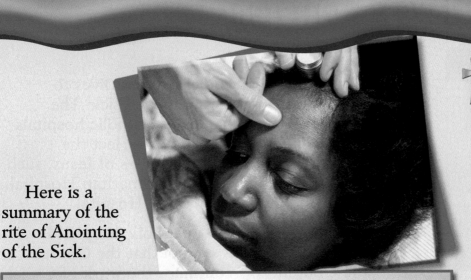

Here is a summary of the rite of Anointing of the Sick.

Our Catholic Identity

Chaplains

A chaplain sometimes serves a hospital. A chaplain can be a priest, deacon, or layperson. Hospital chaplains are trained to participate in the healing mission of Christ. They not only minister to the sick but also spiritually support hospital workers. Parish ministers to the sick often work with chaplains.

Rite of Anointing of the Sick

Only a priest or bishop can administer this sacrament. He meets and prays with the sick or elderly person and with their family and those caring for them. Next he reads from the word of God. Then he leads the celebration of the Liturgy of Anointing. These are the main parts of the celebration.

Litany, or Prayer of Faith

The priest leads all present, who represent the whole Church, in a prayer of faith in response to God's word.

Laying on of Hands

Jesus often laid his hands on sick people (see Luke 4:40). The Church uses this same gesture in this sacrament. It shows that the Church is asking God's blessing on the sick person.

Anointing with Oil

The priest or bishop anoints the sick person with the oil of the sick. First he anoints the sick person's forehead, as he prays, "Through this holy anointing may the Lord in his love and mercy help you with the grace of the Holy Spirit." Then he anoints the person's hands as he prays, "May the Lord who frees you from sin save you and raise you up."

Why do we call Anointing of the Sick a Sacrament of Healing?

Visiting a Friend

A friend is going to receive Anointing of the Sick before a serious surgery. What would you write or say to your friend?

_____

_____

_____

_____

_____

Our Church Makes a Difference

Hospital chaplain visiting with a patient

Catholic Hospitals

From the very beginning of the Church, caring for the sick has been an important ministry of the Church. Catholic hospitals continue this tradition. Each year more than seventy-one million patients are cared for in more than a thousand Catholic hospitals and health care centers in the United States.

Catholic hospitals are often named after saints, such as Saint Frances Cabrini, who dedicated their lives to caring for the sick. The names of Catholic hospitals sometimes reflect the healing stories of Jesus, such as Good Samaritan Hospital and Mercy Hospital.

A Catholic hospital is a symbol that the Church continues the work of Christ the Healer in towns, cities, and countries all over the world. The work of Catholic hospitals reminds us that all the baptized share in the healing work of Christ.

QUESTION *What are some of the ways your parish continues Jesus' work with people who are sick?*

Medical emergency transport helicopter

Guardian angel protecting boy. Mural on exterior of Christus Rosa Hospital, San Antonio, Texas.

What Difference Does Faith Make in My Life?

The Holy Spirit helps you continue the healing work of Jesus. You forgive those who may offend you. You reach out to family, friends, and neighbors when they are sick.

Create a title and design a cover for a music CD about Jesus' healing work among people.

My Faith Choice

This week I will continue the healing work of Jesus. I will

_____

_____.

A Prayer for the Sick

Leader: When we pray for other people, we pray a prayer of intercession. Let us listen to a Gospel story about Jesus healing the servant of an officer in the Roman army. Then pray together a prayer of intercession for people who are sick.

Reader: A reading from the holy Gospel according to Matthew.

All: **Glory to you, O Lord.**

Reader: When [Jesus] entered Capernaum, a centurion approached him and appealed to him, saying, "Lord, my servant is lying at home paralyzed, suffering dreadfully." He said to him, "I will come and cure him." The centurion said in reply, "Lord, I am not worthy to have you enter under my roof; only say the word and my servant will be healed." . . . And Jesus said to the centurion, "You may go; as you have believed, let it be done for you." And at that very hour [his] servant was healed.

MATTHEW 8:5–8, 13

The Gospel of the Lord.

All: **Praise to you, Lord Jesus Christ.**

Leader: Jesus showed us God's love for people who are sick.
Let us pray to God for all the members of our families, for our friends, and for all people who are sick. *(Pause.)*
Bless those who are sick and fill them with new hope and strength.

All: **Lord, have mercy.**

Leader: Support all those who care for the sick.

All: **Lord, have mercy.**

Leader: Quietly give thanks to God who is full of mercy and kindness.

We Remember

What I Have Learned

Circle T if the statement is true. Circle F if the statement is false. Make the false statements true.

1. Penance and Reconciliation and Anointing of the Sick are Sacraments of Service. T F

2. Another name for the Sacrament of Penance and Reconciliation is Reconciliation. T F

3. Confession, contrition, penance, and absolution are all part of the Sacrament of Penance and Reconciliation. T F

4. The Church celebrates Anointing of the Sick with young people, grown-ups, and elderly people. T F

5. All the baptized can administer the Sacrament of Anointing of the Sick. T F

Answer the following.

6. Describe the celebration of the Sacrament of Penance and Reconciliation.

_____

_____

7. Describe the rite of Anointing of the Sick.

_____

_____

8. Compare Jesus' work of forgiveness and healing with the work of the Church on earth.

_____

_____

To Help You Remember

1. God is always ready to forgive us when we sin. We receive God's forgiveness of our sin in the Sacrament of Penance and Reconciliation.

2. The celebration of the Sacrament of Penance and Reconciliation always includes confession of sins, contrition, penance, and absolution.

3. Through Anointing of the Sick, those who are seriously ill, weakened because of old age, or dying are joined to the suffering of Christ and receive strength and courage.

Growing in Faith

One important thing I learned this week is

_____

_____

_____.

This is important because

_____

_____

_____.

What will people see me doing as I live my faith choice this week?

_____

_____

_____

This Week . . .

In chapter 16, "Jesus' Work of Healing," your child learned more about the two Sacraments of Healing, Reconciliation and Anointing of the Sick. Through Reconciliation we receive forgiveness for sins we commit after Baptism. Confession of sins, contrition (or sorrow), penance, and absolution are always a part of the rite of Reconciliation. Throughout his life on earth, Jesus also cured people of bodily illnesses. When he did so, he also reached out to heal their spirits and invite people to grow in faith, trust, and love for God. Through Anointing of the Sick, Christ continues his healing ministry among the sick in the world today.

For more on the teachings of the Catholic Church on the Sacraments of Healing, see *Catechism of the Catholic Church* paragraph numbers 1420–1484 and 1499–1525.

Sharing God's Word

Read together John 20:22–23. Emphasize that bishops and priests today speak in the name of Jesus when they offer God's forgiveness in the Sacrament of Reconciliation, or Penance.

Praying

In this chapter your child prayed a prayer for the sick. Read and pray together this prayer on page 208.

Making a Difference

Choose one of the following activities to do as a family or design a similar activity of your own.

- Invite family members to share stories about forgiving others and being forgiven. Emphasize that when we forgive, we bring healing to others. When we are forgiven, we receive the gift of healing.

- Talk about all the ways your parish continues the healing work of Jesus.

- Talk about how your family continues the healing work of Jesus. Choose one thing you will do this week to continue the healing work of Jesus.

For more ideas on ways your family can live your faith, visit the "Faith First for Families" page at **www.FaithFirst.com**. You will find it helpful to take a look at "Questions Kids Ask."

Called to Serve the Whole Church

We Pray

Praise the LORD, my soul;
    I shall praise the LORD
    all my life,
    sing praise to my God
    while I live.

PSALM 146:2

Father, give those
who serve the Church
the strength to be
witnesses for Christ,
your Son, to others.
                Amen.

*Who are some people who
serve others in your family,
school, or parish?*

People work together in
families, in schools, and
in communities. The
Sacraments of Holy
Orders and Matrimony
call and strengthen some
members of the Church to
serve the whole Church.

*In what ways do those who
receive Holy Orders and
Matrimony serve the
Church?*

Sacrament of Matrimony,
Exchange of Rings

Our Christian Vocation

Imagine you are on a volleyball team. During the match you alone are trying to return the ball. The team would not be very successful. You would be doing the work of six players. This is why all the players on a team need to do their job to get things done.

The Sacraments of Christian Initiation join us to Christ and to all the members of the Church. We receive the call, or **vocation**, to continue the work of Christ, to build up the Church on earth, and to seek the Kingdom of God.

All the baptized—laypeople, religious, and ordained ministers—share in this vocation in different ways. Saint Paul the Apostle taught that all the members of the Church have an important role in the Church. He wrote:

If the whole body were an eye, where would the hearing be? If the whole body were hearing, where would the sense of smell be? But as it is, God placed the parts, each one of them, in the body as he intended. . . .

Now you are Christ's body, and individually parts of it.

1 CORINTHIANS 12:17–18, 27

Saint Paul taught that we are all members of the Body of Christ, the Church. Each member of the Church has a part to play in building up the whole Church.

212

Sacraments at the Service of Communion

Jesus gave the Church two sacraments that consecrate, or set aside, some members of the Church to serve the whole Church. They are the Sacraments of Holy Orders and Matrimony.

The special graces given to those who receive these sacraments help them serve the other members of the Church. Because these two sacraments set aside bishops, priests, deacons, and Christian married couples for the holy purpose of serving the whole Church, they are called **Sacraments at the Service of Communion**.

The lives of everyone in the Church are touched by the service of the Church's ordained baptized ministers and married couples. In Holy Orders baptized men are given the grace to serve the Church as bishops, priests, and deacons. In Matrimony a baptized man and a baptized woman are given the grace to always love each other and to become signs of Christ's love for the Church.

Why are Holy Orders and Matrimony called Sacraments at the Service of Communion?

Discovering Our Vocation

Decode the message to see what we are called to be.

A	.-	G	--.	L	.-..	Q	--.-	V	...-
B	-...	H	....	M	--	R	.-.	W	.--
C	-.-.	I	..	N	-.	S	...	X	-..-
D	-..	J	.---	O	---	T	-	Y	-.--
E	.	K	-.-	P	.--.	U	..-	Z	--..
F	..-.								

Faith Vocabulary

Holy Orders. The Sacrament at the Service of Communion through which a baptized man is consecrated to serve the whole Church as a bishop, priest, or deacon.

The Sacrament of Holy Orders

In **Holy Orders** a baptized man is ordained as a bishop, priest, or deacon. Only bishops can ordain other bishops, priests, and deacons. Bishops share in the fullness of Christ's priesthood and continue the work of the Apostles. They proclaim and preach God's word, lead us in celebrating the sacraments, and guide us in living the Gospel.

Priests are coworkers with their bishop. They preach God's word and lead us in the celebration of the sacraments. Priests stand for Christ and speak in his name.

Deacons help bishops and priests. They proclaim God's word and can baptize and marry people. Sometimes they are married themselves.

Bishop ordaining a priest

Deacon proclaiming Gospel at Mass

Pastor working in parish

214

Celebrating Holy Orders

Here is a summary of
the rite of ordination of a priest.

Laying on of Hands

In silence the ordaining bishop lays his hands on the heads of the candidates to be ordained. Next, all the priests who are present do the same.

Investiture with Stole and Chasuble

Each of the newly ordained priests receives a stole and a chasuble and puts them on.

Prayer of Consecration

The ordaining bishop prays the prayer of consecration. He prays, in part, "Almighty Father, grant to these servants of yours the dignity of the priesthood."

Anointing of Hands

The palms of the hands of the newly ordained priest are anointed with chrism as the bishop prays, "The Father anointed our Lord Jesus Christ through the power of the Holy Spirit. May Jesus preserve you to sanctify the Christian people to offer sacrifice to God."

 QUESTION How do bishops, priests, and deacons serve the Church?

Serving the Church

Write interview questions that you would like to ask a priest about how he serves the Church.

_____

_____

_____

_____

_____

_____

Faith Vocabulary

Matrimony. The Sacrament at the Service of Communion that unites a baptized man and a baptized woman in a lifelong bond, or covenant, of faithful love to serve the Church as a sign of Christ's love for the Church.

The Sacrament of Matrimony

Marriage is a sign of God's faithful and life-giving love for all people. From the very beginning, God created man and woman to marry, share God's love, bring children into the world, and care for the earth.

Many members of the Church have the vocation to marry. They are called to serve God and the Church with one other person whom they love very much. **Matrimony** is the name the Church gives to the Sacrament of Marriage. Matrimony unites a baptized man and a baptized woman in marriage and makes the couple a sign of Christ's love for the Church.

The Christian couple who marries is closer to each other than to anyone else. They form a new family in the Church. In the Sacrament of Matrimony, they receive the grace to live their vocation as a sign of Christ's love for the Church and of God's love for all people.

Here is a summary of the rite of Marriage.

Rite of Marriage

The celebration of Matrimony can take place during Mass or outside of Mass. The celebration of the sacrament takes place right after the Liturgy of the Word. This is what happens during the celebration of the sacrament.

- The bride and groom individually tell the priest or deacon and everyone present they are marrying freely.
- They promise that they will love and honor each other and will be faithful to each other as husband and wife until they die.
- They promise to accept the children God will give them and to raise them according to God's law.
- They usually give each other a ring to wear as a sign of their love and commitment to each other.
- The priest asks God to bless the newly married couple.

Minister of Matrimony

The couple is the minister of the Sacrament of Matrimony. The bishop, priest, or deacon is the official witness of the marriage.

QUESTION *In what ways does a Catholic married couple serve the Church?*

Signs of God's Love

Using each letter in the word LOVE, write a phrase or sentence that tells how the members of your family can be a sign of Christ's love for us.

L is for _____

_____ .

O is for _____

_____ .

V is for _____

_____ .

E is for _____

_____ .

Our Church Makes a Difference

Working Together as a Parish

All the people in a parish—the ordained, the married, the single, and the members of religious communities—are called to share their time and talents with others. All have the responsibility to take part in the work of the Church.

Adults serve the parish in many ways. Some work on the parish council and help organize the work of the parish. Some read the Scriptures at Mass, serve as extraordinary ministers of Holy Communion, or teach as catechists and teachers. Others are sponsors of those who want to become Catholics. Some take care of parish buildings or work with fundraisers that help the parish do its work.

Some adults in the parish care for those who are sick or elderly. Others help people who have financial difficulties or have lost their jobs. Others work with organizations in the civic community to build and repair houses. Some volunteer to serve people who are homeless. A few work with government leaders to get laws passed that help build a more just and fair community. The members of a parish give witness to Jesus through their work in the world. They prepare the way for the coming of the Kingdom of God.

QUESTION *When do you see the members of your parish helping one another live as followers of Jesus Christ?*

What Difference Does Faith Make in My Life?

God calls you to serve others. The things you are doing to help others are preparing you to continue serving the Church when you grow up.

Choose one talent with which God has blessed you. Write it in the center circle. Around the outside center circle, write ways you can use this talent to serve the Church.

Serving the Church

My Faith Choice

This week I will work with others to do the work of the Church. I will

_____

_____ .

Love One Another

Leader: Praying the Scripture guides us in living our faith. Let us listen to God's word and then pray for those who have been called to serve the whole Church.

Reader: A reading from Paul's letter to the Colossians. Put on then, as God's chosen ones, holy and beloved, heartfelt compassion, kindness, humility, gentleness, and patience. . . . And over all these put on love, that is, the bond of perfection. And let the peace of Christ control your hearts, the peace into which you were also called in one body. And be thankful.

COLOSSIANS 3:12, 14–15

The word of the Lord.

All: **Thanks be to God.**

Leader: Let us ask the Holy Spirit to guide those who have been called to serve the Church as bishops, priests, or Christian married couples.

Reader: For all bishops and priests and deacons that they care for God's people with kindness and love as Jesus the Good Shepherd did,

All: **Holy Spirit, kindle the fire of your love in their hearts.**

Reader: For all Christian married couples that their love witnesses the love of Christ for his Church,

All: **Holy Spirit, kindle the fire of your love in their hearts.**

Leader: Let us share with one another a sign of peace to show that we too desire to work together to serve God's people.

All: *Share a sign of peace.*

Humility Kindness Compassion

Gentleness Forgiveness Patience

220

We Remember

What I Have Learned

1. *List reasons why the Sacraments of Holy Orders and Matrimony are called Sacraments at the Service of Communion.*

   _____

   _____

   _____

   _____

   _____

   _____

   _____

Answer the following.

2. Compare the work of the Church with Saint Paul's teaching on the Church as the Body of Christ.

   _____

   _____

3. Describe the vocations of bishops, priests, and deacons.

   _____

   _____

4. Describe the vocation of a Christian married couple.

   _____

   _____

To Help You Remember

1. All the baptized have the vocation to continue the work of Christ. Matrimony and Holy Orders consecrate, or set aside, some members of the Church to serve the whole Church.
2. Holy Orders is the sacrament in which a baptized man is consecrated to serve the whole Church as a bishop, priest, or deacon.
3. Matrimony is the sacrament that unites a baptized man and a baptized woman in a lifelong bond, or covenant, of faithful love to serve the Church.

Growing in Faith

One important thing I learned this week is

_____

_____

_____.

This is important because

_____

_____

_____.

What will people see me doing as I live my faith choice this week?

_____

_____

_____

This Week . . .

In chapter 17, "Called to Serve the Whole Church," your child learned that God calls some members of the Church to serve the whole Church. Through Holy Orders bishops, priests, and deacons are ordained to serve the whole Church by continuing the unique work Jesus entrusted to the Apostles. Through Matrimony a baptized man and a baptized woman are united in a lifelong bond, or covenant, of faithful love and become a sign of Christ's love for the Church. The Sacraments of Holy Orders and Matrimony are called Sacraments at the Service of Communion.

For more on the teachings of the Catholic Church on the Sacraments at the Service of Communion, see *Catechism of the Catholic Church* paragraph numbers 1533–1589 and 1601–1658.

Sharing God's Word

Read together 1 Corinthians 12:12–30. Emphasize that each member of the Church has an important role as a member of the Body of Christ.

Praying

In this chapter your child prayed for those who receive the Sacraments at the Service of Communion. Read and pray together this prayer on page 220.

Making a Difference

Choose one of the following activities to do as a family or design a similar activity of your own.

- Invite family members to share one talent that God has given them. Then ask each person to share how they can use their talent to live as a follower of Christ.

- When you take part in Mass this week, look in the parish bulletin. Find all the ways your parish works together to live as followers of Christ.

- Talk about the work that married couples, bishops, priests, and deacons are set aside to do in Matrimony and Holy Orders. Name ways that married couples and those who receive the Sacrament of Holy Orders are signs of Christ's love. Then choose one way your family can be a sign of Christ's love.

For more ideas on ways your family can live your faith, visit the "Faith First for Families" page at **www.FaithFirst.com**. Click on "Family Prayer" and pray the prayer of the week.

Catholic Social Teaching

"The Invisible Children"

John and his family were watching the evening news on television. The feature story was about three college students who had gone to Africa. They filmed a documentary in Uganda, a country in the middle of a vicious civil war.

The documentary uncovered the story of the "invisible children." These children hid from rebel soldiers so that the rebels would not force them to become soldiers. Many of the children had lost their families and were orphaned. Some were starving. "Wow!" said John. "Can you imagine living like that? They don't even know where their next meal is coming from!"

The report was over. The newscasters broke for a commercial. The first commercial was for the newest iPod. "Oh! I need that!" said John's older sister. The next commercial was for the latest cell phone, complete with video capability. "I need that too!" said John's older sister. "My cell phone is a dinosaur."

"No," John told her. "You want those things. You don't need those things."

223

Making Connections . . .

What we need and what we want are often two different things. Many people around the world do not have what they need. It is important for Christians to know the difference between their needs and wants so that they can share with those who have greater needs.

with Social Studies

Work with a partner. Create ten to twenty cards that illustrate things you think that children your age, living in your community, need and want to be happy. Now sort out the cards in these categories: "Things that are needs," and "Things that are wants."

Working with the same partner, choose a developing country. Create ten to twenty cards that illustrate things you think that children your age, living in that country, need and want to be happy. Sort out these cards as you did before.

Join with another pair of students. Talk about what you discovered.

with Language Arts

Analyze the advertisements from a popular magazine. Discuss how the ads try to convince people that the item being advertised is a need.

with Creative Arts

Create a collage of wants and needs of people around the world. Use pictures and words cut out from magazines, newspaper articles, and other sources of printed media.

➲ **Faith Action** *What actions can you take to help meet the basic needs of others in your community?*

A. Best Response

Read each statement and circle the best answer.

1. What is the liturgy of the Church?
   a. the Church's work of worshiping God
   b. the work of helping others
   c. the gifts of the Holy Spirit
   d. the work of living the Beatitudes

2. Which season of the Church's liturgical year celebrates the Resurrection and our new life in Christ?
   a. Lent
   b. Ordinary Time
   c. Advent
   d. Easter

3. Which one of the following is not a Sacrament of Christian Initiation?
   a. Confirmation
   b. Eucharist
   c. Penance and Reconciliation
   d. Baptism

4. Which of the following is not one of the effects of Baptism?
   a. new life in Jesus Christ
   b. membership in the Body of Christ, the Church
   c. freedom from original sin and all personal sins
   d. ordination to serve the whole Church

5. Which sacrament completes our Baptism?
   a. Anointing of the Sick
   b. Confirmation
   c. Matrimony
   d. Penance and Reconciliation

6. What happened on the first Pentecost?
   a. The disciples prayed with Jesus.
   b. Jesus healed Jairus's daughter.
   c. Jesus was baptized.
   d. The Holy Spirit came upon the Apostles.

7. When did Jesus give us the Sacrament of the Eucharist?
   a. at the wedding feast of Cana
   b. on the feast of Pentecost
   c. at the Last Supper
   d. at the Crucifixion

8. Why do we gather to celebrate Mass?
   a. to do a penance
   b. to receive absolution
   c. to give thanks and praise to God the Father
   d. to be anointed with oil

9. Which one of the following is not a part of the sacrament of Penance and Reconciliation?
   a. confession of sins
   b. doing a penance
   c. contrition for sins
   d. anointing with oil

10. Which of the following are the Sacraments at the Service of Communion?
    a. Baptism and Holy Orders
    b. Holy Orders and Matrimony
    c. Penance and Reconciliation and Anointing of the Sick
    d. Matrimony and Confirmation

B. Words and Phrases

Match the terms in column A with their descriptions in column B.

Column A

_____ 1. Triduum

_____ 2. Lent

_____ 3. Mass

_____ 4. Pentecost

_____ 5. sacrifice

_____ 6. epistles

_____ 7. Corinth

_____ 8. Eucharist

Column B

a. Lord's Supper

b. Jesus dying to save us from sin

c. comes from the Latin word meaning "mission"

d. letters written by Saint Paul and others

e. a city in ancient Greece with followers of Jesus

f. the Holy Spirit coming upon the disciples

g. six weeks of preparation for Easter

h. Holy Thursday, Good Friday, and Easter Vigil

C. What I Have Learned

Write three things you learned in this unit.
Share them with the group.

_____

_____

_____

Look at the list of faith terms in "Words to Know" on page 138.
Circle the faith terms you know now.

D. From a Scripture Story

Saint Paul reminded the early Church in Corinth of the true meaning
of the Eucharist. Use words or drawings to complete the following.

Saint Paul's Teaching about the Eucharist	What Happens at the Eucharist

How do we live a life of holiness?

Getting Ready

What I Have Learned

What is something you already know about these faith terms?

conscience

_____

_____

The Beatitudes

_____

_____

holiness

_____

_____

Words to Know

Put an X next to the faith terms you know. Put a ? next to the faith terms you need to know more about.

Faith Vocabulary

_____ moral decisions

_____ Sermon on the Mount

_____ grace

_____ actual grace

_____ the Catholic Letters

_____ Ten Commandments

_____ the Covenant

_____ chastity

_____ justice

Questions I Have

What questions would you like to ask about God's gift of grace?

_____

_____

_____

_____

A Scripture Story

John's message of God's love

How do you show God's love?

Making Christian Decisions

We Pray

Make known to me
   your ways, LORD;
teach me your paths.

PSALM 25:4

Lord God, make us
ready to live the
Gospel and eager
to do your will. Amen.

*What are some decisions
that you make every day?*

Every day you make
choices and decisions.
Your choices tell people
a lot about you. Think
about some of the
decisions you have made.

*How do you know if your
decision is a good one?*

Choosing to Live a Holy Life

Faith Focus

Why is it important to make moral decisions?

Faith Vocabulary

moral decisions.
The decisions and choices we make to live as children of God and followers of Jesus Christ.

Choosing What Is Good

Choosing friends to spend our time with, taking part in our parish or community service projects, helping out at home or at school—these are all choices that tell people something about us.

God made us to know him, to love him, and to serve him. **Moral decisions** are the choices we make to live as children of God and followers of Jesus Christ.

Moral decisions bring us closer to living the life that God created us to live. They build up our relationships with God, the Church, and others. Moral decisions strengthen our character and lead us toward the happiness God created us to have.

Our intellect, free will, and feelings can help us make moral decisions.

Intellect

God has given us the marvelous ability to learn. He has blessed us with the gift of our intellect. Our intellect gives us the ability to learn more about God, ourselves, others, and the world in which we live.

Free Will

God created us out of love and has given us the gift of a free will. Our free will is the power God gives us to make our own decisions and to love him and others. We can choose to do what we know is good or evil. We can choose to love God or turn away from his love.

Feelings

Our feelings, or emotions, are neither good nor bad. They can help us do good, or they can weaken us to do evil.

loving thing to do or say. We struggle to overcome temptation. Temptation is all that moves us to make decisions that lead us away from living as children of God.

Choosing to Live a Good Life

Sadly, we live in a world in which original sin has weakened our intellect and will. We do not always use our feelings to help us choose what we know is the good or

The Holy Spirit always helps and guides us to make good decisions, to overcome temptation, and to live a holy life. We just need to remember to ask for help.

 What do you think about when making a decision?

Signs of a Good Decision

Design a collage of phrases that describes making a decision to live as a follower of Jesus Christ.

Faith Vocabulary

conscience. The gift of God that is part of every person and that guides us to know and judge what is right and wrong.

The Gift of Conscience

Maybe you have wondered, How can I know what is right and what is wrong?

What is God's will and what is not God's will? What is it that says, "It's okay" or "Stop right there"? That ability to know and judge what is good and what is evil comes from our **conscience.**

When we read the Gospel story about Saint Peter denying that he was a follower of Jesus, we see how a conscience works. Three times Saint Peter was asked, "Do you know Jesus? You are one of his followers." "No!" "No!" "No!" Peter insisted.

> Then Peter remembered the word that Jesus had said to him, "Before the cock crows twice you will deny me three times." He broke down and wept. MARK 14:72

Saint Peter's conscience made him aware that he had done something wrong. He was sorry, and he wept.

Forming a Good Conscience

Every person is born with a conscience. Just as we train and develop our gifts to play a sport, do math, use computers, play a musical instrument, or dance or sing, we also need to develop our ability to make moral decisions. We need to train and develop our conscience. Here are some ways we can develop or train our conscience.

- Pray to the Holy Spirit.
- Take part in the celebration of the sacraments, especially the Eucharist and Reconciliation.
- Read, study, and pray the Bible, especially the Gospels.
- Study what the Catholic Church teaches about how we should live.
- Learn from the lives of others, such as the saints, who have lived holy lives.
- Ask the advice of our parents and other adults who teach us about our faith.

The ability to use and follow our conscience can also become weakened. We can develop a bad conscience. We can listen to the many other voices that try to lead us away from living as Jesus taught.

We have a serious responsibility to work hard at forming a good conscience. This is something we have the responsibility to do our whole life long.

 How can we train and develop our conscience?

Training My Conscience

Choose one of the ways we can train our conscience. Make a plan of how you will use it to train your conscience.

_____

_____

_____

_____

Faith Vocabulary

moral virtues. Spiritual powers, or habits, that give us the strength to do what is right and good and to live holy lives.

cardinal virtues. The four virtues of prudence, justice, fortitude, and temperance.

The Cardinal Virtues

The more we train our voice to sing or practice our serve in tennis, the more improvement we see and the better we do. We develop good habits, or ways of doing things that seem natural. People may comment, "He has a natural singing voice" or "She has a natural serve."

The same is true in following a well-trained conscience and making moral decisions. The more we cooperate with the grace of the Holy Spirit and we work at making moral decisions, the better we become at it. We develop **moral virtues**. Moral virtues are spiritual powers, or habits, that give us the strength to do what is right, avoid what is wrong, and live a holy life.

There are four moral virtues that are called cardinal virtues. The word *cardinal* comes from a word meaning "to hinge on." Our moral life and moral decision-making hinge on these virtues. They help us live as Jesus taught. The four cardinal virtues are prudence, justice, fortitude, and temperance.

Prudence

Prudence helps us evaluate situations and judge them wisely. Prudence helps us know whether our decisions will lead us to do good or evil.

Justice

Justice directs us to give to God what rightfully belongs to him. It also guides us to give to our neighbors what rightfully belongs to them.

Fortitude

Fortitude keeps us steady in doing what is good. Fortitude keeps us going in the right direction, especially when difficulties arise.

Temperance

Temperance helps us balance our lives. This cardinal virtue helps us use and not abuse things. Temperance guides us to enjoy things within correct limits and in a way that is not harmful to us or others.

Our moral life and moral decision-making hinge on the cardinal virtues. They help us live as followers of Jesus Christ.

How do the four cardinal virtues help you make decisions to live as a follower of Jesus?

NAME THE VIRTUES

Read this situation. Then name the cardinal virtue that is at work.

Devan really enjoys playing his electronic games. He could play with them all the time. But he makes sure to do his school work and play with his friends. He does not let playing electronic games take the place of these important things.

This is a description of the virtue of

_____ .

Create your own situation. Ask a friend to name the virtue you are describing.

Making a Retreat

The word *retreat* has many meanings. One meaning is "a quiet place." Catholics often set aside time to go to a quiet place. While they are there, they think and pray about the way they are living their faith. Sometimes Catholics go away to a retreat house. They stay there for a day, overnight, a few days, a week, or longer.

Retreat houses organize retreats for adult women and men, for married couples, and for singles. They also hold retreats for youth groups and young people preparing for Confirmation. Catholics make a retreat so they take time to grow in their relationship with God and plan ways to live holy lives.

QUESTION How does your parish help you grow in your love for God and for others?

Chapel, St. Benedict's Lodge, Dominican Retreat Center, McKenzie Bridge, Oregon

What Difference Does Faith Make in My Life?

Each day you try to grow as a Catholic and make decisions to live the life that God asks you to live.

You are the commentator of a student talk show, "Decisions! Decisions!" Today the topic is "Helpful Decisions Made by Fifth Graders." Create a dialogue you might have with a student about making moral decisions and the good consequences that come from those decisions.

Decisions! Decisions!

_____

_____

_____

_____

_____

_____

_____

_____

_____

_____

My Faith Choice

This week I will try to be more aware of how I go about making moral decisions. Before I make an important decision I will

_____

_____ .

An Examination of Conscience

An examination of conscience is like a miniretreat. Set aside time each day. Use this examination of conscience.

1. Sit in a comfortable place. Remember that God is with you.
2. Spend time thinking about the day.
3. Answer these questions:
   a. How have I shown or not shown love and respect for God?
   b. How have I shown or not shown love and respect for myself?
   c. How have I shown or not shown love and respect for other people?
   d. How have I used or misused the gift of God's creation?
4. Spend some time talking to God. Ask him to help you make better decisions.
5. Promise that you will try to do your best.
6. Pray the Act of Contrition
   My God,
   I am sorry for my sins
   with all my heart.
   In choosing to do wrong
   and failing to do good,
   I have sinned against you
   whom I should love above all things.
   I firmly intend, with your help,
   to do penance,
   to sin no more,
      and to avoid whatever leads me to sin.
      Our Savior Jesus Christ
      suffered and died for us.
      In his name, my God, have mercy.

We Remember

What I Have Learned

Fill in the circle next to each correct answer.

1. A _____ is a spiritual power, or habit, that helps us do what is right, avoid what is wrong, and live a holy life.

   ○ temptation   ○ conscience   ○ virtue

2. Our _____ is our ability to know God, our self, and other people.

   ○ intellect   ○ free will   ○ soul

3. A _____ is the gift of God that is part of every person and helps us know and judge what is right and wrong.

   ○ virtue   ○ free will   ○ conscience

Answer the following.

4. Describe why it is important to train our conscience.

   _____

   _____

   _____

   _____

5. Choose two of the cardinal virtues. Explain how each of the virtues you chose helps you live a holy life.

   _____

   _____

   _____

   _____

Growing in Faith

One important thing I learned this week is

_____

_____

_____.

This is important because

_____

_____

_____.

What will people see me doing as I live my faith choice this week?

_____

_____

_____

This Week . . .

In chapter 18, "Making Christian Decisions," your child learned about the importance of making moral decisions. Such decisions guide us in living as children of God and followers of Christ. Each of us has been given a conscience, an intellect, a free will, and feelings, or emotions. All these natural gifts give us the ability to make decisions that guide us in living holy lives. Throughout our entire life we cooperate with the grace of the Holy Spirit and work at forming a good conscience and developing virtues. The cardinal virtues of prudence, justice, fortitude, and temperance strengthen our desire and ability to choose what is good, to overcome the temptation to do evil, and avoid doing what is not good.

For more on the teachings of the Catholic Church on conscience, cardinal virtues, and making moral decisions, see *Catechism of the Catholic Church* paragraph numbers 1699–1709, 1716–1724, 1730–1742, 1762–1770, 1776–1794, and 1803–1811.

Sharing God's Word

Read together Psalm 25:4. Emphasize that the four cardinal virtues play a pivotal role in helping us make good decisions to live holy lives.

Praying

In this chapter your child learned one form of an examination of conscience. Use this examination of conscience. Follow the steps on page 238.

Making a Difference

Choose one of the following activities to do as a family or design a similar activity of your own.

- Invite family members to share the things that help them develop a good conscience. Encourage each other to make decisions to live holy lives.

- An examination of conscience helps us reflect on our moral decisions. Talk about why it is important to think about our moral decisions before, during, and after we make them.

- Identify ways your family can help one another make decisions to live a holy life. Choose one thing you will do this week to help each other.

For more ideas on ways your family can live your faith, visit the "Faith First for Families" page at **www.FaithFirst.com**. Click on "Make a Difference" for ideas on how your family can share God's love with others this week.

The Beatitudes
A Scripture Story

We Pray

Bless the LORD, my soul;
  all my being, bless his
    holy name!

PSALM 103:1

Father,
send the Holy Spirit
to guide us to live
as faithful members
of your holy people.
Amen.

Where do you think true happiness comes from?

Everyone wants to be happy. Everyone spends their whole life seeking happiness. Jesus taught the Beatitudes to help us learn the true meaning of happiness.

What are the Beatitudes?

Saint Elizabeth Ann Seton, stained glass

Faith Focus

How does the Sermon on the Mount help us live as Christians?

Faith Vocabulary

Sermon on the Mount. The teachings of Jesus that are grouped together in chapters 5, 6, and 7 of the Gospel of Matthew.

Beatitudes. The sayings or teachings of Jesus that are found in the Sermon on the Mount that describe both the qualities and actions of people blessed by God.

Flock of sheep on Mount of Beatitudes, Galilee

The Sermon on the Mount

Jesus taught his disciples many things. He gave them concrete guidelines on how he wanted them to live. Saint Matthew has gathered many of these teachings of Jesus in chapters 5, 6, and 7 of his Gospel. This part of Matthew's Gospel is called the **Sermon on the Mount.**

The Sermon on the Mount begins with the **Beatitudes.** The word *beatitude* means "blessedness" or "happiness." The Beatitudes are the sayings or teachings of Jesus that describe both the qualities and the actions of people blessed by God.

The words *blessed* and *kingdom* are repeated throughout the Beatitudes. Jesus' listeners knew both of these words very well. They are the key to understanding Jesus' teachings in the Beatitudes.

Blessed

The Jewish people of Jesus' time used the word *blessed* in praying the Psalms, which they prayed daily. They addressed God as "Blessed." They also described people who trusted and hoped in God above all else as "blessed." When Jesus taught "Blessed are . . . ," the people knew that these were powerful and special words.

The Kingdom

The word *kingdom* also had special meaning for Jesus' listeners. The Jewish people living in Jesus' time were under the rule of the Romans. They wanted to be free of that rule. They prayed that God would establish the kingdom he had promised to Abraham, Moses, and David.

Jesus' disciples and other Jews who listened to Jesus hoped that he would bring about that kingdom. So when Jesus spoke of the Kingdom of God, they listened attentively. What they did not yet understand was that the Kingdom of God that Jesus was announcing was not a kingdom of power on earth. It was a different kind of kingdom.

QUESTION *How does understanding the meaning of the words blessed and kingdom help us live as Jesus' followers?*

Happiness is...

Describe some of the ways you seek happiness. Share how these ways are ways that God would call "blessed."

Reading the Word of God

Faith Focus

What do the Beatitudes teach us?

The Beatitudes

Matthew's Gospel teaches that Jesus traveled throughout Galilee and Judea, preaching the good news of the coming of the Kingdom of God. One day a crowd followed Jesus up a mountainside in Galilee. Seeing the crowd, Jesus began to teach them. He said:

Blessed are the poor in spirit,
for theirs is the kingdom of heaven.
Blessed are they who mourn,
for they will be comforted.
Blessed are the meek,
for they will inherit the land.
Blessed are they who hunger and thirst for righteousness,
for they will be satisfied.
Blessed are the merciful,
for they will be shown mercy.
Blessed are the clean of heart,
for they will see God.
Blessed are the peacemakers,
for they will be called children of God.
Blessed are they who are persecuted for the sake of righteousness,
for theirs is the kingdom of heaven."

MATTHEW 5:3–10

Jesus concluded by telling his listeners that living the Beatitudes would not be easy. He said:

"Blessed are you when they insult you and persecute you and utter every kind of evil against you [falsely] because of me. Rejoice and be glad, for your reward will be great in heaven. Thus they persecuted the prophets who were before you."

MATTHEW 5:11–12

Jesus told his disciples that they would need courage to be "poor in spirit," to "mourn," to "hunger and thirst for righteousness," to be "merciful," to be "clean of heart," and to be "peacemakers." He warned them that people would make fun of them and persecute them. But if they trusted him and lived as he taught them, they would discover true happiness. Their reward would be great in the kingdom—the Kingdom of Heaven.

 What does Jesus promise to those who are blessed in God's eyes?

Beatitudes in Action

The headline "Workers Meet to Settle Salary Demands" might describe the Beatitude "Blessed are the Peacemakers." Make up your own headlines for two other Beatitudes.

Headline: _____

Beatitude: _____

_____

_____

Headline: _____

Beatitude: _____

_____

Faith Focus

How does each of the Beatitudes help us make decisions to live as Christians?

Participants signing up for Walk for Hunger, Walk for Hunger Wall, Boston, Massachusetts

The Blessed

There are Christians you know or you have read about who are mourning or who are being persecuted. Yet they do not seem to be as upset as we might think they would be. There is something strong about them. It seems Jesus was talking about people just like them when he taught the Beatitudes. By understanding the meaning of each of the Beatitudes, we can better understand the teachings of Jesus on what it means to be truly blessed, or happy.

The Poor in Spirit

People who are poor in spirit place all their trust in God. They know that all they have—no matter how much or how little—is from God.

Those Who Mourn

People who mourn are those who have suffered a loss in their lives. They are strong because they know God is always with them. They comfort others and help those who are suffering.

The Meek

People who are meek are considerate. They do not push their own wishes on others. They treat others kindly and respectfully.

Those Who Hunger and Thirst for Righteousness

People who hunger and thirst for righteousness are people who work to build the kind of world God wants. They work so that everyone is treated fairly and justly.

The Merciful

People who show others mercy reach out and help people. They see people as God sees them. They are generous and kind. They forgive others as they know God forgives them.

The Clean of Heart

People who are clean of heart place God above everyone and everything else in their lives.

The Peacemakers

People who work for peace solve problems without harming anyone. They devote themselves to building the kind of world in which all may live as children of God.

Those Persecuted for Righteousness

When things are the way God wants them to be, they are "right." People who work for righteousness do what God wants, even when it is difficult to do so.

The Beatitudes are guides for living as Jesus taught us to live. All our actions are to show that we live for the kingdom that Jesus announced. The rewards promised to the blessed will be fully received in the Kingdom of God.

 What do the Beatitudes teach about the Kingdom of God?

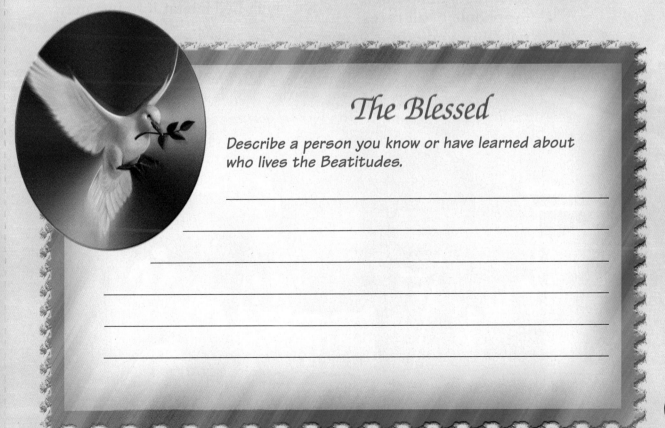

The Blessed

Describe a person you know or have learned about who lives the Beatitudes.

_____

_____

_____

_____

_____

Habitat for Humanity

Habitat for Humanity International is a Christian housing organization. It brings together Catholic and other Christian volunteers to work together for justice and righteousness. They build "simple, decent, and affordable housing in partnership with those in need of adequate housing."

Habitat for Humanity volunteers have built more than 175,000 homes all over the world. This includes more than 50,000 in the United States. These homes are for people who cannot afford to buy a home of their own.

Habitat for Humanity volunteers build homes for people of all races, religions, and ethnic groups.

Their work is a sign of God's love for all people and helps all people place their trust in him. You can imagine the happiness that families feel when they move into a home built by Habitat for Humanity.

 How does your parish help to build a better world by living the Beatitudes?

What Difference Does Faith Make in My Life?

When you live the Beatitudes, you are a sign to others of what it means to be blessed by God. You have your eyes on living in the Kingdom of Heaven.

Each of these actions is one way of living a Beatitude. Think about the two actions described below. Name the Beatitude each puts into action. Then write one way you have lived that Beatitude.

Living the Beatitudes

Action	Beatitude	How I Lived It
1. You are kind to someone others are picking on.	_____	_____
	_____	_____
	_____	_____
	_____	_____
2. You listen to someone you disagree with. Together you solve your problem.	_____	_____
	_____	_____
	_____	_____
	_____	_____

My Faith Choice

I believe that the Holy Spirit calls me to live the Beatitudes. This week I will

_____

_____ .

Prayer to Live the Beatitudes

Leader: In a prayer of petition, we ask God to help us live for the Kingdom of God. Pray this prayer of petition. Ask God to help you live the Beatitudes.

Loving Father, send us the Holy Spirit.
Teach us to be poor in spirit

All: **that we will receive the gift of the Kingdom of Heaven.**

Leader: Teach us to mourn

All: **that we will receive the gift of your comfort.**

Leader: Teach us to be meek

All: **that we will inherit the earth.**

Leader: Teach us to hunger and thirst for righteousness

All: **that we will be satisfied.**

Leader: Teach us to be merciful

All: **that we will be shown mercy.**

Leader: Teach us to be clean of heart

All: **that we will see you.**

Leader: Teach us to be peacemakers

All: **that we will be called children of God.**

Leader: Teach us to have courage when we are treated harmfully because of our love for you

All: **that we will receive the gift of the Kingdom of Heaven.**

BASED ON MATTHEW 5:3–10

Leader: Let us pray the Lord's Prayer together.

We Remember

What I Have Learned

Match the parts of the Beatitudes.

___ 1. "Blessed are the meek,

___ 2. "Blessed are the peacemakers,

___ 3. "Blessed are the poor in spirit,

___ 4. "Blessed are the clean of heart,

___ 5. "Blessed are they who mourn,

a. for theirs is the kingdom of heaven."

b. for they will see God."

c. for they will be comforted."

d. for they will inherit the land."

e. for they will be called children of God."

Answer the following.

6. Describe the meaning of the word *blessed* that begins each Beatitude.

_____

_____

7. Describe the kingdom promised to those who live the Beatitudes.

_____

_____

8. Compare living the Beatitudes with working to prepare the way for the Kingdom of God.

_____

_____

_____

1. The Beatitudes name ways Jesus wants his disciples to live.

2. The Beatitudes describe the qualities and actions of people blessed by God.

3. The Beatitudes guide us to prepare the way for the coming of the Kingdom of God, which will come about at the end of time.

Growing in Faith

One important thing I learned this week is

_____

_____

_____ .

This is important because

_____

_____

_____ .

What will people see me doing as I live my faith choice this week?

_____

_____

_____

This Week . . .

In chapter 19, "The Beatitudes: A Scripture Story," your child learned about the Beatitudes that are found in the Sermon on the Mount in Matthew's Gospel. The Beatitudes name qualities, actions, and rewards of those blessed by God. The disciples of Jesus are called to live in such a way that we witness to the coming of the Kingdom of Heaven. We are to be living signs of the blessedness, or happiness, God wishes for all.

For more on the teachings of the Catholic Church on the human vocation to beatitude, or happiness, see *Catechism of the Catholic Church* paragraph numbers 1716–1724.

Sharing God's Word

Read together Matthew 5:3–12. Emphasize that Jesus taught the Beatitudes to identify people who were truly blessed by God.

Praying

In this chapter your child prayed a prayer of petition, asking God for the grace to live the Beatitudes. Read and pray together this prayer on page 250.

Making a Difference

Choose one of the following activities to do as a family or design a similar activity of your own.

- We are blessed by God when we are peacemakers. Name ways that you can live as peacemakers at home, at school, at work, and in your community.

- Write each of the Beatitudes on an index card and put the cards in a container near the entrance to your home. Each day this week have each family member choose a card, read it, place it back into the container, and try to put the Beatitude they chose into practice that day.

- In the Sermon on the Mount, Jesus taught that happiness comes from living as God created us to live. Talk about why living as a child of God is the only way to find true happiness.

For more ideas on ways your family can live your faith, visit the "Faith First for Families" page at **www.FaithFirst.com**. Click on "Contemporary Issues" to find an article on an especially interesting topic.

Live as Children of Light

20

We Pray

The LORD is my light and
my salvation.

PSALM 27:1

God, loving Father,
fill our hearts with
light and lead us
to your Son.   Amen.

*What makes every person
special?*

God created us to be holy.
When you think of a holy
person, who do you think
of? We live holy lives when
we live our Catholic faith.

*What are the qualities of
a holy person?*

Our Call to Holiness

Faith Focus

How do we live a holy life?

Faith Vocabulary

holiness. The quality, or condition, of a person who is living in communion with and in the right relationship with God, others, and with all of his creation; being in the state of grace.

Created in God's Image

The Blessed Virgin Mary, Saint Francis of Assisi, and Blessed Mother Teresa of Calcutta are holy people. What about you? Did you know that you are holy too? God created every person to be holy. He created us in his image and likeness. We are to be holy because we have been created in the image of God, the Holy One.

"Be holy because I [am] holy."
1 PETER 1:16

Through Baptism, every Christian is called to a life of **holiness**. Holiness is sharing in the very life of God. As the newly baptized are dressed with a white garment, the priest or deacon says,

(Name) you have become a new creation, and have clothed yourself in Christ. See in this white garment the outward sign of your Christian dignity. With your family and friends to help you by word and example, bring that dignity unstained into the everlasting life of heaven.
RITE OF BAPTISM FOR CHILDREN

Living a life of holiness includes trying our best to live as children of God.

254

Jesus, Model of Holiness

Jesus is the "Holy One of God" (Mark 1:24). Jesus lived and taught the way to the Father, the way of holiness. After he taught his disciples the Beatitudes, Jesus told his disciples that they were to be lights in the world. He said:

"You are the light of the world. . . . [Y]our light must shine before others, that they may see your good deeds and glorify your heavenly Father." MATTHEW 5:14, 16

At the Last Supper Jesus told his disciples what it meant to be a light in the world. He said:

"As the Father loves me, so I also love you. . . . This I command you: love one another."
JOHN 15:9, 17

Our choices—our words and actions—are to show our love for God and for one another. Each day we ask the Holy Spirit to help us try our best to love, forgive, and care for others as Jesus showed us.

 What does it mean to live a holy life?

Living as Children of God

God the Father sent us a gift to help us live holy lives. Solve this code to discover God's gift.

A · −	H · · · ·	O − − −	V · · · −
B − · · ·	I · ·	P · − − ·	W · − −
C − · − ·	J · − − −	Q − − · −	X − · · −
D − · ·	K − · −	R · − ·	Y − · − −
E ·	L · − · ·	S · · ·	Z − − · ·
F · · − ·	M − −	T −	
G − − ·	N − ·	U · · −	

"_____ _____ _____ _____

_____ _____ _____ _____

_____ _____ _____ _____ _____

_____ _____ _____ _____ _____ _____ _____ _____ ." JOHN 14:26

Faith Vocabulary

actual grace. The gift of God's presence with us to help us live as children of God and followers of Christ.

Living by God's Grace

At Baptism we are joined to Christ, the Holy One of God. We receive the gift of the Holy Spirit and become adopted sons and daughters of God the Father. We receive God's grace to live a holy life.

At Baptism our parents and godparents received a candle lighted from the Easter candle as the priest or deacon said:

Parents and godparents, this light is entrusted to you to be kept burning brightly. These children of yours have been enlightened by Christ. They are to walk always as children of the light. May they keep the flame of faith alive in their hearts. When the Lord comes, may they go out to meet him with all the saints in the heavenly kingdom.

RITE OF BAPTISM FOR CHILDREN

Our parents share with us the gift of life and their love and faith in Jesus Christ. Through Baptism God shares the gift of his life and love with us. We call this gift sanctifying grace. The word *sanctifying* means "making holy." Through this grace all that separates us from God is taken away. Sin is forgiven. We are made holy.

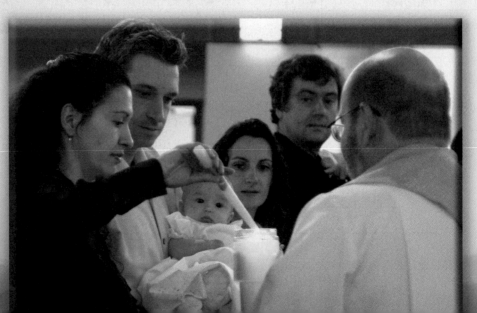

Throughout our whole life God also gives us the gift of his help to live holy lives. We call this help from God **actual grace**. The Holy Spirit teaches us and helps us make moral decisions to live as followers of Jesus Christ. It is because of the grace of the Holy Spirit that we can live as children of God and followers of Jesus. In speaking of his life and work, Saint Paul wrote:

Of this I became a minister by the gift of God's grace that was granted me in accord with the exercise of his power. To me, the very least of all the holy ones, this grace was given, to preach to the Gentiles the inscrutable riches of Christ, and to bring to light [for all] what is the plan of the mystery hidden from ages past in God who created all things.

EPHESIANS 3:7–9

When we take part in the celebration of the sacraments, especially the Eucharist, we strengthen our love for God. We receive his grace to live holy lives. Reading the Bible and praying also help us cooperate with God's grace to live holy lives as his children.

 What might you do that shows you are saying yes to God's gift of grace?

Choosing What We Know Is Good

Write a prayer in this space. Ask the Holy Spirit to help you try your best to live as a child of God.

_____

_____

_____

_____

Faith Vocabulary

mortal sin. A serious
failure in our love and
respect for God, our
neighbor, creation,
and ourselves. Three
things are necessary
for a sin to be
mortal, namely,
(1) the thing we do or
say must be gravely
wrong; (2) we must
know it is gravely
wrong; and (3) we
must freely choose it.

Choosing the Way to Holiness

Think about what it means to become friends. Someone cannot force us to be their friend. God loves us so much that he does not force us to be his friend. He does not force us to love him and live a holy life.

We can choose to live the Great Commandment, or we can choose not to live it. We can choose to love God above all else, or we can choose not to do so. We can choose to love our neighbor as Jesus taught, or we can choose not to do so. When we freely choose not to love God, others, and ourselves, we sin. We choose not to live the way of holiness.

The decision to sin can begin with a temptation. Sin can begin with a thought or desire to do something we know is wrong. Then the choice is made. We can freely do what we know God does not want us to do. We can freely and deliberately choose to do what we know is against God's will. We can sin.

Kinds of Sin

All sin offends God and hurts us. All sins are not the same. Some sins are more serious than others. Looking at sins this way, the Church divides sins into two types—mortal sin and venial sin.

Mortal Sin

A **mortal sin** is a serious, or grave, sin that separates us from God and results in our losing the gift of sanctifying grace. Three things are necessary to commit a mortal sin. They are:

1. The thing we choose to do or not to do must be very seriously wrong.
2. We must know what we choose to do or not to do is seriously wrong.
3. We must freely choose to do what we know is seriously wrong.

Venial Sin

A **venial sin** is less serious than a mortal sin. A sin is a venial sin when one, two, or three of the things named for a sin to be a mortal sin are missing. Venial sins damage and weaken our love for God and for others. They do not break our relationship with God. Ignoring our venial sins or failing to be sorry for them can lead us to more serious sins.

Keeping our eyes focused on God and trying our best to live a holy life is the best way to make moral decisions. It is the best way to say yes to God in big things and in little things.

 What results from committing a sin?

BE HOLY

Look up and read John 15:9–14. Write a sentence to summarize what it says about living a holy life.

_____

_____

_____

Venerable Father Casey

God invites everyone to share in his life and love. He invites everyone to live a holy life. Sometimes people who live holy lives are named saints, or canonized, by the Church. The Church has named Bernard Casey a Venerable of the Church. This is the first step in naming him a saint.

Bernard Casey was the sixth child of a family of ten boys and six girls. They lived on a farm in Wisconsin near the Mississippi River. At the age of twenty-one, he entered St. Francis Seminary in Milwaukee. Five years later he received the name

Venerable Father Solanus Casey, top left, in Detroit Soup Kitchen

Solanus when he entered the Franciscan Capuchin Order.

After he was ordained a priest, Father Solanus devoted his life to serving the sick and the poor in many places in the United States. In 1929 during the Depression when most families were hungry and without money, he worked with his brother Franciscans to set up the Detroit Soup Kitchen. The work of this soup kitchen continues today.

Father Solanus Casey truly loved others as Jesus loved him. One day before he died, he said, "I looked on my whole life as giving, and I want to give until there is nothing left."

> **QUESTION** *Think of a person you know who is living a holy life. How is that person making a difference in the lives of other people?*

Venerable Father Solanus, top left, passing out bread

What Difference Does Faith Make in My Life?

You are holy and are called to live a holy life.

Faced with these situations, what are some good choices that would help you grow in holiness?

Growing in Holiness

A friend of yours makes the team but you do not. How might you react?

I would _____

_____

_____

Your parents really want you to go someplace with the family, but you want to go somewhere with your friends. How would you feel? What would you do?

I would feel _____

_____

I would _____

_____

_____

My Faith Choice

This week I will look for ways to make choices that will help me grow in holiness. I will

_____

_____.

Praying a Psalm

Leader: The Psalms are prayers of the People of God. Some Psalms share thoughts and feelings of God's people as they struggle to live a holy life.

Let us pray these Psalm verses and ask God to help us walk the way of holiness that Jesus taught.

All: **All the paths of the LORD are faithful love.**

Group 1: Make known to me your ways, LORD;
teach me your paths.

Group 2: Guide me in your truth and teach me,
for you are God my savior.

All: **All the paths of the LORD are faithful love.**

Group 1: Remember your compassion and love, O LORD;

Group 2: for they are ages old.

All: **All the paths of the LORD are faithful love.**

Group 1: Good and upright is the LORD,

Group 2: who shows sinners the way.

All: **All the paths of the LORD are faithful love.**

Group 1: [The LORD] guides the humble rightly,

Group 2: and teaches the humble the way.

All: **All the paths of the LORD are faithful love.**

Group 1: Let honesty and virtue preserve me,

Group 2: I wait for you, O LORD.

All: **All the paths of the LORD are faithful love.**

PSALM 25:4–6,8–9, 21

We Remember

What I Have Learned

All these statements are false. Rewrite each one so that it is true.

1. Only Christians are called to live holy lives.

   _____

2. Sin is saying yes to God.

   _____

3. Mortal sin is less serious than venial sin.

   _____

4. Venial sin is a serious sin that separates us from God's love.

   _____

5. Sanctifying grace is the help God gives us to make a decision to live a holy life.

   _____

Answer the following.

6. Describe the meaning of the Scripture teaching "Be holy because I [am] holy" (1 Peter 1:16).

   _____

   _____

7. Compare sanctifying grace and actual grace.

   _____

   _____

8. Describe the effects of sin.

   _____

   _____

To Help You Remember

1. When we live as images of God, we live holy lives.

2. When we sin, we choose not to live holy lives.

3. The grace of God helps us live holy lives.

Growing in Faith

One important thing I learned this week is

_____

_____

_____.

This is important because

_____

_____

_____.

What will people see me doing as I live my faith choice this week?

_____

_____

_____

This Week . . .

In chapter 20, "Live as Children of Light," your child learned more about the call of every person to live a holy life. Christians are called to live the way of holiness Jesus lived and taught his disciples to live. Through Baptism we receive the gift of sanctifying grace, the gift of holiness. We are made sharers in the life and love of God the Father, the Son, and the Holy Spirit. We are joined to Christ and receive the gift of the Holy Spirit and the graces to live as children of God the Father. When we freely choose not to live as we know God wants us to live, we sin. We can accept or reject God's invitation and his help to live a holy life.

For more on the teachings of the Catholic Church on sin and grace, see *Catechism of the Catholic Church* paragraph numbers 1846–1869 and 1987–2016.

Sharing God's Word

Read together 1 Peter 1:15–16. Emphasize that God created every person to be holy.

Praying

In this chapter your child prayed a prayer based on Psalm 25. Read and pray together this prayer on page 262.

Making a Difference

Choose one of the following activities to do as a family or design a similar activity of your own.

- Cooperating with God's grace helps us grow in holiness. Name some people who help you make choices to live a holy life.

- Ask each family member to think of a person who they believe lives a holy life. Then have family members share how those people are making a difference in the lives of others.

- Ask each family member to share the name of their favorite saint. Together research the lives of your family's favorite saints on the *Catholic Encyclopedia* Web site. Talk about why that person was named a saint, a model of holiness.

For more ideas on ways your family can live your faith, visit the "Faith First for Families" page at **www.FaithFirst.com**. Click on "Family Prayer." Plan to pray this prayer together this week.

God Is Love
A Scripture Story

21

We Pray

Give thanks to the LORD,
who is good,
whose love endures
forever.

PSALM 118:1

Father of all goodness,
may we live our life
in Christ, your Son,
with joy and express it
in love.   Amen.

What are some ways you share your thoughts and feelings?

We share our thoughts and feelings with one another in many ways. God speaks to us about himself in the Bible. The First Letter of John in the New Testament tells us, "God is love" (1 John 4:16).

Why do you think God wants us to know this about himself?

265

Bible Background

How does reading the First Letter of John help us understand what it means to love God?

Faith Vocabulary

Catholic Letters. The seven New Testament letters that bear the names of the Apostles John, Peter, Jude, and James.

The New Testament Letters

Prayerfully reading the Scriptures with other people or alone helps us come to know and love God. The Church has named the forty-six books of the Old Testament and the twenty-seven books of the New Testament as the inspired word of God.

While the Gospels are the heart of the New Testament, they were not the first books of the New Testament that were written. Many of the letters in the New Testament were written before the four Gospels. In addition to the four Gospels, the New Testament contains the Acts of the Apostles, the Book of Revelation, and twenty-one

Saint Paul, stained glass

letters. The New Testament includes the:

- thirteen letters, or epistles, of Saint Paul the Apostle
- seven Catholic Letters
- Letter to the Hebrews

Letters of Saint Paul

The letters of Saint Paul the Apostle include the:

- Letter to the Romans
- First and Second Letter to the Corinthians
- Letter to the Galatians
- Letter to the Ephesians
- Letter to the Philippians
- Letter to the Colossians
- First and Second Letter to the Thessalonians
- First and Second Letter to Timothy
- Letter to Titus
- Letter to Philemon

The Catholic Letters

The **Catholic Letters** were written for all Christians. The word *catholic* means "universal" or for "everyone." The seven Catholic Letters in the New Testament are the:

- Letter of James
- First Letter of Peter
- Second Letter of Peter
- First Letter of John
- Second Letter of John
- Third Letter of John
- Letter of Jude

Each of these seven letters has the name of an Apostle in its title. The Church teaches that these letters pass on to us the authentic teachings of the Apostles.

 What are the different kinds of writings in the New Testament?

Sharing the Good News of Jesus

Look up and read 1 John 2:3–6. Compare the message of this passage with the message of John 15:9–14. Write your comparison here.

_____

_____

_____

_____

_____

_____

Reading the Word of God

Faith Focus

How does reading the First Letter of John help us come to know who God is?

God Is Love

Three of the seven Catholic Letters are attributed to Saint John the Apostle. This means that they share his teachings with us. The First Letter of John helps us understand the depth of God's love for us. In this letter we read:

Beloved, let us love one another, because love is of God; everyone who loves is begotten by God and knows God. Whoever is without love does not know God, for God is love. . . .

God is love, and whoever remains in love remains in God and God in him. . . . If anyone says, "I love God," but hates his brother, he is a liar; for whoever does not love a brother whom he has seen cannot love God whom he has not seen. This is the commandment we have from him: whoever loves God must also love his brother.

1 JOHN 4:7–8, 16, 20–21

This letter is a wonderful testimony of the faith of the Church in God. Saint John the Apostle passes on the faith of the early Church in who Jesus, the Incarnate Son of God, revealed God to be. The early Church professed, "God is love."

In this way the love of God was revealed to us: God sent his only Son into the world so that we might have life through him. In this is love: not that we have loved God, but that he loved us.

1 JOHN 4:9–10

As we read the First Letter of John, we listen to God tell us about himself. We also listen to God tell us about who we are.

See what love the Father has bestowed on us that we may be called the children of God. Yet so we are.   1 JOHN 3:1

We are children of God. We are to love one another if we are to live in God's love.

QUESTION How does 1 John 4:9–10 help us understand the connection between loving God and loving our neighbor?

What Does It Mean to Say God Is Love?

Describe what would change in the world if everyone really understood and lived the message of the First Letter of John.

_____

_____

_____

_____

_____

_____

_____

Understanding the Word of God

Faith Vocabulary

theological virtues.
The virtues of faith, hope, and love (charity); gifts of God that enable us to live a life of holiness, or a life in communion with the Holy Trinity.

Love of God and Others

Love is a word that we use very often—and in many different ways. We see it in big, brightly colored letters on birthday and Valentine's Day cards. We use it to sign letters and cards. But the real meaning of love is not very easy to understand. What does the love revealed by Jesus mean? The First Letter of John teaches what Christian love is. John teaches that love is of God and "God is love" (1 John 4:8).

God gives us a special gift that gives us the power to love him. It is the gift of the theological virtue of love. The **theological virtues** of faith, hope, and love enable us to live a life of holiness and to share in the life and love of the Holy Trinity. The theological virtue of love gives us the power to return to God the love he shares with us. It gives us the power to make God's love the most important thing in our lives.

How do we know that God's love and life are really in us? How can we tell that we are growing in his love?

We know that God's love is taking hold of us by the way that we treat others. John tells us that we are called to love others as God loves us. We are to care for one another in ways that are real and not just in words. If people are hungry, we give them food. If people are troubled, we comfort them. If people are homeless, we find them shelter.

In giving us his Son, God the Father gave us the generous gift of his love. If we are to live as children of God, we must imitate this divine generosity of God's love. We do not ask, "What's in it for me?" before we help someone. Once we realize how much God loves us, we can begin to love others as he loves them—and us.

 What can you do to show that you are a child of God, who is love?

Our Catholic Identity

Christian Martyrs

The word *martyr* means "witness." Christian martyrs are witnesses for Christ. They make the greatest sacrifice of all to live the Great Commandment. Because of their love for God and people, they freely choose to suffer death rather than stop loving God and their neighbors.

Showing God's Love

Write about one sign of God's love you experienced recently.

_____

_____

_____

_____

_____

_____

_____

_____

_____

_____

_____

Witnesses for Christ

From the first days of the Church, Christians have lived as Christ and given their lives out of love for God and people. Here are but a few of the thousands of Christian martyrs who have willingly risked and given up their lives as they proclaimed the good news of God's love for all people:

• Ursuline Sister Dorothy Kazel, Maryknoll Sisters Ita Ford and Maura Clarke, and lay missionary Jean Donovan were shot and killed in 1980 for working with the poor and preaching the Gospel in El Salvador in Central America.

• Sister Aloysius Maria, a Missionary of Charity, was killed by rebels in Sierra Leone in 1999.

• Father Albino Saluhakku, a priest of the diocese of Huambo in Angola, and two catechists working with him were killed in 1999.

• Bishop Benjamin de Jesus, a member of the Oblates of Mary Immaculate, was gunned down in 1998 outside the cathedral in Jolo in the Philippines.

• Marist Brothers Servando Mayor Garcia, Miguel Angel Isla Lucio, Fernando de la Fuente, and Julio Rodriguez Jorge were murdered in 1995 in Eastern Zaire by Rwandan militants while working with Rwandan refugees.

Benjamin de Jesus, OMI (1940–1998), bishop of Jolo, Philippines

Sister Maura Clarke, MM (1931–1980)

QUESTION *Who do you know who is suffering in your community? How can you work with others to help them?*

What Difference Does Faith Make in My Life?

Each day your deeds and words show your love for God.

Create a picture story of your actions speaking loudly about God's love.

ACTIONS SPEAK LOUDER THAN WORDS

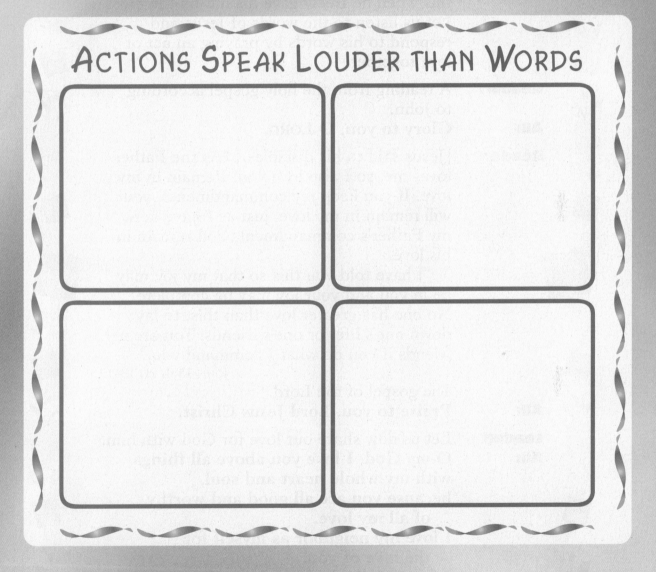

My Faith Choice

This week I will show that I love God.
I will

_____

_____.

An Act of Love

Leader: God created us to share in his love and to share that love with others. Jesus reminded us of this when he taught about the Great Commandment. He most clearly revealed this when he freely gave his life on the cross. Let us listen to the words of Jesus and respond to his words by praying an act of love together.

Reader: A reading from the holy gospel according to John.

All: **Glory to you, O LORD.**

Reader: [Jesus said to his disciples,] "As the Father loves me, so I also love you. Remain in my love. If you keep my commandments, you will remain in my love, just as I have kept my Father's commandments and remain in his love.

"I have told you this so that my joy may be in you and your joy may be complete. . . . No one has greater love than this, to lay down one's life for one's friends. You are my friends if you do what I command you."

JOHN 15:9–11, 13–14

The gospel of the Lord.

All: **Praise to you, Lord Jesus Christ.**

Leader: Let us now share our love for God with him.

All: **O my God, I love you above all things,
with my whole heart and soul,
because you are all good and worthy
    of all my love.
I love my neighbor as myself for
    the love of you.
I forgive all who have injured me,
and I ask pardon of all whom
    I have injured.
Amen.**

What I Have Learned

Circle the word or phrase that completes each sentence correctly.

1. There are _____ Catholic Letters.
   a. two   **b. five**   **c. seven**

2. The Catholic Letters are part of the _____.
   a. New Testament   **b. Old Testament**
   c. *Catechism of the Catholic Church*

3. The Catholic Letters each have the name of an _____.
   a. Evangelist b. Apostle   c. pope

4. The Catholic Letters are addressed to _____ Christians.
   a. all   **b. some**   **c. no**

5. The First Letter of _____ tells us that a person cannot love God and hate other people.
   a. John   **b. Paul**   **c. Matthew**

Answer the following.

6. Describe the importance of the name of an Apostle being in the title of each of the Catholic Letters.

   _____

   _____

7. Describe the theological virtue of love.

   _____

   _____

8. Use the expression "Actions speak louder than words" to describe the First Letter of John's teaching on Christian love.

   _____

   _____

To Help You Remember

1. The seven Catholic Letters in the New Testament were written to all Christians.

2. The First Letter of John reveals to us that "God is love."

3. If we truly love God, we love others as God loves them.

Growing in Faith

One important thing I learned this week is

_____

_____

_____.

This is important because

_____

_____

_____.

What will people see me doing as I live my faith choice this week?

_____

_____

_____

This Week . . .

In chapter 21, "God Is Love: A Scripture Story," your child learned about the Catholic Letters in the New Testament, in particular the First Letter of John. The First Letter of John reveals that "God is love" (1 John 4:8). As children of God, who is love, we are to love others. If we say we love God and do not love others, we are liars.

For more on the teachings of the Catholic Church on the attributes, or qualities, of God that he has revealed about himself, see *Catechism of the Catholic Church* paragraph numbers 199–221.

Sharing God's Word

Read together 1 John 4:7–21. Emphasize that in this passage John teaches "God is love, and whoever remains in love remains in God and God in him."

Praying

In this chapter your child learned to pray an act of love. Read and pray together this prayer on page 274.

Making a Difference

Choose one of the following activities to do as a family or design a similar activity of your own.

- Make a banner with the words "Whoever loves God must also love his brothers and sisters." Decorate the banner and hang it in your home where it can remind everyone of the importance of loving one another.

- We show our love for God by loving others. Research the ways your parish shows its love for God by loving others.

- Talk about how your family puts your love for God into action. Choose one thing you can do this week to put your love for God into action as a family.

For more ideas on ways your family can live your faith, visit the "Faith First for Families" page at **www.FaithFirst.com**. Check out "Bible Stories." Read and discuss the Bible story this week.

Living Our Covenant with God

We Pray

LORD, teach me the way
    of your laws. . . .
Give me insight to
    observe your
    teaching,
  to keep it with all
    my heart.

PSALM 119:33–34

Father, blessed be your
Son, Jesus, whom you
sent to show us how
we can love you. Amen.

*Which of the Ten
Commandments can
you name?*

Rules help us respect one
another and live together
as a community. The Ten
Commandments outline
our responsibilities to love
and respect God, others,
and ourselves.

*Why is it important for all
people to obey the Ten
Commandments?*

Moses carrying stone
tablets containing the
Ten Commandments,
stained glass

Living as the People of God

Faith Focus

What are the Ten Commandments?

Faith Vocabulary

Ten Commandments. The laws of the Covenant God revealed to Moses and the Israelites on Mount Sinai.

St. Catherine's Monastery at the foot of Mount Sinai, Egypt

Living the Covenant

Stop on red. Go on green. These are simple traffic rules. What happens if these rules are not followed? Stop signs control the flow of traffic. They also point to our responsibility to respect our own lives and the lives and property of others.

The **Ten Commandments** guide us in living responsibly the Covenant God has made with his people. They guide us in making moral decisions. Each one of the Ten Commandments, in its own way, helps us express our love and respect for God, for other people, for ourselves, and for creation.

The story of the revelation of the Ten Commandments is part of a bigger story. It is part of the story of the Covenant that God made with his people. It is part of the Exodus.

The Bible tells us that after Moses led the Israelites out of slavery in Egypt, they journeyed for forty years in the desert in search of the land God promised them. The days and years were hot and long. The people often were thirsty, hungry, and tired. They grew angry with God, with Moses, and with one another. They complained about their freedom. Some even wished to go back to Egypt and slavery.

The Ten Commandments

Sacred Scripture tells us that God saw all that was happening to his people, so he called Moses up to the mountain. There he gave Moses the Ten Commandments to guide his people in living the Covenant.

After Moses came down from the mountain, he stood before the Israelites and explained:

"These then are the commandments . . . which the LORD, your God, has ordered that you be taught to observe. . . . Hear then, Israel, and be careful to observe them, that you may grow and prosper the more, in keeping with the promise of the LORD." DEUTERONOMY 6:1, 3

Jesus fulfilled these laws revealed by God to Moses. They guide us in living the new and everlasting Covenant, which God has made with us in Christ. They give direction to our lives as followers of Jesus. They guide us in making choices that help us live as children of God and followers of Christ.

 How does living the Ten Commandments help you live as a follower of Christ?

Eye Witness Report

Imagine you are witnessing Moses coming down from the mountain. What do you see? What do you hear? How do you feel? Write your report in this space.

_____

_____

_____

_____

_____

_____

_____

The First Three Commandments

Like Moses and the Israelites, many people have made long journeys to be free to worship God. You are familiar with the story of the *Mayflower* and the Pilgrims. These Christians braved the stormy waters of the Atlantic Ocean to live in a land where they could worship God without being persecuted.

The First, Second, and Third Commandments describe our privilege and responsibility to worship God. Everyone should be free to worship God according to their conscience.

The First Commandment

I am the LORD your God: you shall not have strange gods before me.
BASED ON EXODUS 20:2–3

The First Commandment called the Israelites to have faith and trust in the one true God. Sometimes it was very difficult for the Israelites to practice their religion. Other nations

New citizens of the United States swearing loyalty at a naturalization ceremony

sometimes tried to force them to worship their false gods. When other nations seemed wealthier and more powerful, many Israelites wondered, "Are these gods more powerful than the Lord our God?"

Through the First Commandment, God calls us to worship him alone. He calls us to believe in him, hope in him, and love him above all else. We are not to let things such as money and popularity become more important to us than God.

The Second Commandment

"You shall not take the name of the LORD, your God, in vain." EXODUS 20:7

The Second Commandment teaches us to use God's name truthfully. We use God's name in vain when we take an oath and then lie under the oath. When we do this, we commit perjury.

We also use God's name in vain when we curse or swear or use the names *God* or *Jesus* in anger or in any other inappropriate way. When we speak God's name in these ways, we are not showing our love or respect for God.

People trust us when we take an oath and call on God to witness to the truth of what we are saying or promising. Friendships, families, schools, communities, and countries are built on promises people keep.

 QUESTION

What does it mean to love and honor God above all else?

A World Built on the Commandments

Describe what might happen when the First and Second Commandments are lived and when they are not lived.

FIRST COMMANDMENT

When We Live It

_____

_____

_____

When We Do Not Live It

_____

_____

_____

SECOND COMMANDMENT

When We Live It

_____

_____

_____

When We Do Not Live It

_____

_____

_____

Faith Vocabulary

Lord's Day. The name Christians give to Sunday, the day of the Lord's Resurrection.

The Third Commandment

Remember to keep holy the LORD's Day.
BASED ON EXODUS 20:8

Each weekend all across the United States of America, people exercise their freedom to worship God. People walk or drive to their church, synagogue, or mosque. People of all faiths exercise their right to worship God.

For the Israelites and the Jewish people today, the seventh day of the week, Saturday, is the Sabbath, the day of rest, the **Lord's Day.** For Christians, Sunday is the Lord's Day. It is the day on which Jesus was raised from the dead. It is the first day of the week, the first day of the new creation of the world in Christ. Taking part in Mass on the Lord's Day, either on Saturday evening or Sunday, is a serious responsibility for Catholics.

Catholics who do not have a serious reason for not participating in Mass, such as an illness, and deliberately choose not to fulfill this responsibility commit a serious sin.

Together as the Body of Christ, we gather to thank and praise God for all his blessings. We remember everything God has done, is doing, and will do out of his love for us.

The Lord's Day is a time set aside to worship God the Creator. We need to rest from unnecessary work. It is to be a time to pay closer attention to the things of God. It is a time to enjoy our families and to help us begin the week with a fresh and holy start on this the first day of the week. It is a time to make sure all the work we do is God's work. It is a time to nourish our faith and our life.

Weekends are a very busy time for families today. We need to make sure that taking part in the celebration of Mass is the center of all our weekend activities.

 How do Catholics keep the Lord's Day holy?

The Day of Faith

Describe what you can do to celebrate the Lord's Day as a day of faith.

_____

_____

_____

_____

_____

_____

Holy Days of Obligation

Catholics around the world set aside the Lord's Day to give public witness to God and his loving plan of salvation. They also gather and celebrate God's love on holy days of obligation. All Catholics have the responsibility to celebrate these days by taking part in the celebration of the Eucharist.

In some places these days are celebrated with processions and festivals.

Special costumes are worn, and statues are carried through the streets. Sometimes there is singing and dancing. These celebrations remind Catholics and all who witness them that God is the Father of all people. He invites everyone to respond to his love with faith and trust.

 How does celebrating holy days of obligation invite us to grow in our love for God?

Fishermen carrying statue of Madonna of Portosalvo to celebrate the feast of the Assumption, Ragusa, Sicily, Italy

Candles illuminating a cemetery, All Saints' Day, Lacombe, Louisiana

Christmas, Bethlehem, Israel

What Difference Does Faith Make in My Life?

You are growing in your love for God each day. Many things you do show others that God is at the center of your life.

In each part of the circle write one thing you can do to help make God the center of your life.

The Center of My Life

GOD

My Faith Choice

This week I will keep Sunday as a holy and special day dedicated to the Lord. I will

_____

_____ .

You Are God

Leader: The Te Deum ("You Are God") is an ancient hymn of the Church. This great hymn of praise of God was written in the fourth century.

Let us raise up our voices in joyful blessing and praise of God.

All: **You are God: we praise you.**

Group 1: You are God: we praise you;
you are God: we acclaim you;

Group 2: you are the eternal Father:
all creation worships you.

All: **You are God: we praise you.**

Group 1: To you all angels, all the powers of heaven,
cherubim and seraphim, sing in endless praise:

Group 2: holy, holy, holy Lord, God of power and might,
heaven and earth are full of your glory.

All: **You are God: we praise you.**

Group 1: The glorious company of apostles praise you.
The noble fellowship of prophets praise you.
The white-robed army of martyrs praise you.

Group 2: Throughout the world the holy Church
acclaims you:
Father, of majesty unbounded,
your true and only Son, worthy of all worship,
and the Holy Spirit, advocate and guide.

All: **You are God: we praise you.**

We Remember

What I Have Learned

Match the terms in column A with their descriptions in column B.

Column A

_____ 1. First Commandment

_____ 2. Second Commandment

_____ 3. Third Commandment

Column B

a. Keep the Lord's Day as a holy day.

b. Use God's name truthfully and respectfully.

c. Worship only God and love him above all things.

Answer the following.

4. Describe why Sunday is the Lord's Day for Christians.

_____

_____

_____

5. Describe the responsibilities Catholics have to keep Sunday holy.

_____

_____

_____

_____

To Help You Remember

1. God revealed the Ten Commandments to guide us in making moral decisions.

2. The First, Second, and Third Commandments describe our privilege and responsibility to worship God.

3. The Lord's Day is a holy day and a time to rest from our work. Sunday is the Lord's Day for Christians.

Growing in Faith

One important thing I learned this week is

_____

_____

_____.

This is important because

_____

_____

_____.

What will people see me doing as I live my faith choice this week?

_____

_____

_____

This Week . . .

In chapter 22, "Living Our Covenant with God," your child learned more about the Ten Commandments. The Ten Commandments guide us in living the Covenant that binds God and humankind. The First, Second, and Third Commandments describe our privilege and responsibility to worship, respect, and reverence God as God. The First Commandment calls us to believe in, hope in, and love God above all else. The Second Commandment teaches the fundamental human responsibility to respect God by only calling on his name truthfully to witness to what we do and say. The Third Commandment obliges us to worship God together at Mass and to nourish our relationship with both him and our family.

For more on the teachings of the Catholic Church on the First, Second, and Third Commandments, see *Catechism of the Catholic Church* paragraph numbers 2083–2132, 2142–2159, and 2168–2188.

Sharing God's Word

Read together Exodus 19:1–20 and 20:1–17. Emphasize that God gave Moses the Ten Commandments to guide his people in making decisions to live the Covenant.

Praying

In this chapter your child learned to pray the hymn Te Deum. Read and pray together this prayer on page 286.

Making a Difference

Choose one of the following activities to do as a family or design a similar activity of your own.

• The First, Second, and Third Commandments teach us to show our love and respect for God. Talk about how you show your love and respect for God during Mass, and how you show your love and respect for God at home.

• The Third Commandment teaches us to keep holy the Lord's Day, Sunday. How does this Commandment help us grow in faith? How does this Commandment help our parish grow in faith?

• Talk about how your family makes Sunday a special and holy day. Choose one thing you can do this week to make Sunday a day for the Lord.

For more ideas on ways your family can live your faith, visit the "Faith First for Families" page at **www.FaithFirst.com**. Click on "Games" and make learning fun for your child.

Love Your Neighbor as Yourself

We Pray

Make known to me
   your ways, LORD;
   teach me your paths.
                    PSALM 25:4

O God, we love you
above all things.
You are all-good
and worthy of all love.
We love our neighbor
as ourselves for the
love of you.   Amen.

*What are some of the ways
we show respect for one
another?*

We show our respect for
people by the way we
treat them. Jesus taught
that we show respect
for God and for people
by living the Great
Commandment. The
Ten Commandments
help us live the Great
Commandment.

*Which of the Ten
Commandments teach us
to love and respect one
another?*

Faith Focus

How do the Fourth and Fifth Commandments help us live the Great Commandment?

Faith Vocabulary

obey. To follow the commands of others who have rightful authority in our lives and who are helping us live according to God's laws.

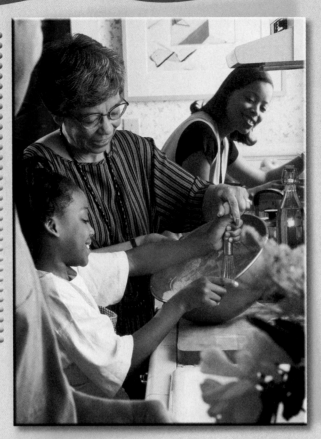

Our neighbor is every living person other than ourselves. God calls us to love everyone. All people are our neighbors in God's eyes. The Fourth through the Tenth Commandments teach us about our love for others and for ourselves.

The Fourth Commandment

"Honor your father and your mother."
EXODUS 20:12

In the First Letter of John, we read that our love for God, which the first three Commandments teach about, and our love for other people cannot be separated. To use a common expression, "They are two sides of one coin."

Jesus reminded the lawyer who asked him which was the greatest of the Commandments that there is one Great Commandment, which has two inseparable parts. We are to love God *and* we are to love our neighbors as we love ourselves.

This Commandment teaches us to love and honor the members of our family, especially our parents. One way we honor our parents and all those who have the authority and responsibility to care for us is to **obey** them. We are to follow the guidance of those who are helping us live according to God's laws.

The family is the first and most important group in society. The heart of our family is the love, honor, and respect that bind parents and children. It is our responsibility to deepen this honor and love for as long as we live.

The Fifth Commandment

"You shall not kill."
EXODUS 20:13

Every human life is sacred. The Fifth Commandment teaches us to respect and treat as sacred the life of every person. We have a serious responsibility both to take care of our own life and health and to protect the lives and health of others. This is true regardless of the age, race, gender, health, physical ability, and mental ability of a person.

Acts of violence toward others or ourselves are acts against the teaching of the Fifth Commandment. Video and computer games, movies and DVDs, athletic competition, and bullying in school tempt us to see violence as okay! But violence toward others and toward ourselves is against how God wants us to treat one another.

The Fifth Commandment also requires us to honor and respect our spiritual life and the spiritual lives of others. We are not to give scandal to others. This means that we are not to deliberately do or say anything that leads people away from their love of God and neighbor. Jesus was quite clear on this. He taught:

"Whoever causes one of these little ones who believe in me to sin, it would be better for him to have a great millstone hung around his neck and to be drowned in the depths of the sea."
MATTHEW 18:6

 What do the Fourth and Fifth Commandments teach?

Choosing Life, Not Violence

List the names of several popular movies and videos. Explain how each promotes or does not promote the teaching of the Fifth Commandment.

_____

_____

_____

_____

Faith Focus

How do the Sixth and Ninth Commandments help us live the Great Commandment?

Faith Vocabulary

chastity. The virtue that is the good habit of respecting and honoring our sexuality and that guides us to share our love with others in appropriate ways.

The Sixth and the Ninth Commandments

"You shall not commit adultery."
"You shall not covet your neighbor's wife."

EXODUS 20:14, 17

You know the biblical account of creation very well. In that story God tells us many important things about ourselves. First, God creates every person in his image and likeness. All life is sacred. Second, God creates us male and female. God has given each person the gift of being either a boy or a girl who will grow to be a man or a woman. This gift is the gift of our sexuality. Third, everything and everyone God creates is good.

The Sixth and Ninth Commandments help us respect our own sexuality and the sexuality of others. A good word to describe this respect is *reverence*. Reverence is the virtue that enables us to honor someone or something as holy.

The Sixth and Ninth Commandments teach that we are to express and share our friendship and love for others in appropriate ways. **Chastity** is the virtue that helps us live these two Commandments.

The Sixth and Ninth Commandments also teach about the sacredness, or holiness, of the love between a husband and a wife. A husband and a wife are to love and honor each other their whole life long. They are to live and keep the promises they made to each other when they married:

I, *name*, take you, *name*, to be my wife (husband). I promise to be true to you in good times and in bad, in sickness and in health. I will love and honor you all the days of my life.

FROM RITE OF MARRIAGE

All people are to respect and support married couples in living and keeping their promises to each other. The Ninth Commandment teaches that other people are to help married people grow in love. They are not to do or say things that tempt married people to be unfaithful or break up a marriage or a family.

 What do the Sixth and Ninth Commandments teach?

WHAT ARE YOU WATCHING?

Think about some of today's popular TV shows about friendship and marriage. Give some examples of how TV sitcoms show or do not show what the Sixth and Ninth Commandments teach.

Faith Focus

How do the Seventh, Eighth, and Tenth Commandments help us live the Great Commandment?

Faith Vocabulary

justice. One of the moral, or cardinal, virtues; the good habit of giving to God and to all people what is rightfully due to them.

People of Justice and Mercy and Truth

"Millions Open Their Hearts and Wallets To Aid Tsunami Victims." "After Thirty Years on Death Row Prisoner Freed: Witness Lied!" You often see and hear news stories similar to these. They are about mercy, justice, and honesty.

Jesus taught clearly about justice and mercy. In the Beatitudes he taught:

"Blessed are they who hunger and thirst for righteousness. . . . Blessed are the merciful."
MATTHEW 5:6, 7

When we are merciful and just, we are blessed by God. We are living as images of God who is always just and merciful. We bring God's blessings to others.

Tsunami relief, loading medical supplies, Port Klang, Kuala Lumpor, Malaysia

The Seventh Commandment

"You shall not steal."
EXODUS 20:15

The Seventh Commandment teaches that we are to be people of **justice**. We are to give God and others what is their due. We are to be generous and kind to others as God is to us. We are to respect and use God's gift of creation wisely. We are to be good stewards of creation.

When we cheat or steal or misuse creation, we are not living as children of God. If we take things without permission or damage things that belong to others, we are to make reparation. We are to return or replace what we have taken or damaged. When we do this, we are acting justly.

The Eighth Commandment

"You shall not bear false witness against your neighbor." EXODUS 20:16

God the Father is always faithful and trustworthy. His word to us is always true. Jesus, the Son of God, is the Word of God, who is "full of grace and truth" (John 1:14). The Holy Spirit is "the Spirit of truth" (John 15:26) who testifies to Jesus.

The Eighth Commandment teaches us to be people of the truth. We are to respect the reputation, or good name, of others. We are not to lie. We are not to join with others and gossip and spread false rumors about people.

The Tenth Commandment

You shall not covet your neighbor's goods.
BASED ON EXODUS 20:17

The Tenth Commandment reminds us that God is the source of all blessings. This Commandment helps us value and respect all the good things that we and other people have that are gifts from God. Just as our gifts have been generously given to us by God, we are to share them generously and freely with others—especially with people in need.

 What role does justice, mercy, and truth have in the life of a follower of Christ?

What Do You Do?

List ways you can live a just and truthful life.

_____

_____

_____

_____

_____

_____

_____

United States Conference of Catholic Bishops

The Catholic bishops in the United States help us live the command to love God and our neighbors. One way they do this is through the teachings of the United States Conference of Catholic Bishops (USCCB).

The USCCB was formed in 1966 to guide Catholics in living their faith. The bishops have spoken out about nuclear weapons and peace, abortion and capital punishment, economic justice, hunger and fair housing, and the dignity and rights of the elderly and people with disabilities.

The bishops, through the USCCB, help Catholics live as responsible citizens. They remind us of the principles of the Gospel so we can work together to love others justly and with mercy as Jesus taught.

QUESTION *What are some ways you see your parish community building a better world by living the Ten Commandments as Jesus taught?*

What Difference Does Faith Make in My Life?

The Holy Spirit teaches and helps you live the Ten Commandments each day. You pray. You respect and honor your parents and teachers. You treat your classmates and friends with respect. You share with others. You are honest. You are fair and kind to others.

Write a story, draw a picture, or outline a skit that shows ways you and other fifth graders can live the Ten Commandments.

Loving and Respecting Others

 My Faith Choice

Each day I have many opportunities to show my love for others as Jesus taught. This week I will

_____

_____.

Prayer of Saint Francis of Assisi

Leader: Saint Francis of Assisi's prayer for peace is a favorite of Christians. Let us pray this prayer and ask God to guide us in living as his children, loving one another as Jesus taught.

Lord, make me an instrument of your peace.

All: **Lord, make me an instrument of your peace:**

Group 1: where there is hatred, let me sow love;

Group 2: where there is injury, pardon;

Group 1: where there is doubt, faith;

Group 2: where there is despair, hope;

Group 1: where there is darkness, light;

Group 2: where there is sadness, joy.

All: **Lord, make me an instrument of your peace.**

Leader: O divine Master, grant that I may not so much seek

Group 1: to be consoled as to console,

Group 2: to be understood as to understand, to be loved as to love.

Group 1: For it is in giving that we receive, it is in pardoning that we are pardoned,

Group 2: it is in dying that we are born to eternal life.

All: **Lord, make me an instrument of your peace.**

We Remember

What I Have Learned

Using the Fourth through Tenth Commandments, write the number of the Commandment that names these moral principles.

_____ 1. Respect the gift of sexuality.

_____ 2. Live as a just and honest person.

_____ 3. Respect the good name of others.

_____ 4. Reverence and respect all life.

_____ 5. Share our blessings with others.

_____ 6. Honor and respect parents and those in authority.

_____ 7. Be faithful in marriage.

Answer the following.

8. Describe how the virtue of obedience helps us live the Fourth Commandment.

_____

_____

9. Describe how the virtues of reverence and chastity help us live the Sixth and Ninth Commandments.

_____

_____

10. Describe how the virtues of justice and mercy help us live the Seventh and Tenth Commandments.

_____

_____

To Help You Remember

1. The Fourth Commandment teaches us that we are to honor and respect our parents and those who have legitimate authority over us. The Fifth Commandment teaches that we are to respect all life as sacred.

2. The Sixth and Ninth Commandments teach that we are to live a chaste life.

3. The Seventh, Eighth, and Tenth Commandments teach that we are to be truthful, just, merciful, kind, and generous.

Growing in Faith

One important thing I learned this week is

_____

_____

_____.

This is important because

_____

_____

_____.

What will people see me doing as I live my faith choice this week?

_____

_____

_____

This Week . . .

In chapter 23, "Love Your Neighbor as Yourself," your child learned more about the teachings of the Ten Commandments. The Fourth Commandment teaches us to honor our parents by respecting and obeying them. The Fifth Commandment teaches us to respect the life of every person as sacred regardless of age, race, gender, health, physical ability, or mental ability. The Sixth and Ninth Commandments teach that we are to share our love for others in a faithful and chaste manner. The Seventh Commandment teaches us to be just and merciful and to use God's creation fairly and wisely. The Eighth Commandment teaches us to live truthful lives. The Tenth Commandment teaches us to respect the good things that we and others have as gifts from God.

For more on the teachings of the Catholic Church on the Fourth through Tenth Commandments, see *Catechism of the Catholic Church* paragraph numbers 2196–2246, 2258–2317, 2331–2391, 2401–2449, 2464–2503, 2514–2527, and 2534–2550.

Sharing God's Word

Read together Matthew 5:17–20. Emphasize that Jesus fulfilled the Ten Commandments.

Praying

In this chapter your child prayed the Prayer of Saint Francis of Assisi. Read and pray together this prayer on page 298.

Making a Difference

Choose one of the following activities to do as a family or design a similar activity of your own.

• The Ten Commandments teach that we are to honor and respect ourselves and others. Name ways that honoring and respecting others help us grow in faith.

• Watch TV together and keep track of the Ten Commandments that are kept and broken as you watch each show.

• The Fourth Commandment teaches that we are to honor our mother and father. Discuss ways your family can grow in honoring one another.

For more ideas on ways your family can live your faith, visit the "Faith First for Families" page at **www.FaithFirst.com**. Check out this week's "Just for Parents" article.

Catholic Social Teaching

It's Not Always Easy

Jessie was excited. A new shopping mall had just opened. Everyone was planning to meet there Saturday afternoon. Jessie couldn't wait. She had been saving her money to spend on some new clothes for herself. She wanted the latest labels and fashions.

That night Jessie announced to her mother that she was going to the mall on Saturday afternoon. "No, remember Grandma's birthday party? That is where we will be on Saturday afternoon," said Jessie's mom. "Your grandma turns eighty. It will be very special for her to see her grandchildren."

"If I don't go to the mall, Sally will get the jacket, and then I won't be able to!" Jessie said, trying to get out of going to the party.

"Jessie, you are coming with us on Saturday. I think maybe you have a thing or two to think about. What is more important to you? A jacket or people?"

We Treat All Life as Sacred

Each person has the basic dignity of being a child of God. It is our responsibility to protect that dignity and defend the rights that flow from that dignity.

301

Making Connections . . .

Even though Jessie's grandmother is elderly and has trouble remembering things, she has a right to live with dignity. This includes simple things such as celebrating her birthday. But sometimes, like Jessie, we are mixed up about what is most important and deserving of our respect.

with Math and Science

Conduct a survey of your friends and family. Have them share the five most important things in their lives. Create a bar graph illustrating what you find out. Discuss the conclusions you can draw on how the data supports or does not support respect for others.

with Language Arts

Write a letter to Jessie telling her what you feel about the situation. Help Jessie put things in perspective to see what is most important. Then rewrite the story on the previous page to include an ending that demonstrates how Jessie shows respect for human dignity.

with Social Studies

The ancestors of Jessie's grandmother had come to the United States from Europe during the immigration period from 1789 to 1850. Learn about the history of your ancestors. Find out how and when your ancestors came to the United States and how they were treated when they arrived.

⊃ **Faith Action** *Reach out to an elderly person in your community. Let him or her know that you care.*

Name _____

A. Best Response

Read each statement and circle the best answer.

1. Which one of the following do we use to make moral decisions?
   - a. intellect
   - b. feelings
   - c. free will
   - d. all of the above

2. Developing a well-formed conscience is the responsibility of _____.
   - a. young people
   - b. the elderly
   - c. adults
   - d. all of the above

3. _____ is a moral virtue.
   - a. Fortitude
   - b. Hope
   - c. Love
   - d. Faith

4. In the Beatitudes, peacemakers are called _____.
   - a. children of God
   - b. Apostles
   - c. disciples of Jesus
   - d. members of the Church

5. We have been created in the image and likeness _____.
   - a. of God
   - b. of the angels
   - c. of Adam and Eve
   - d. none of the above

6. "Keep holy the Lord's Day" is the _____ Commandment.
   - a. Fourth
   - b. First
   - c. Third
   - d. Sixth

7. Using God's name with respect is a teaching of the _____ Commandment.
   - a. First
   - b. Eighth
   - c. Fourth
   - d. Second

8. The Eighth Commandment teaches us to _____.
   - a. be people of truth
   - b. honor our parents
   - c. use God's gift of creation wisely
   - d. respect and protect human life as sacred

9. _____ grace is the gift of God sharing his life and love with us.
   - a. Actual
   - b. Sanctifying
   - c. Spiritual
   - d. Christian

10. The First Letter of John reveals that God is _____.
    - a. hope
    - b. love
    - c. forgiveness
    - d. none of the above

B. Matching Words and Phrases

Match the terms in column A with their descriptions in column B.

Column A

_____ 1. mortal sin

_____ 2. sanctifying grace

_____ 3. love

_____ 4. actual grace

_____ 5. venial sin

Column B

a. God sharing the gift of his life and love

b. the gift of God's help to live a holy life

c. separates us from God's love

d. weakens our love for God

e. virtue that helps us keep God at the center of our life

C. What I Have Learned

Write three things you learned in this unit. Share them with the group.

_____

_____

_____

Look at the list of faith terms in "Words to Know" on page 228. Circle the terms you know now.

D. From a Scripture Story

What does the First Letter of John teach us about love? Describe how you can witness John's teachings.

John's Teachings	Witnessing John's Teachings
_____	_____
_____	_____
_____	_____
_____	_____
_____	_____
_____	_____

Unit 4 • We Pray

What kinds of prayers do we pray?

Getting Ready

What I Have Learned

What is something you already know about these faith terms?

The prayer of Jesus

_____

_____

The Church as a people of prayer

_____

_____

The Our Father

_____

_____

Words to Know

Put an X next to the faith terms you know. Put a ? next to the faith terms you need to know more about.

Faith Vocabulary

_____ Psalms

_____ chant

_____ personal prayer

_____ communal prayer

_____ prayer of praise

_____ disciple

Questions I Have

What questions would you like to ask about developing the habit of prayer?

_____

_____

_____

_____

A Scripture Story

Jesus teaching the Our Father

Why does the Church pray the Our Father?

Jesus, Our Model of Prayer

We Pray

Hear my cry, O God,
listen to my prayer!

PSALM 61:2

Lord God,
may all that we do
begin and end in you.
Amen.

When do you spend time with your friends?

Everyone enjoys spending time with friends. We enjoy talking with our friends and doing things with them. That is what we do when we pray. We spend time with God and share our thoughts and feelings with him.

In your own words, describe what praying means to you.

The Prayer of the People of God

Faith Focus

Why was the Old Testament tradition of prayer important in the life of Jesus?

Faith Vocabulary

Psalms. The prayer songs found in the Old Testament Book of Psalms, or the Psalter.

chant. Plainsong; a simple type of song with only one melody line, using the rhythm of the spoken word.

The Prayer of Jesus

Recall for a moment the Gospel account of Mary and Joseph finding Jesus in the Temple. Jesus was twelve years old, and the Holy Family had traveled to Jerusalem to celebrate Passover. When it was time for them to return home, Mary and Joseph could not find Jesus. After looking for three days, they found him in the Temple where he was:

> . . . sitting in the midst of the teachers, listening to them and asking them questions.   LUKE 2:46

After being reunited with Mary and Joseph, Jesus returned home with them to Nazareth. There he "advanced [in] wisdom and age and favor before God and man" (Luke 2:52).

We know from the Gospels that Jesus often prayed. Like all young children, he probably first learned about prayer at home. The teachers in the synagogue in Nazareth and in the Temple in Jerusalem also taught him the prayers of the Jewish people.

The Prayer of Abraham

God invited Abraham to believe in him, the one true God, and to trust in him and leave his homeland. Jesus would have learned about the prayer life of Abraham from listening to the Scriptures.

The Old Testament gives many accounts that Abraham was a person of prayer. He shared his thoughts and feelings with God. He prayed for himself and for others. The Church honors Abraham as "our father in faith" (Eucharist Prayer I).

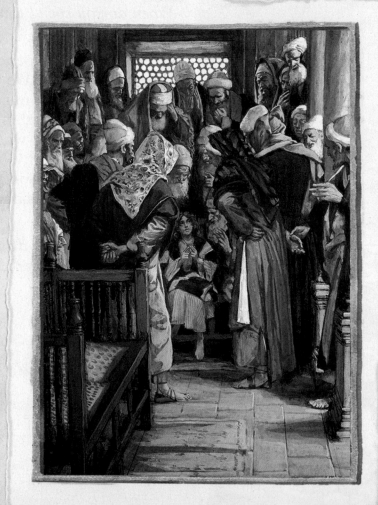

Jesus Sitting in the Midst of the Doctors. James J. Tissot (1836–1902), French painter.

The Psalms

Jesus joined with his family, friends, and neighbors to pray the **Psalms**. The Psalms are prayer songs that the Jewish people prayed to share their thoughts and feelings with God. There are one hundred fifty Psalms in the Book of Psalms in the Old Testament.

The Church prays the Psalms every day at Mass and in the Liturgy of the Hours. Sometimes we **chant**, or sing, the Psalms. The verses of the responsorial psalm at Mass are sometimes sung this way. We raise up our prayer to God in song.

 What can we learn about prayer from the Old Testament?

A page of a fifteenth-century illuminated Bible. This page illustrates Psalm 7 and shows David in prayer.

Lifting Up Your Voice in Prayer

Think about your day. In this space create a psalm verse that you might pray often throughout the day.

_____

_____

_____

_____

Faith Vocabulary

Transfiguration. The mysterious change in appearance of Jesus in the presence of Peter, James, and John during which Jesus speaks with Moses and the Prophet Elijah; the manifestation of the divinity of Jesus Christ.

Jesus Prayed Always

There are some times when we pray "naturally." For example, when someone we care about is really sick, or when something "great" has just happened to us, we seem to want to pray.

The Gospels tell us that when Jesus was about to do something important, he talked it over with his Father. He prayed. The Gospels make that point time and time again.

Jesus' Work on Earth

Saint Luke tells us that when Jesus began his work on earth, he prayed. Luke writes that while Jesus "was praying, heaven was opened and the holy Spirit descended upon him" (Luke 3:21–22).

Choosing the Apostles

Before choosing the Apostles, Jesus "departed to the mountain to pray, and he spent the night in prayer to God"

(Luke 6:12). When he came down, "he chose Twelve, whom he also named apostles" (Luke 6:13).

The Transfiguration

After Saint Peter confessed his belief that Jesus was the Messiah, Luke tells us:

> [Jesus] took Peter, John, and James and went up the mountain to pray.   LUKE 9:28

It was during this time of prayer that the **Transfiguration** took place. At the Transfiguration it was revealed that Jesus was indeed the Son of God. Luke tells us "Then from the cloud came a voice that said, 'This is my chosen Son'" (Luke 9:35).

Jesus' Passion— Suffering and Death

After the Last Supper, Jesus went to the Garden of Gethsemane on the Mount of Olives to pray. We read:

> After withdrawing about a stone's throw from [his disciples] and kneeling, he prayed, saying, "Father, if you are willing, take this cup away from me; still, not my will but yours be done."   LUKE 22:41–42

The Transfiguration (oil on panel). Pietro Perugino (c. 1445–1523), Italian painter.

The Crucified Savior (wood carving), artist unknown

Faith-Filled People

Jude Thaddeus

Saint Jude Thaddeus was the cousin of Jesus and the brother of the Apostles Saint James the Lesser and Saint Simon the Zealot. His mother, Mary Clopas, stood by Mary's side at the foot of the cross and anointed the body of Jesus after he died. The feast day of Saint Jude, Apostle and martyr, is October 28.

Jesus' whole life was a life of prayer. Jesus' life on earth, which began in prayer, also ended in prayer. Describing the very moment of Jesus' death, Luke writes:

Jesus cried out in a loud voice, "Father, into your hands I commend my spirit"; and when he had said this he breathed his last.　LUKE 23:46

QUESTION What does the Gospel tell us about the prayer life of Jesus?

TIME TO PRAY

Think about your day. Draw hands on the watch to identify a time of the day when it is important for you to pray. Illustrate or write about why it is important.

Faith Vocabulary

trust. To know that a person will always do what is good and best for us.

Trust and Confidence

When someone is really listening to us, we somehow feel like talking. Jesus showed us that God always listens to us when we pray. Jesus taught that we should always pray with **trust** and confidence. In Mark's Gospel we read:

And as [Jesus] was leaving Jericho with his disciples and a sizable crowd, Bartimaeus, a blind man, the son of Timaeus, sat by the roadside begging. On hearing that it was Jesus of Nazareth, he began to cry out and say, "Jesus, son of David, have pity on me." And many rebuked him, telling him to be silent. But he kept calling out all the more, "Son of David, have pity on me." Jesus stopped and said, "Call him." So they called the blind man, saying to him, "Take courage; get up, he is calling you." He threw aside his cloak, sprang up, and came to Jesus. Jesus said to him in reply, "What do you want me to do for you?" The blind man replied to him, "Master, I want to see." Jesus told him, "Go your way; your faith has

Jesus Healing the Blind Man, stained glass

saved you." Immediately he received his sight and followed him on the way.

MARK 10:46–52

In the Gospel story about Bartimaeus, the man born blind, Jesus revealed that God always hears and listens to our prayers. Jesus stopped, listened, and answered Bartimaeus' prayer. Like Bartimaeus, we trust and have confidence that God always listens to our prayers.

The Holy Spirit

Sometimes we find it too hard to pray. We just do not know what to say. When we feel this way, we need to remember, believe, and trust that we do not pray alone. The Holy Spirit moves us to pray, teaches us to pray, and gives us the grace to pray.

The Holy Spirit helps us pray with confidence and trust. There is no time and no place that we cannot stop and pray. God is always with us. He is always listening.

 How does the Holy Spirit help us pray?

Placing Trust in God

Look up two of these Scripture passages. Write what these passages tell about putting faith and trust in God.

Psalm 4:2–9	Isaiah 12:1–6
Mark 10:46–52	Luke 11:9–13

_____

_____

_____

_____

_____

_____

_____

Our Church Makes a Difference

Christian Role Models

Role models help us make good decisions. The saints of the Church are role models whose lives teach us how to make decisions to live our faith. Saints have lived and preached the Gospel in every part of the world. Here are some of the people named saints by Pope John Paul II.

Europe. Sister Teresa Benedicta of the Cross (1891–1942), was a victim of the Holocaust. She became a Carmelite sister who devoted her life to prayer. Arrested in 1942, she died in the gas chamber at Auschwitz.

Asia. Andrew Dung Lac (1785–1839) and one hundred sixteen others who served the people of Vietnam were martyred by the government of Vietnam.

South America. Born in Paraguay, Roque Gonzalez de Santa Cruz (1576–1628), Alphonsus Rodriquez (1598–1628), and John de Castillo (1596–1628) worked with the tribal people of Paraguay and southern Brazil. They were the first Americans to be beatified as martyrs.

North America. Rose Philippine Duchesne (1769–1852) came to the United States from France in 1918. She and other members of her religious order worked with orphans and Native Americans. The Potowatami called her "the woman who prays always." Her name is included in the Pioneer Hall of Fame in the state capitol of Missouri.

Saints and people in prayer, tapestry, Cathedral of Our Lady of the Angels, Los Angeles, California

Who is your favorite saint? How can learning more about that saint make a difference in the way you live as a follower of Jesus?

What Difference Does Faith Make in My Life?

Your family and other people have helped you learn to pray. God always listens when you pray.

Describe one important time in your life when you prayed and how praying helped you.

My Life of Prayer

One important time in my life when I prayed was

_____

_____

_____.

Praying helped me because

_____

_____

_____.

My Faith Choice

This week I will spend some time each night thinking about and thanking God for my day.

Litany of the Saints

The saints pray for us. Mary is the greatest saint. Think of each of these saints and how much they want you to live as a child of God. Then ask them to pray for you.

Mary and Jesus

Holy Mary, Mother of God	pray for us.
Saint Joseph	pray for us.
Saint John the Baptist	pray for us.
Saint Peter and Saint Paul	pray for us.
Saint Mary Magdalene	pray for us.
Saint John the Evangelist	pray for us.
Saint Agnes	pray for us.
Saint Perpetua and Saint Felicity	pray for us.
Saint Francis and Saint Dominic	pray for us.
Saint Clare	pray for us.
Saint Martin de Porres	pray for us.
Saint Teresa Benedicta	pray for us.
Saint Andrew Dung Lac	pray for us.
Saint Alphonsus Rodriquez	pray for us.
Saint Rose Duchesne	pray for us.
All holy men and women	pray for us.

Saint Claire of Assisi

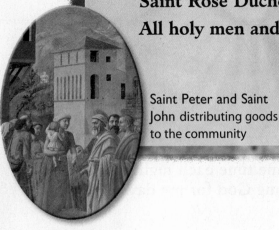

Saint Peter and Saint John distributing goods to the community

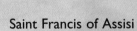

Saint Francis of Assisi

What I Have Learned

1. *Circle the words in the puzzle that tell about prayer. Use the words to tell someone why praying is important to you.*

```
C V G T R U S T B I H K
L C O N F I D E N C E T
T Y U L I S T E N U R E
T P T H O U G H T I R R
C D F E E L I N G S T U
Y H O L Y S P I R I T R
R W J E S U S T P L O K
```

Answer the following.

2. Describe the prayer life of Jesus while he lived on earth.

_____

_____

3. Explain the place of the virtues of trust and confidence in prayer.

_____

_____

4. Compare the place of the Psalms in the prayer of Jesus with the prayer of the Church.

_____

_____

To Help You Remember

1. The Old Testament tells about the prayer of Abraham, of King David, and of the Jewish people.

2. Jesus' life on earth was a life of prayer. The Gospels tell us that Jesus prayed before and during important events in his life.

3. Jesus revealed that God always listens to our prayers. He taught that we are to pray with confidence and trust.

Growing in Faith

One important thing I learned this week is

_____

_____

_____.

This is important because

_____

_____

_____.

What will people see me doing as I live my faith choice this week?

_____

_____

This Week . . .

In chapter 24, "Jesus, Our Model of Prayer," your child learned about prayer, especially prayer in the Old Testament and the prayer of Jesus. Jesus' whole life was a life of prayer. Through the help of the Holy Spirit, we lift up our minds and hearts to God and share our thoughts and feelings with him. We pray to God, trusting and confident that he always listens to us and does what is best for us.

For more on the teachings of the Catholic Church on prayer in the Old Testament and the prayer of Jesus, see *Catechism of the Catholic Church* paragraph numbers 2558–2589 and 2598–2617.

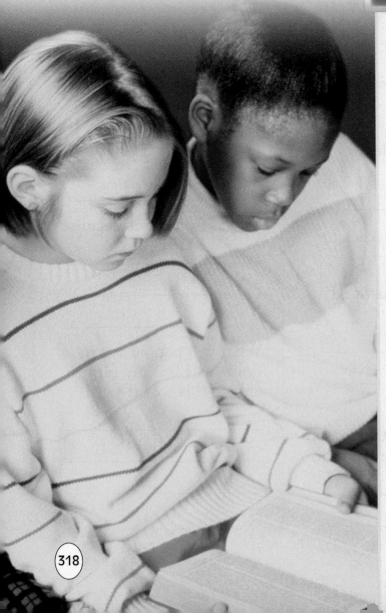

Sharing God's Word

Read together Matthew 6:5–8 and 7:7–11. Emphasize that when we pray we should pray with trust and confidence.

Praying

In this chapter your child prayed a brief litany of the saints. Read and pray together the prayer on page 316.

Making a Difference

Choose one of the following activities to do as a family or design a similar activity of your own.

- Pray at the beginning and at the end of each day. Gather in the morning to ask God's blessings on your family. Gather in the evening to thank him for the blessings of the day.

- Saints are our role models. Ask each family member to name a saint who is a role model for them and explain why that saint is a role model.

- Praying helps us make moral decisions. Discuss some examples of decisions a family would talk about with God. Talk about how prayer can help us make good decisions.

For more ideas on ways your family can live your faith, visit the "Faith First for Families" page at **www.FaithFirst.com**. Take a look at "Just for Parents" this week.

People of Prayer

25

We Pray

I rejoiced when they said
   to me,
 "Let us go to the house
   of the LORD."

PSALM 122:1

God, Father, Son,
and Holy Spirit,
we love you.
We praise you.
We bless you.
We give you glory.

Amen.

*What is one good habit
you have?*

Good habits come from
doing good things over
and over again. Praying is
a good habit we all need
to develop.

*What are some of your
favorite times and places
to pray?*

*People at Prayer,
stained glass*

319

The Habit of Praying

Faith Focus

How does praying regularly help us become a person of prayer?

Faith Vocabulary

personal prayer.
Spending time alone with God.

communal prayer.
Praying with others.

Pray Always

Habits are ways of doing things. Working at and developing the habit of prayer is vital for a Christian. Praying on a regular basis builds up our relationship with God. Remember, praying does not have to be difficult. Prayer is as easy as talking and listening to God. It is lifting our minds and hearts to God alone or with others.

We can pray anytime and anyplace. When we make prayer a regular part of our daily lives as Jesus did, we are developing the habit of prayer.

Morning Prayer

A good starting point in developing a habit of prayer is praying when we wake up in the morning. We can thank God for bringing us to a new day. We can ask his help to live out the day with faith, care, and respect for other people. We can ask God to help us make responsible choices throughout the day to live as his children.

Mealtime Prayer

Another good time to pray is at mealtimes. Praying before and after meals thanks God for his loving care for us. It is also a prayer asking God to bless people in need.

Nighttime Prayer

At the end of our day, we can thank God for the opportunities that he has given us during the day. We ask God to forgive us for our sins. We ask him to protect us and the people we love.

Personal and Communal Prayer

Sometimes we pray by ourselves. Each one of us sometimes wants to be alone with God. We have special reasons to thank and praise him. We have special needs we want to talk about with him. Praying alone is called **personal prayer**.

At other times, we pray together with other people. We pray with our family at mealtimes. We pray with the Church at Mass and on many other occasions, such as Baptisms, marriages, and when we are ill. Praying with others is called **communal prayer**.

Whether we pray alone or with others we need to pray often each day. When we pray often, we are doing what Saint Paul the Apostle urges us to do, "Pray without ceasing" (1 Thessalonians 5:17). We become more and more aware that God is walking with us, side-by-side through life.

 How might you develop the habit of prayer?

Paul the Apostle's Advice on Prayer

Use this code to decipher Saint Paul's teaching about prayer.

B = A	G = G	M = H	Q = C	T = N	X = T
C = Y	H = S	N = U	R = L	V = W	Y = M
D = O	J = I	O = D	S = E	W = V	Z = R
F = T	K = P	P = K			

KZBC   VJFMDNX   QSBHJTG

_ _ _ _ _ _ _ _ _ _ _ _ _ _ _ _ _ _ .

JT BRR QJZQNYHXBTQSH

_ _ _ _ _ _ _ _ _ _ _ _ _ _ _ _ _ _

GJWS XMBTPH

_ _ _ _ _ _ _ _ _ .   1 THESSALONIANS 5:17–18

Faith Focus

How do different types
of prayers help us
to pray?

Faith Vocabulary

prayer of adoration.
Acknowledging that
God alone is the
Creator and source
of all that is.

Kinds of Prayer

Many of our prayers can be in our own words—simply speaking to God out loud or silently in our hearts and minds. At other times we might pray a prayer the Church has been saying for a long time, such as the Our Father or the Nicene Creed.

There are many different kinds of prayers and ways of praying. When we think about what we say in our prayers, we discover that there are five different kinds of prayers. There are prayers of blessing and adoration, prayers of praise, prayers of thanksgiving, prayers of petition, and prayers of intercession.

Blessing and Adoration

In our prayer of blessing and adoration, we tell God that he is important to us above all else. We pray:

[L]et us bow down
    in worship;
let us kneel before the
    LORD who made us.
PSALM 95:6

Praise

Our prayer of praise tells God that we trust in his goodness and greatness and in his love and faithfulness. We pray:

Praise the LORD, all you
    nations!
Give glory, all you
    peoples! PSALM 117:1

Thanksgiving

Our prayer of thanksgiving tells God that he is the source of all that is good. We tell God that we depend on him above all else and that we are grateful to him. We pray:

It is good to give thanks
    to the LORD.
                PSALM 92:2

Petition

Our prayer of sorrow, or contrition, is a prayer of petition. We ask God for the gift of his mercy for having offended him and others. We pray:

Have mercy on me, God, in your goodness. . . .

A clean heart create for me, God; renew in me a steadfast spirit.
PSALM 51:3, 12

Intercession

In prayers of intercession we bring the needs of others and the needs of the Church and the world to God. We pray:

May God be gracious to us and bless us; may God's face shine upon us. PSALM 67:2

Every time we pray, the Holy Spirit helps us pray. As members of the Body of Christ, we join our prayer with the prayer of Jesus. We pray to the Father in Jesus' name through the power of the Holy Spirit.

QUESTION *What kind of prayer do you pray most frequently? Why?*

We Lift Up Our Hearts

In this space list or draw the things you wish to thank God for right now. Then decide on one way you will show your thanks.

Why do Catholics pray
with and to Mary?

Magnificat. Mary's
canticle of praise
to God.

We Pray to Mary

Why do children go to
their mother for help when
they have a problem? Why
do children smile, hug their
mother, and say "Thank
you"? Why do children often
ask their mother to speak to
another family member on
their behalf? If you can
answer these questions,
you already know why, as
Catholics, we pray to Mary.

The prayer of Christians
is addressed primarily
to God the Father, God
the Son, and God the Holy
Spirit. Catholics also share
thoughts and feelings in
prayer with Mary and the
other saints. Mary loves and
cares for us as a mother
loves and cares for her
children. Mary is the Mother
of the Church.

When we share our
thoughts and feelings with
Mary, we trust she always
welcomes and listens and
responds to our prayers.
We believe Mary shares our
prayers with Jesus, her Son,
and asks him to help us.

May Crowning,
honoring Mary

Holy Family, wood carving

Our Lady of Guadalupe shrine,
Saint John the Evangelist
Church, Los Angeles,
California

The Magnificat

The New Testament records one prayer that Mary said. It is called the **Magnificat**. In the Magnificat, Mary praises and thanks God for his many blessings. It is a wonderful example of a prayer of praise. Mary prayed:

"My soul proclaims the greatness of the Lord;
    my spirit rejoices in God my savior.
For he has looked upon his handmaid's lowliness;
    behold, from now on will all ages call me blessed.
The Mighty One has done great things for me,
    and holy is his name.
His mercy is from age to age
    to those who fear him.
He has shown might with his arm,
    dispersed the arrogant of mind and heart.
He has thrown down the rulers from their thrones
    but lifted up the lowly.
The hungry he has filled with good things;
    the rich he has sent away empty.
He has helped Israel his servant,
    remembering his mercy,
according to his promise to our fathers,
    to Abraham and to his descendants forever."

LUKE 1:46–55

 How does praying the Magnificat teach us to pray?

The Visitation. Bartholomaeus Bruyn the Elder (1493–1555), German painter.

Praising God

Write your own prayer of praise of God.

_____

_____

_____

_____

_____

Our Church Makes a Difference

Contemplatives

There are religious communities of men and religious communities of women in the Church who dedicate their lives to praying. These religious are called contemplatives. Contemplatives live in convents, monasteries, or abbeys. They organize their day so that everything they do centers around prayer. They set aside times for praying during the day and night. The work they do to support themselves and the religious community never interferes with the work of praying.

Trappists in prayer

The monks of the Abbey of Gethsemane in Trappist, Kentucky, are contemplatives. They gather seven times a day to pray the Liturgy of the Hours, which is the "work of God." In addition, each monk spends time every day prayerfully reading the Scriptures, the writings of the saints, and other writings.

The monks of the Abbey of Gethsemane earn their living by making cheese, fruitcake, and fudge. They also care for guests who come there to make a retreat.

QUESTION *When does your parish gather to pray? How might your family center its life around prayer?*

Trappist baking fruit cakes

What Difference Does Faith Make in My Life?

The Holy Spirit teaches you how to pray and helps you pray. Remember, you can pray anywhere and anytime.

Complete these sentences to help you discover how easy it is to pray throughout the day.

Growing as a Person of Prayer

I will tell God, "I love you."

I will praise God for _____.

I will thank God for _____.

I will ask God for _____.

My Faith Choice

This week I will try my best to pray several times each day. I will

_____

_____.

The Angelus

Leader: The Angelus is a prayer that was developed many centuries ago. By praying the Angelus, we honor Mary and remember the mystery of the Incarnation. Let us pray the Angelus together.

The Angel of the Lord declared unto Mary,

All: **And she conceived of the Holy Spirit.**
Hail, Mary, full of grace,
the Lord is with thee.
Blessed art thou among women
and blessed is the fruit of thy womb, Jesus.
Holy Mary, Mother of God,
pray for us sinners,
now and at the hour of our death. Amen.

Leader: "Behold the handmaid of the Lord:
All: **Be it done unto me according to your Word."**
Hail Mary . . .

Leader: And the Word was made flesh,
All: **And dwelt among us.**
Hail Mary . . .

Leader: Pray for us, O holy Mother of God,
All: **That we may be made worthy**
of the promises of Christ.

Leader: Let us pray.
Pour forth, we beseech you, O Lord,
your grace into our hearts: that we, to
whom the Incarnation of Christ your Son
was made known by the message of an Angel,
may by his Passion and Cross be brought
to the glory of his Resurrection.
Through the same Christ our Lord.
All: **Amen.**

We Remember

What I Have Learned

Use each letter in the word *pray* to describe something about prayer. The letter "Y" has been done for you.

1. _____ **P** _____

2. _____ **R** _____

3. _____ **A** _____

4. Pray alwa**Y**s _____

Answer the following.

Describe each of the following kinds of prayer:

5. Blessing and adoration _____

_____

6. Praise _____

_____

7. Thanksgiving _____

_____

8. Intercession _____

_____

9. Petition _____

_____

To Help You Remember

1. Praying throughout the day helps us develop the habit of prayer and become people of prayer.

2. The Church prays five different types of prayer: blessing and adoration, praise, thanksgiving, intercession, and petition.

3. Christians pray to Mary, the Mother of the Church. We are confident that Mary shares our prayers with her Son.

Growing in Faith

One important thing I learned this week is

_____

_____

_____.

This is important because

_____

_____

_____.

What will people see me doing as I live my faith choice this week?

_____

_____

_____

This Week . . .

In chapter 25, "People of Prayer," your child learned about the importance of developing the habit of prayer. The Holy Spirit invites us to pray throughout the day. We pray five basic kinds of prayer— blessing and adoration, praise, thanksgiving, petition, and intercession. The prayer of Christians is primarily addressed to God the Father through the power of the Holy Spirit in the name of Jesus, the Son of God. The Church also prays to Mary, the Mother of the Church, and to the other saints. We are confident and trust that Mary shares our prayers with her Son.

For more on the teachings of the Catholic Church on Christian prayer, see *Catechism of the Catholic Church* paragraph numbers 2623–2643, 2650–2660, and 2663–2677.

Sharing God's Word

Read together Luke 1:46–55, the Magnificat. Emphasize that the Magnificat is a prayer of praise.

Praying

In this chapter your child prayed the Angelus. Read and pray together this prayer on page 328.

Making a Difference

Choose one of the following activities to do as a family or design a similar activity of your own.

- At mealtimes this week think about how God has blessed you. Pray the Magnificat, Mary's prayer of praise to God, for your family mealtime prayer each evening.

- Make a banner with the words "Anywhere, Anytime!" Decorate and hang the banner where it can serve as a reminder to the whole family to pray to God anywhere and anytime.

- Talk about the importance of prayer in the life of a Christian family. Choose one thing you will do this week to make prayer a regular part of every day.

For more ideas on ways your family can live your faith, visit the "Faith First for Families" page at **www.FaithFirst.com**. Click on "Family Prayer," and pray the prayer together this week.

Lord, Teach Us to Pray

A Scripture Story

We Pray

As the heavens tower
 over the earth,
 so God's love towers
 over the faithful.
PSALM 103:11

**God, Father and
 Creator,
 you are blessed
 and the source
 of everything that
 is good.   Amen.**

Who teaches you to pray?

We learn to pray from
others. We first learn to
pray with our families.
Jesus taught his disciples
to pray.

*When his disciples asked
Jesus to teach them to pray,
what did he teach them?*

331

Bible Background

Faith Focus

What is the importance of Jesus preaching on a mountain?

Faith Vocabulary

Mount Sinai.
One of several mountain peaks in the Sinai Peninsula in Egypt, also called Mount Horeb, on which God revealed himself to Moses.

Hillside near Sea of Galilee

Matthew's Gospel

Some books tell stories. Some books are collections of famous sayings. Other books, like almanacs, are collections of facts. Matthew's Gospel is a collection of the teachings and events of Jesus' birth, life, Passion, death, and Resurrection. It concludes with the Risen Jesus sending his disciples out to make disciples of all people and promising to always be with them.

Matthew's Gospel was written around A.D. 70. It uses many phrases and images that had special meaning for his Jewish listeners and readers who had become Jesus' disciples. One of those images is Jesus teaching on a mountain.

Mountain in Galilee

Mountains played an important role in the history of the Jewish people. The mountain was a special place of God's presence. It was on a mountain, **Mount Sinai,** that God spoke to Moses and entered into the Covenant with Moses and the Israelites.

332

In Matthew's Gospel the account of Jesus teaching his disciples to pray the Our Father is found in the Sermon on the Mount. It takes place on a mountainside. As God revealed himself to Moses on a mountain, Jesus teaches his disciples on a mountain. This emphasizes the importance of this teaching.

Many believe that the Our Father in Matthew's Gospel was a prayer the first Christians had often prayed. Praying the Our Father had become part of what they did when they gathered for prayer.

QUESTION Why is the Our Father such an important prayer for all Christians?

Praying to God the Father

Look up and read John 17:1–26 and think about Jesus' prayer. Write your own prayer to God the Father.

_____

_____

_____

_____

_____

_____

_____

_____

_____

_____

Reading the Word of God

Why is the Our Father a prayer that shows our trust in God?

The Our Father

Imagine you are sitting with the disciples on the mountainside in Galilee and listening to Jesus. You are learning much about what it means to live as his disciple. Then Jesus begins teaching about prayer. He says:

"This is how you are to pray:
Our Father in heaven,
  hallowed be your name,
  your kingdom come,
  your will be done,
    on earth as in heaven.
  Give us today our daily
    bread;

and forgive us our
    debts,
  as we forgive our
    debtors;
  and do not subject us
    to the final test,
  but deliver us from
    the evil one."
                    MATTHEW 6:9–13

Jesus invites us to pray to his Father with great trust. God the Father is our Father too.

Detail from *Christ on the Mountain*. C. Arnold Slade (1892–1961), American painter.

334

The Lord's Prayer

The Our Father is called the Lord's Prayer. It is the prayer that Jesus, our Lord, taught us. It is the prayer of all Christians.

We pray the Our Father when we welcome new members into the Church. Every time we celebrate the Eucharist, we pray the Lord's Prayer to prepare to receive Holy Communion. We pray it every day in the Liturgy of the Hours. We pray it at work and in our homes. We may pray it to begin our day and to end our day.

 When do you pray the Our Father?

Glory to God, Our Father

Decorate the frame with words and symbols and colors that show your love, honor, and respect for God the Father.

> *For the kingdom, the power and the glory are yours, now and forever.*

Understanding the Word of God

A Summary of the Gospel

The Our Father, or Lord's Prayer, has been called a summary of the Gospel. Praying the Our Father teaches us to pray and to live as disciples of Jesus.

OUR FATHER

We do not pray *my* Father but *our* Father. We belong to God as his children. He is our Abba. We are all united, one people, because he is the Father of all people.

WHO ART IN HEAVEN

This does not mean God is far away. It means God, our Father, is glorious and majestic. He is above and beyond everything and everyone else in this world.

HALLOWED BE THY NAME

Hallowed means "very holy" and "very honored." We want all the peoples of the world to know and love God, the Creator and Redeemer of the universe.

THY KINGDOM COME

Jesus' death, Resurrection, and Ascension opened up the way for God's kingdom to take hold of the world. We live in hope and wait with trust for the day when God's kingdom of justice and peace and of love and wisdom announced by Jesus will come about. We prepare for the coming of the kingdom by living as children of God as Jesus taught.

THY WILL BE DONE

God's will is that all people will be saved in Jesus. We pray that we will follow God's will and live as Jesus taught.

GIVE US THIS DAY OUR DAILY BREAD

Each day and every moment of our lives we depend on God to give us life. We place our trust in him. We ask him to give us all we need. We put our words into action by living the Corporal and Spiritual Works of Mercy.

FORGIVE US OUR TRESPASSES AS WE FORGIVE THOSE WHO TRESPASS AGAINST US

Jesus is the Savior of the world. The heart of his work on earth was the forgiveness of sins. We ask God to forgive us. We promise to forgive all people who hurt us.

LEAD US NOT INTO TEMPTATION

We ask God for strength to overcome all that tries to lead us away from God's love. We ask God to help us choose to live the Gospel and the Commandments as Jesus taught.

DELIVER US FROM EVIL

We ask God to free us from whatever and whoever would keep us separated from him now and forever. We ask for the grace to help us live with God forever in heaven.

QUESTION *How can praying the Our Father teach you to pray?*

Living the Our Father

Draw ways you can put the words of the Our Father into practice.

Young volunteers helping to gather green sea turtle eggs

Caring for God's Creation

When we call God our Father, we are showing that all creation belongs to him. God has given us the responsibility to care for one another and for the world. This responsibility includes the responsibility to use creation to do the work of God and give glory to him.

We are to be good stewards of God's creation. A steward is someone who has responsibility to care for what belongs to someone else.

QUESTION *How are the people in the pictures acting as good stewards of creation?*

338

What Difference Does Faith Make in My Life?

Each time you pray the Our Father, the Holy Spirit helps you grow as a child of God. You learn both how to pray and how to live the Gospel.

Write or draw something you could do to help others understand that God is the Father of all people.

God Is Our Father

My Faith Choice

This week I will think about how I can act as a son or daughter of God, the loving Father of all people. I will

_____

_____.

The Lord's Prayer

Leader: The Our Father, or Lord's Prayer, is the prayer of all Christians. Let us listen to the words of Jesus, which he prayed at the Last Supper.

Reader: A reading from the holy gospel according to John.

All: **Glory to you, O Lord.**

Reader: [Jesus said,] "I pray not only for them, but also for those who will believe in me through their word, so that they may all be one, as you, Father, are in me and I in you, that they also may be in us, that the world may believe that you sent me."

JOHN 17:20–21

The gospel of the Lord.

All: **Praise to you, Lord Jesus Christ.**

Leader: Together, let us join hands and pray as Jesus taught us:

All: **Our Father, who art in heaven,
hallowed be thy name;
Thy kingdom come;
Thy will be done on earth
   as it is in heaven.
Give us this day our daily bread;
and forgive us our trespasses
as we forgive those who trespass
   against us;
and lead us not into temptation,
but deliver us from evil.
Amen.**

Leader: Let us share a sign of peace
to show that we are all children
of God, our Father.

We Remember

What I Have Learned

1. Imagine that you were on the mountain listening as Jesus taught the disciples the Our Father. Create a headline and write a news report describing what happened. Use these and other words and phrases in your report.

> worship   trust
> forgive   justice   love

_____
_____
_____
_____
_____

Answer the following.

2. Compare the role of mountains in Moses' life with mountains in Jesus' life.

_____
_____

3. Describe the Our Father as the prayer of all Christians.

_____
_____

4. Explain what is meant by calling the Our Father a summary of the Gospel.

_____
_____

To Help You Remember

1. Jesus taught his disciples to pray the Our Father.

2. When we pray the Our Father, we place our trust in God the Father as Jesus did.

3. The Our Father is a summary of the Gospel. Praying the Our Father teaches us what it means to be children of God.

Growing in Faith

One important thing I learned this week is

_____
_____
_____.

This is important because

_____
_____
_____.

What will people see me doing as I live my faith choice this week?

_____
_____
_____

This Week . . .

In chapter 26, "Lord, Teach Us to Pray: A Scripture Story," your child learned about the Our Father. In Matthew's Gospel, Jesus' teaching the Our Father, or Lord's Prayer, to the disciples is part of the Sermon on the Mount. Many biblical scholars think that the version of the Our Father in Matthew's Gospel is close to the version the early Church prayed. The Lord's Prayer has been called a summary of the Gospel. When we pray the Our Father, the Holy Spirit teaches us both how to pray and how to live the Gospel.

For more on the teaching of the Catholic Church on the Our Father, see *Catechism of the Catholic Church* paragraph numbers 2759–2856.

Sharing God's Word

Read together Matthew 6:9–13. Emphasize that the Our Father is also called the Lord's Prayer. It is the prayer that Jesus, our Lord, taught us.

Praying

In this chapter your child prayed the Lord's Prayer. Read and pray together the prayer on page 340.

Making a Difference

Choose one of the following activities to do as a family or design a similar activity of your own.

• When you participate in Mass this weekend, pay close attention to the praying of the Lord's Prayer. Imagine you are with Jesus as he teaches you to pray it.

• Jesus reminded us that God is our Father. Every member of your family is a child of God. Choose one thing you can do this week to live as God's children.

• Use the Lord's Prayer for family prayer this week. Pray it every day.

For more ideas on ways your family can live your faith, visit the "Faith First for Families" page at **www.FaithFirst.com**. "Gospel Reflections" will continue to change each week over the summer. Don't forget to check it out.

Catholic Social Teaching

Getting the Job Done—Together

It is time for the fifth grade's annual Invention Showcase. Every year, each fifth grader creates an invention that goes on display for the whole school community at the Invention Showcase. Even though students work on their projects as individuals, it takes the whole class to set up the auditorium for the showcase.

This year, a number of students—those who volunteered to make the Invention Showcase banner and those who volunteered to set up the refreshment tables—are not getting their jobs done. In thirty minutes the parents will be arriving. Unless everyone pitches in, the Invention Showcase will not be ready on time.

We Live in Community

As Christians, we are active members of our communities. We participate and contribute to the well-being of all members. This is our responsibility as Christians.

Making Connections . . .

As members of various groups, we have responsibilities. Several members of the fifth grade class, who are preparing for the Invention Showcase, are not participating as they agreed to. They are not meeting their responsibilities. This will affect the whole group.

with Language Arts

Interview friends and family members to find out what groups they enjoy working with the most. Ask them why and what makes that group work so well. Then write a description of the children setting up the Invention Showcase. Describe how the fifth graders could be working together as a group to complete their goal of setting up for the showcase.

with Math and Science

Identify two different situations in nature in which living things and their environment are interdependent. Describe how you and your family are interdependent. Discuss why interdependence is important in a family and in a class.

with Creative Arts

Design a cartoon with speech bubbles that illustrates a group of people not participating together well. Have a character pop up in your cartoon that makes comments that will encourage the other characters in your cartoon to join in with the group.

➲ **Faith Action** *This week, look for ways to cooperate with each other while learning in your classroom.*

Name _____

A. Best Response

Read each statement and circle the best answer.

1. Jesus prayed the ____ .
   a. Psalms   b. Nicene Creed
   c. Apostles' Creed   d. Hail Mary

2. Jesus taught us to pray ____ .
   a. with trust   b. with confidence
   c. out of love   d. all of the above

3. Jesus taught his disciples the ____ .
   a. Glory Prayer   b. Creed
   c. Our Father   d. Act of Contrition

4. Asking God to forgive us is a prayer of ____ .
   a. praise   b. thanksgiving
   c. petition   d. adoration

5. A prayer of ____ tells God that he alone is God.
   a. praise   b. intercession
   c. blessing and adoration   d. thanksgiving

6. A prayer of ____ tells God that he is the source of all that is good.
   a. praise   b. intercession
   c. blessing and adoration   d. thanksgiving

7. A prayer of ____ tells God we trust in his faithfulness.
   a. praise   b. intercession
   c. blessing and adoration   d. thanksgiving

8. ____ prayer is praying with other people.
   a. Communal   b. Personal
   c. Private   d. Daily

9. The prayer of Christians is addressed primarily to ____ .
   a. Mary   b. God the Father
   c. the saints   d. the Holy Spirit

10. The Our Father is a summary of the ____ .
    a. Ten Commandments   b. Gospel
    c. creed   d. sacraments

B. Matching Words and Phrases

Match the parts of the Lord's Prayer in column A
with their descriptions in column B.

Column A

_____ 1. Our Father who art
in heaven

_____ 2. Hallowed be thy name

_____ 3. Thy will be done

_____ 4. Give us this day
our daily bread

_____ 5. Forgive us our
trespasses as we
forgive those who
trespass against us

Column B

a. God is glorious beyond all that
he has created.

b. We ask God to forgive us and we
forgive others.

c. We pray that we will always do
what God wants us to do.

d. We depend on God each day.

e. God's name is holy and honored.

C. What I Have Learned

Write three things you learned in this unit.
Share them with the group.

_____

_____

_____

Look at the list of faith terms in "Words to Know" on
page 306. Circle the terms that you know now.

D. From a Scripture Story

The Book of Psalms contains prayers of praise, blessing and
adoration, thanksgiving, petition, and intercession. Choose two
of these kinds of prayers. Write your own psalm verse for each.

_____   _____

_____   _____

_____   _____

Why are the celebrations of the Church's liturgical year important?

The Liturgical Year

The Year of the Lord

From the days of the early Church, the Church has celebrated Sunday as the Lord's Day.

The Church celebrates the paschal mystery on the first day of the week, known as the Lord's Day or Sunday. This follows a tradition handed down from the apostles and having its origin from the day of Christ's resurrection. Thus Sunday must be ranked as the first holy day of all.

ROMAN MISSAL, "GENERAL NORMS FOR THE LITURGICAL YEAR AND THE CALENDAR," 4

In addition to the celebration of Sunday, the Church celebrates a cycle of seasons, solemnities, feasts, and memorials. The lessons in this unit focus on the seasons of the liturgical year. This page lists the solemnities and feasts of Jesus and of Mary that the Church in the United States of America celebrates throughout the year.

Solemnities and Feasts of Jesus Christ

Epiphany
   Sunday between January 2 and January 8
Baptism of the Lord
   Sunday after Epiphany
Presentation of the Lord
   February 2
Annunciation
   March 25
The Body and Blood of Christ
   Sunday after Holy Trinity

Sacred Heart
   Friday following Second Sunday after Pentecost
Transfiguration
   August 6
Triumph of the Cross
   September 14
Christ the King
   Last Sunday in Ordinary Time
Christmas
   December 25

Solemnities, Feasts, and Memorials of the Blessed Virgin Mary

Mary, Mother of God
   January 1
Our Lady of Lourdes
   February 11
Visitation
   May 31
Immaculate Heart of Mary
   Saturday following Second Sunday after Pentecost
Our Lady of Mount Carmel
   July 16
Assumption
   August 15

Queenship of Mary
   August 22
Birth of Mary
   September 8
Our Lady of Sorrows
   September 15
Our Lady of the Rosary
   October 7
Presentation of Mary
   November 21
Immaculate Conception
   December 8
Our Lady of Guadalupe
   December 12

Faith Focus

What does the season of Advent help us prepare for?

The Word of the Lord

These are the Gospel readings for the First Sunday of Advent. Choose this year's reading. Read and discuss it with your family.

Year A
Matthew 24:37–44

Year B
Mark 13:33–37

Year C
Luke 21:25–28,
34–36

What You See

The Advent wreath is made of evergreens and four candles. The candles are lighted successively each week of Advent to symbolize the coming of Christ, the Light of the world.

Preparing for the Coming of the Lord

New things happen all the time. In the spring we see new life everywhere. In school we learn new things every day. Watching TV we learn things about the world that we never knew before.

Advent begins a new year for Christians. It is a new year and a new time to renew our love for God and for one another. It is a time to accept the Holy Spirit's invitation and grace to prepare ourselves to make room in our hearts for Jesus.

Saint John the Baptist announced, "Prepare the way for the Lord." During the four weeks of Advent we do just that. We listen to the Scripture readings each Sunday and are reminded to prepare for the coming of the Lord in our lives. For the Lord not only came on that first Christmas but also comes to us every moment of every day. He will come again in glory at the end of time.

During Advent we welcome Jesus into our lives every day. Then we will truly be ready to welcome him with great joy at Christmas.

Lighting the Advent wreath on the Third Sunday of Advent

Awaiting the Lord's Coming

Look up these stories in your Bible. Each is about a person whose words and example help prepare us for the Lord's coming. In the spaces write the name of the person in each story.

Read Mark 1:1–8. Who first used the words, "Behold, I am sending my messenger ahead of you; / he will prepare your way"? MARK 1:2

_____

Read Luke 1:46–56. Who said yes to God and sang these words, "My soul proclaims the greatness of the Lord"? LUKE 1:46

_____

Read Matthew 1:18–25. Who believed Isaiah's words, "Behold, the virgin shall be with child and bear a son, / and they shall name him Emmanuel"? MATTHEW 1:23

_____

Read Matthew 3:1–7. Who announced Jesus' coming and preached repentance by saying, "Prepare the way of the Lord"? MATTHEW 3:3

_____

These are the Gospel readings for the Second Sunday of Advent. Choose this year's reading. Read and discuss it with your family.

Year A
Matthew 3:1–12

Year B
Mark 1:1–8

Year C
Luke 3:1–6

Prepare the Way!

The lights go down. The music begins to roar and fills the arena. The voice of the announcer is loud and clear. Quickly, the spirit of the hometown crowd is raised. The players are introduced one by one as we cheer. The announcer has done his job. We are prepared.

Saint John the Baptist was the son of Elizabeth and Zechariah. At the birth of John, his father sang a canticle, or song of praise, to describe the work his son would do. Zechariah said:

"And you, child, will be called prophet of the Most High, for you will go before the Lord to prepare his ways, to give his people knowledge of salvation." LUKE 1:76–77

When Saint John grew up, he went into the desert to prepare to do his work. One day he came down to the banks of the Jordan River and announced the coming of the Messiah. The Messiah was the One whom God had promised to send to save his people. Saint John preached, "Turn back to God and change your ways." Many listened to John the Baptist and changed their ways.

Telling Others About Jesus

Many people help you come to know Jesus Christ. When they do, they are like John the Baptist. In this space draw or write an announcement that will help others come to know Jesus.

Faith Focus

How does listening to the message of Isaiah the Prophet help us celebrate Advent?

The Word of the Lord

These are the Gospel readings for the Third Sunday of Advent. Choose this year's reading. Read and discuss it with your family.

Year A
  Matthew 11:2–11

Year B
  John 1:6–8, 19–28

Year C
  Luke 3:10–18

God's Promised One

In times past, God chose certain people to speak in his name. We call these people prophets. The writings of Isaiah the Prophet are often read during Advent.

Isaiah spoke many wonderful words that filled people's hearts with hope. As they were suffering at the hands of the Assyrians, who were trying to conquer the world, God's people wanted a leader who would help them survive. Isaiah promised that God would send a leader to help them.

This is how the Book of Isaiah the Prophet describes this new leader:

The spirit of the LORD shall
    rest upon him:
  a spirit of wisdom and
    of understanding,
A spirit of counsel and of
    strength,
  a spirit of knowledge and
    of fear of the LORD.
            ISAIAH 11:2

But he shall judge the
    poor with justice,
  and decide aright for
    the land's afflicted. . . .
Justice shall be the band
    around his waist,
  and faithfulness a belt
    upon his hips. . . .

There shall be no harm or
    ruin on all my holy
    mountain;
  for the earth shall be
    filled with knowledge
    of the LORD,
  as water covers the sea.
            ISAIAH 11:4, 5, 9

Isaiah was speaking about Jesus. Jesus is the Promised One who Isaiah said would bring peace to all people. When Jesus began his work on earth, he went into the synagogue and read from the writings of Isaiah. When he finished reading, Jesus rolled up the scroll and announced that he was the One whom Isaiah spoke about many years ago.

Jesus, God's Promised One

Solve the puzzle using the alpha grid on the right. The shape from the lines of the grid and the number of dots inside the shape indicate which letter to use. Look at the example. The first symbol is [·]. Find this shape [ ] on the grid. Notice that the dot is in the first position. This means that G is the first letter. Work through the O and D. Now decode this message from Isaiah the Prophet.

ABC	JKL	STU
DEF	MNO	VWX
GHI	PQR	YZ

Example: G o d

"_ _ _ _   _ _ _ _ _

_ _ _ _   _ _ _

_ _ _ _ _ _ _ _ ." Matthew 1:23

354

Faith Focus

How do the words and actions of Mary help us celebrate Advent?

The Word of the Lord

These are the Gospel readings for the Fourth Sunday of Advent. Choose this year's reading. Read and discuss it with your family.

Year A
   Matthew 1:18–24

Year B
   Luke 1:26–38

Year C
   Luke 1:39–45

Hill country near Nazareth, showing the type of land Mary would have traveled to visit Elizabeth

Mary's Song of Joy

When something exciting happens to us, we cannot wait to share it. When friends begin to tell us about something good that has happened to them, we cannot wait to hear more about it. That is just how Elizabeth, the mother of John the Baptist, and Mary felt before their sons were born.

Mary and Elizabeth both believed they were very blessed by God. Through both their children, God would fulfill his promises to his people. The time God's people were waiting for had finally come.

We listen carefully each Advent as we retell the story of Mary and Elizabeth as they prepare for the birth of their sons. The Gospel according to Luke tells us that the angel Gabriel announced to Mary that her child "will be called holy, the Son of God" (Luke 1:35). At the same time, Gabriel told Mary that Elizabeth was going to have a child too. Hearing that news, Mary traveled into the hill country to visit Elizabeth.

Seeing Mary approaching her home, Elizabeth praised God for blessing Mary. She greeted Mary, saying, "Most blessed are you among women, and blessed is the fruit of your womb. . . . Blessed are you who believed that what was spoken to you by the Lord would be fulfilled" (Luke 1:42, 45). During Advent, Christians throughout the world remember this event. In languages spoken throughout the whole world we praise and thank God the Father for sending his only Son to come to live among us.

God Among Us

Complete the sentences to show that you believe that God truly does live among us. The first two sentences have already been completed.

We recognize you in the poor and the homeless.

We recognize you when someone helps us know you better.

We recognize you in _____

_____

_____ .

We recognize you when _____

_____

_____ .

We recognize you where _____

_____

_____ .

Christmas

Faith Focus

Why do we say that Jesus is the Prince of Peace?

The Word of the Lord

These are the Gospel readings for Mass on Christmas Day. Choose one reading. Read and discuss it with your family.

John 1:1–18 or
John 1:1–5, 9–14

What You See

Evergreen trees and wreaths are Christmas symbols. The circle of the evergreen wreath is a sign of God's never-ending love for us.

Shout for Joy!

Imagine a world filled with peace and harmony. Think of a world in which no family is homeless and all children eat well each and every day. What would that world be like? The Son of God became one of us and lived among us to show us how to build such a world. It is a task we will need to work at until Jesus comes again at the end of time.

During the Christmas season we remember and celebrate that "a savior has been born for you who is Messiah and Lord" (Luke 2:11). Joining with the angels, we sing:

"Glory to God in the highest / and on earth peace to those on whom his favor rests." LUKE 2:14

Jesus is the Prince of Peace, who makes all things new. Announcing the kingdom of peace, Isaiah the Prophet says:

The calf and the young lion shall browse together,
with a little child to guide them.
ISAIAH 11:6

When Jesus was born, God's plan for all people to live in peace was born again too. All creatures, even those who now treat each other as enemies, are called to live together in peace. Jesus is the Prince of Peace. With him we work to build a world of peace. We work at preparing for the coming of the Kingdom of God.

Making All Things New

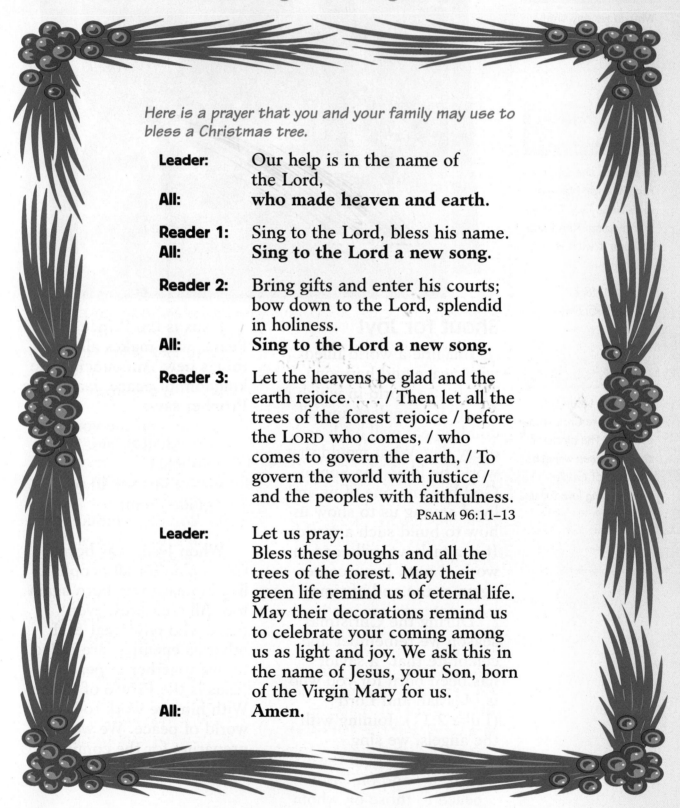

Here is a prayer that you and your family may use to bless a Christmas tree.

Leader: Our help is in the name of the Lord,

All: who made heaven and earth.

Reader 1: Sing to the Lord, bless his name.

All: Sing to the Lord a new song.

Reader 2: Bring gifts and enter his courts; bow down to the Lord, splendid in holiness.

All: Sing to the Lord a new song.

Reader 3: Let the heavens be glad and the earth rejoice. . . . / Then let all the trees of the forest rejoice / before the LORD who comes, / who comes to govern the earth, / To govern the world with justice / and the peoples with faithfulness.

PSALM 96:11–13

Leader: Let us pray:
Bless these boughs and all the trees of the forest. May their green life remind us of eternal life. May their decorations remind us to celebrate your coming among us as light and joy. We ask this in the name of Jesus, your Son, born of the Virgin Mary for us.

All: Amen.

Faith Focus

Why do we call Lent the Church's springtime?

The Word of the Lord

These are the Gospel readings for the First Sunday of Lent. Choose this year's reading. Read and discuss it with your family.

Year A
Matthew 4:1–11

Year B
Mark 1:12–15

Year C
Luke 4:1–13

What You See

During Lent the color of the vestments is purple or violet. Purple is a symbol of sorrow and penance. We remember Jesus' Passion and prepare to celebrate his Resurrection.

The Church's Springtime

Spring is a season of rebirth and renewal. During springtime flowers begin to grow. Leaves begin to sprout and cover the bare branches of winter. Ice and snow begin to melt. Flowing down mountainsides, streams fill the forests with sounds of new life. Nature begins its long return from death to new life.

Lent is the Church's sacred springtime. It is a season of rebirth and renewal. It is the time when people make final preparations to receive new life in Christ in Baptism. It is a time that the baptized renew the new life they have received in Baptism.

During Lent we walk with Jesus and stand with him as we meditate on his Passion and death. Lent is also a time when we look forward to the Resurrection at Easter.

During Lent we strengthen our decision to be faithful to the Great Commandment, which calls us to love God and love our neighbor as ourselves. We make decisions that increase our efforts to

- give alms, or share our time, talents, and other gifts with which God has blessed us;
- fast, or eat less, and share in the sufferings of Jesus; and
- pray, or talk things over with God more often.

Throughout Lent we make personal decisions to fulfill our baptismal promise. We also join with other members of the Church to work and pray together. We support one another in our celebration of Lent. We look forward to Easter and the celebration of our new life in Christ.

Finding Out About the Season of Lent

Find a classmate who can help you complete these statements about Lent. Write your answers in the spaces provided and have your classmate put his or her initials on the lines.

The color used to celebrate Lent is

_____. Initials:_____

A Lenten devotion is

_____. Initials:_____

Lent lasts this many days:

_____. Initials:_____

Lent begins on

_____. Initials:_____

Lent ends on

_____. Initials:_____

Lent is a season of

_____. Initials:_____

The Second Week of Lent

How does the Church renew and prepare for Baptism during Lent?

The Word of the Lord

These are the Gospel readings for the Second Sunday of Lent. Choose this year's reading. Read and discuss it with your family.

Year A
   Matthew 17:1–9

Year B
   Mark 9:2–10

Year C
   Luke 9:28–36

What You Hear

Before the Gospel reading the Alleluia is sung in every season except Lent. During Lent only a Psalm verse is used before the reading of the Gospel.

Baptismal Commitment

Baptism celebrates your birthday as a Christian. Through Baptism you were joined to Christ and became a member of his Church.

As we listen to the Scripture readings during Lent, we hear many images that describe Jesus. He is "living water," "the light of the world," and "the resurrection and the life."

These images help us understand our Baptism and what it means to be a member of the Body of Christ, the Church.

We call the Body of Christ that has gathered for worship the worshiping assembly. The assembly is divided into three groups of people:
- the faithful,
- penitents, and
- catechumens.

The faithful are the baptized members of the Church who seek to renew themselves. The penitents are those who have separated themselves from the Church and who seek to return to the Church once again. The catechumens are those who seek to become members of the Church. For catechumens Lent is a time to prepare for the celebration of the Sacraments of Christian Initiation—Baptism, Confirmation, and Eucharist.

Throughout Lent all the members of the Church pray for and help one another. Together we prepare to renew and celebrate our newness of life in Christ at Easter.

Supporting One Another During Lent

During Lent you join with your parish to help the catechumens prepare for their initiation into the Church. In this space create a message you could share with the catechumens in your parish.

_____

_____

_____

_____

_____

_____

_____

_____

_____

_____

Faith Focus

How does prayer help the Church renew and prepare for Baptism during Lent?

The Word of the Lord

These are the Gospel readings for the Third Sunday of Lent. Choose this year's reading. Read and discuss it with your family.

Year A
> John 4:5–42 or
> John 4:5–15, 19–26, 39, 40–44

Year B
> John 2:13–25

Year C
> Luke 13:1–9

Listening to God

Think about the many ways you like to pray. You can pray alone or with others. You can pray aloud or quietly in your heart.

God has revealed that he is always near. He is always at our side, listening to us and waiting for us to speak to him. This is what praying is really all about—talking with and listening to God.

Lent is a special time for growing as a person of prayer. During Lent we think about the many stories in the Bible that tell about God's forgiveness. As we listen to God's word, we ask him to forgive our sins and to help us make better decisions to live as followers of Jesus Christ. Praying the word of God, alone or with other people, helps us open our hearts to God.

Scripture tells us, "Be still before the LORD; / wait for God" (Psalm 37:7). Praying Scripture keeps us, in a special way, in God's presence. We try to be still and become more aware of his presence with us. We listen to the Holy Spirit, who lives in our heart and speaks to us.

Praying the Psalms

Psalm 37 uses the Hebrew alphabet to help people remember God's blessings. Use as many letters of our alphabet as you can to name your blessings.

Praise God, who is good to us,
    whose kindness endures forever.
Praise God for

A nimals. They bring joy to our lives.

B _____

_____

_____

_____

_____

_____

    I will praise and thank God all my life,
      from beginning to end, from A to Z. Amen.

How does Lent help us remember to live as followers of Jesus?

The Word of the Lord

These are the Gospel readings for the Fourth Sunday of Lent. Choose this year's reading. Read and discuss it with your family.

Year A
    John 9:1–41 or
    John 9:1, 6–9,
        13–17,
        34–38

Year B
    John 3:14–21

Year C
    Luke 15:1–3, 11–32

What You Hear

As we get closer to remembering the time of Jesus' suffering and death, the music we hear becomes less joyful.

Changing to Do Better

Most of us like to learn new words. Here is a new word—*metanoia*. It means "a change of heart." You often have to change the way you do something to learn to do it better. For example, if you learn how to take better notes, you study better. What have you changed that has helped you do something better?

During Lent the Church helps us live the Gospel better. One thing we try to do is work harder at being more generous with the gifts God has given us. We look at the ways we may be treating others selfishly. We treat others as we want them to treat us. Remembering that God is merciful and gracious, we try to be kinder and more forgiving.

We look at how we are using and caring for creation. We turn away from using resources and creatures of the world carelessly. We work harder at becoming more careful in our use of water, food, and the other gifts of the earth.

Jesus told us that we are to be lights in the world. During Lent we think more about ways to do this. When we are self-giving and generous, we are filled with the light and love of God. We are letting our light shine as Jesus asked.

Lights in the World

LEADER: Dear brothers and sisters, as we continue to celebrate Lent, let us consider how we can live as lights in the world.

READER 1: God made all things and shares his life and love with us.

ALL: **Let us live as lights in the world.**

READER 2: God asks that we learn to live the Gospel better.

ALL: **Let us live as lights in the world.**

LEADER: Take out a small piece of paper. Write down one action that will help you live as a light in the world. *(Pause.)* Let us pray:

READER 3: In our need, Spirit of God,

ALL: **be our helper.**

READER 4: In our weakness, Spirit of God,

ALL: **be our power.**

READER 5: In our life as followers of Christ, Spirit of God,

ALL: **be our life, now and forever more. Amen.**

Faith Focus

Why is the cross of Christ central to our celebration of Lent?

The Word of the Lord

These are the Gospel readings for the Fifth Sunday of Lent. Choose this year's reading. Read and discuss it with your family.

Year A
    John 11:1–45 or
    John 11:3–7, 17,
        20–27,
        33–45

Year B
    John 12:20–33

Year C
    John 8:1–11

Remembering the Passion and Death of Jesus

Sometimes bad things happen to us. These things might hurt our feelings or harm our bodies or both. But sometimes something good comes out of a bad experience. You may fail a test, but good can come out of your failing. This experience can encourage you to work harder to learn more and do better on the next test.

From Jesus' death on the cross came new life. Lent helps us remember that we share in the new life that came out of Jesus' suffering and death.

Christians give the cross a place of honor in our churches and in our lives. During Lent, Catholics put aside time to kneel before the crucifix and thank God for his great love for us. On the Fridays of Lent, many parish communities pray the Stations of the Cross. On their own, some people set aside a time to walk with Jesus and meditate on his journey to death and through his death to his Resurrection. We look at our own life and ask, "How are we sharing in Jesus' suffering and in his Resurrection?"

Youth praying the Stations of the Cross during World Youth Day, Denver, Colorado

367

Follow Me

As the youth columnist for your local Catholic newspaper, you receive these letters in the mail. How would you answer them?

I play the flute pretty well. Our parish wants musicians to play during Holy Week. I don't think I'm good enough. What do you think?

Deaundra Flutist

Dear Deaundra,

My grandpa wants me to come and visit him. He is lonely, but he tells the same stories over and over and over. How can I get out of this?

Jason Bored

Dear Jason,

I love chocolate! I gave it up for Lent, but I ate a whole bag of chocolate-covered peanuts last night. Now that I've eaten chocolate, why should I continue to give it up?

Failing Pepe

Dear Pepe,

I ruined my friend's CD. I don't have any money to get her a new one. What can I do? I really want to wait until I have the money before I tell her.

Puzzled Huan Yue

Dear Huan Yue,

Palm Sunday of the Lord's Passion

Faith Focus

Why do we say that Holy Week is a celebration of being forgiven and growing in forgiveness?

The Word of the Lord

These are the Gospel readings for Palm Sunday of the Lord's Passion. Choose this year's reading. Read and discuss it with your family.

Year A
Matthew 26:14–27:66 or Matthew 27:11–54

Year B
Mark 14:1–15:47 or Mark 15:1–39

Year C
Luke 22:14–23:56 or Luke 23:1–49

What You See

Palm branches, or palm fronds, are blessed and carried in procession and are held high as we listen to the reading of "The Passion of our Lord Jesus Christ."

Carrying palm fronds in entrance procession, liturgy for Palm Sunday

A Forgiven and a Forgiving People

Forgiving others and being forgiven by others are two very important things in our relationship with others. A forgiving word or look and a hug or a smile for someone who has been hurt helps families grow closer. An apology to someone we have hurt can make a friendship stronger. Forgiveness, reconciliation, and new life are what the life and work of Jesus Christ were all about.

Holy Week begins the center of the story of God's plan of forgiveness. On Palm Sunday of the Lord's Passion we listen to how Jesus was cheered when he rode into Jerusalem on a donkey. Only a few days later the cheering of the crowds would turn into jeering. Jesus would be crucified so we could be forgiven.

Throughout his life on earth, Jesus taught that we are to have forgiving hearts. We are to forgive as God forgives—not once, not twice, but over and over again. We are to be merciful and forgiving—"seventy times seven times," as many times as necessary.

369

Holy Week invites us to think about how we are living as a forgiving people. But we are to do more than think. We need to ask the Holy Spirit to strengthen and guide us to act as a forgiving people. As followers of Jesus Christ we continue his work of forgiveness throughout our lives.

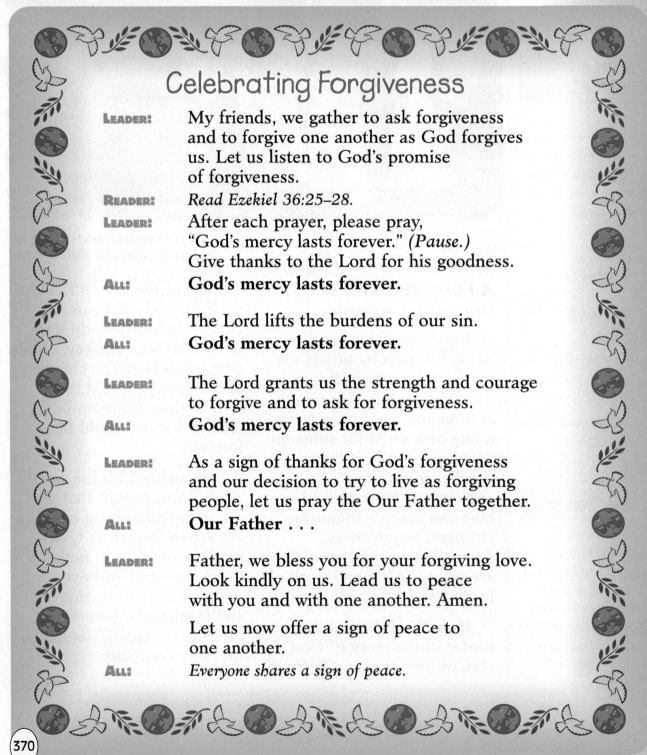

Celebrating Forgiveness

LEADER: My friends, we gather to ask forgiveness and to forgive one another as God forgives us. Let us listen to God's promise of forgiveness.

READER: *Read Ezekiel 36:25–28.*

LEADER: After each prayer, please pray, "God's mercy lasts forever." *(Pause.)* Give thanks to the Lord for his goodness.

ALL: **God's mercy lasts forever.**

LEADER: The Lord lifts the burdens of our sin.

ALL: **God's mercy lasts forever.**

LEADER: The Lord grants us the strength and courage to forgive and to ask for forgiveness.

ALL: **God's mercy lasts forever.**

LEADER: As a sign of thanks for God's forgiveness and our decision to try to live as forgiving people, let us pray the Our Father together.

ALL: **Our Father . . .**

LEADER: Father, we bless you for your forgiving love. Look kindly on us. Lead us to peace with you and with one another. Amen.

Let us now offer a sign of peace to one another.

ALL: *Everyone shares a sign of peace.*

into the fresh aroma of new, green life. What signs of spring and new life fill the places where you live and play?

Signs of the new life we have in Christ fill our churches during Easter. At the Easter Vigil the newly lighted Easter candle stands tall and shines in the darkness. Standing and holding lighted candles that flood the church with light, the worshiping assembly listens as the Church proclaims:

Exult, all creation around God's throne!
Jesus Christ, our King, is risen!

Faith Focus

Why is Easter the most important season of the Church's year?

The Word of the Lord

These are the Gospel readings for Easter Sunday. Choose this year's reading. Read and discuss it with your family.

Year A
John 20:1–9 or
Matthew 28:1–10 or
Luke 24:13–35

Year B
John 20:1–9 or
Mark 16:1–8 or
Luke 24:13–35

Year C
John 20:1–9 or
Luke 24:1–12 or
Luke 24:13–35

This Is the Day

There is something special about the farm when crops begin to grow and fill the field. The air is filled with new scents as the smell of winter dirt is transformed

Das Lamb. Paul Klee (1879–1940), Swiss expressionist painter. The New Testament uses the title *Lamb of God* for Christ.

Everyone rejoices. Easter is the Church's season of new life. On Easter Sunday the Church around the world breaks into joyful song and sings,

"This is the day the Lord has made; let us rejoice and be glad."

RESPONSORIAL PSALM, EASTER SUNDAY

We fill our homes and lives with signs of joy and new life. Flowers and candles decorate our homes. Special foods remind us that this is a life-giving feast. Throughout this day and for fifty days afterward, our celebration of Easter continues. We sing aloud and in the quiet of our hearts, "Alleluia! Alleluia! Alleluia!"

Alleluia! Christ Is Risen

Create a design for an Easter banner in this space. Then, using your design, work with your family to create the banner and hang it in your home.

Faith Focus

How does the story of Saint Thomas the Apostle help us live our Baptism?

The Word of the Lord

This is the Gospel reading for the Second Sunday of Easter. Read and discuss it with your family.

John 20:19–31

What You See

One of the Easter symbols is the Paschal, or Easter, candle. It is lighted at the Easter Vigil and throughout the Easter season. After Pentecost the lighted Easter candle is used at the celebration of Baptism and funerals to symbolize the Resurrection.

Doubting Thomas? Faithful Thomas?

Eyewitness reportings of events are the most believable. When our friends describe with enthusiasm and in detail things or events they have seen, we become part of their story. It is almost as if we were there. What is an event that you have witnessed and told your friends about?

All four of the Evangelists tell about the witnesses who first learned about Jesus' Resurrection. Mary Magdalene, Mary the mother of James and John, and Salome were the first to come to the empty tomb. Only after hearing the women describe what they had seen did Saint Peter and the other disciples go to the tomb and witness the empty tomb for themselves.

Later the Risen Lord appeared to the disciples. Saint Thomas the Apostle was not present with the others when the Risen Jesus first appeared to them. Because he, at first, so strongly refused to believe in the Resurrection, people who refuse to believe what others know to be true are called "doubting Thomases."

Stained-glass window of "Doubting Thomas" from the Franciscan Chapel in Jerusalem. According to tradition, the chapel is at the site where the Last Supper took place.

Saint Thomas did not remain a doubter; he too became a strong believer in the Risen Jesus. When the Risen Lord appeared a second time, Thomas loudly and clearly professed his faith. He said, "My Lord and my God!"

Our Baptism began our life in the Risen Lord. The Holy Spirit whom we received at Baptism invites us to live our faith. We proclaim our faith in Jesus loudly and clearly in our words and actions.

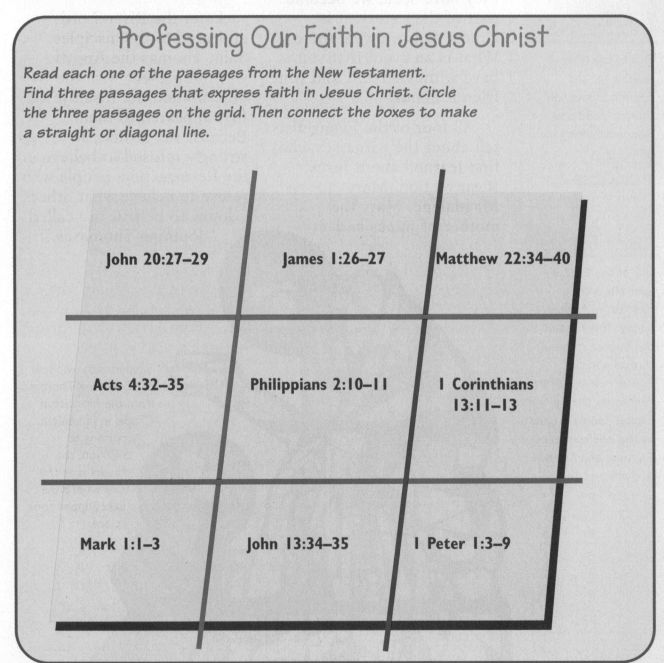

Professing Our Faith in Jesus Christ

Read each one of the passages from the New Testament. Find three passages that express faith in Jesus Christ. Circle the three passages on the grid. Then connect the boxes to make a straight or diagonal line.

John 20:27–29	James 1:26–27	Matthew 22:34–40
Acts 4:32–35	Philippians 2:10–11	I Corinthians 13:11–13
Mark 1:1–3	John 13:34–35	I Peter 1:3–9

Road to Emmaus. The journey from Jerusalem to Emmaus is about seven miles.

Faith Focus

What happened when the Risen Jesus blessed, broke, and shared bread with the two disciples he traveled with to Emmaus?

The Word of the Lord

These are the Gospel readings for the Third Sunday of Easter. Choose this year's reading. Read and discuss it with your family.

Year A
    Luke 24:13–35

Year B
    Luke 24:35–48

Year C
    John 21:1–19 or
    John 21:1–14

The Road to Emmaus

Good news is great to receive. When we receive it, we just cannot help sharing it. When was the last time you received good news? How did you feel? Did you tell anyone else?

The Gospel according to Luke tells us about two disciples who had not yet heard the good news of Jesus' Resurrection. They were puzzled by reports that Jesus had been raised from the dead and had been seen by many. As they were walking from Jerusalem to Emmaus, they were joined by a "stranger." The stranger was the Risen Jesus, but they did not recognize him.

The two disciples started telling the stranger about Jesus. The Risen Jesus began explaining the Scriptures, which they knew so well, to help them understand everything that had happened.

Finally, as the sun began to set, they were approaching Emmaus, the village where the disciples lived. Amazed and interested in what the "stranger" was telling them, they invited the Risen Jesus to stay with them. While they were eating, Jesus took bread, blessed, and broke it. Then he shared it with them. At that moment the disciples suddenly recognized the stranger to be the Risen Jesus, who immediately disappeared. The disciples hurried back to Jerusalem to tell the other disciples the good news of what had happened to them (see Luke 24:13–35).

Each week at Mass we listen to the Scriptures and share in the Eucharist, the bread and wine that have become the Body and Blood of Christ. Fed by the word of God and the Eucharist, we are sent forth into our homes, neighborhoods, and schools. We tell others about Jesus and the good news of God's love for us.

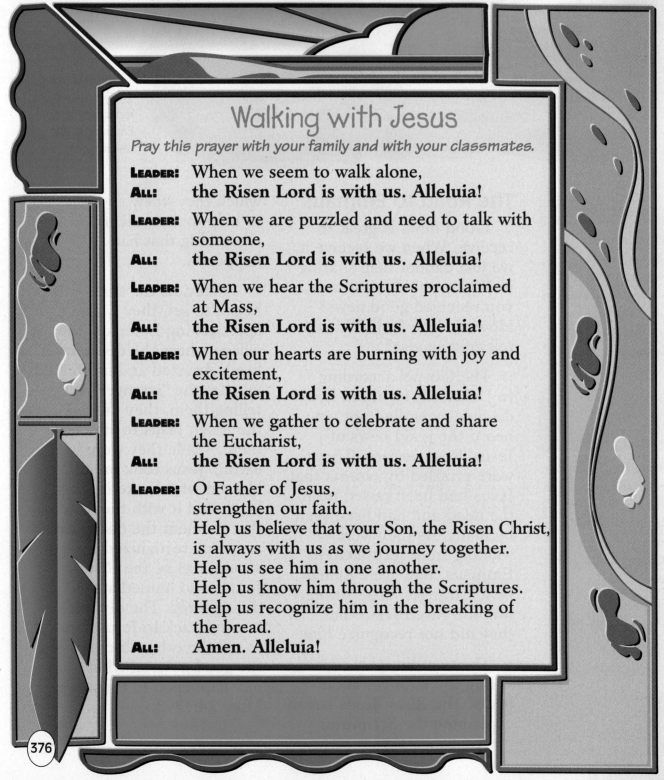

Walking with Jesus

Pray this prayer with your family and with your classmates.

LEADER: When we seem to walk alone,

ALL: the Risen Lord is with us. Alleluia!

LEADER: When we are puzzled and need to talk with someone,

ALL: the Risen Lord is with us. Alleluia!

LEADER: When we hear the Scriptures proclaimed at Mass,

ALL: the Risen Lord is with us. Alleluia!

LEADER: When our hearts are burning with joy and excitement,

ALL: the Risen Lord is with us. Alleluia!

LEADER: When we gather to celebrate and share the Eucharist,

ALL: the Risen Lord is with us. Alleluia!

LEADER: O Father of Jesus,
strengthen our faith.
Help us believe that your Son, the Risen Christ, is always with us as we journey together.
Help us see him in one another.
Help us know him through the Scriptures.
Help us recognize him in the breaking of the bread.

ALL: Amen. Alleluia!

The Fourth Week of Easter

The Good Shepherd

Faith Focus

How does the image of the Good Shepherd help us understand our relationship to Jesus?

The Word of the Lord

These are the Gospel readings for the Fourth Sunday of Easter. Choose this year's reading. Read and discuss it with your family.

Year A
    John 10:1–10

Year B
    John 10:11–18

Year C
    John 10:27–30

What You See

The priest wears white vestments during the Easter season. White is a symbol of joy and life. We rejoice in Jesus' Resurrection.

Teams have coaches. Schools have principals. Governors are the leaders of our states, and the president is the leader of our country. Good leaders are important. They remind us of the principles and goals of the groups we belong to. Think of a leader you admire. What leadership qualities does this person have?

In the Old Testament the image of a shepherd is often used to describe the leader of God's people. Today we call our bishops the shepherds of the Church. In the Scriptures the word *shepherd* is also used for God. God is the true shepherd of his people. Jesus uses this image

Shepherd tending flock near Bethlehem

to describe his relationship to us. He said:

"I am the good shepherd, and I know mine and mine know me, just as the Father knows me and I know the Father; and I will lay down my life for the sheep."
JOHN 10:14–15

Fifteenth-century mosaic of the Good Shepherd

377

Remembering that Jesus sacrificed his life for them and all people, the early Church used the image of the Good Shepherd to express her faith in Jesus Christ, the Good Shepherd who gave his life for us.

Through the gifts of faith and Baptism, we choose Jesus to be our shepherd. Through him we share in the life and love of God.

Design a mosaic that shows Jesus is the Good Shepherd.

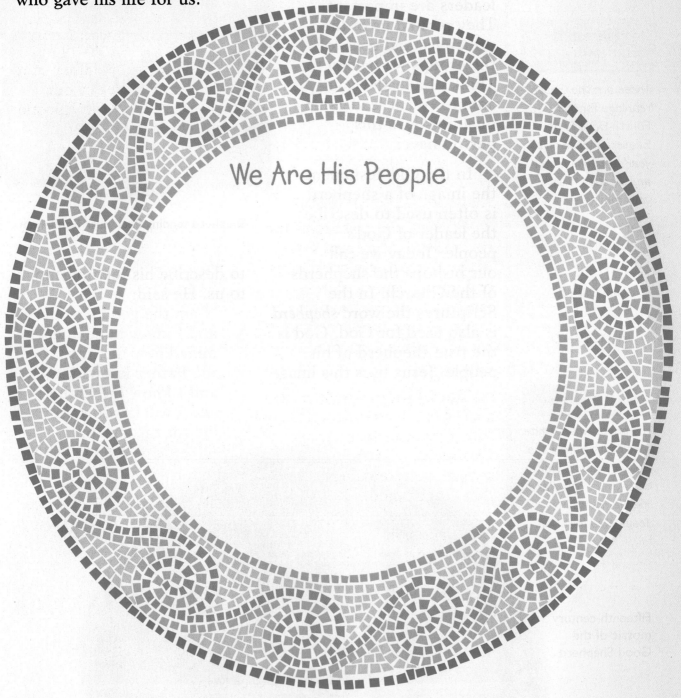

We Are His People

America's first mission (1565), Saint Augustine, Florida

Faith Focus

How can we remember that Jesus is the center of the lives of all who have been baptized?

The Word of the Lord

These are the Gospel readings for the Fifth Sunday of Easter. Choose this year's reading. Read and discuss it with your family.

Year A
  John 14:1–12

Year B
  John 15:1–8

Year C
  John 13:31–35

Remembering Jesus

Each family celebrates its memories in different ways. Many families collect photos or home videos. Other families have parties and invite family members and friends to share food and memories.

The Church gathers and shares her memories of the Risen Jesus in many ways. During the Easter season we remember that Christ died, rose from the dead, and will come again in glory. He is always at the center of all our celebrations.

Singing Psalm 118 during Easter helps us recall that in Baptism we share in the gift of new life God has given us. We sing:
  I shall not die, but live, and declare the works of the Lord.

RESPONSORIAL PSALM, EASTER SUNDAY

To help us remember that Jesus is the center of our lives, Saint Peter the Apostle used the image of a cornerstone. He wrote:
  Come to him, a living stone. . . . [L]et yourselves be built into a spiritual house to be a holy priesthood to offer spiritual sacrifices acceptable to God through Jesus Christ. For it says in scripture:
  "Behold, I am laying a stone in Zion, a cornerstone, chosen and precious."

1 PETER 2:4–6

Our Lord of Good Ending Church, Salvador, Brazil

379

A cornerstone of a building is the stone around which all other stones are built. Christ is the center of the Church. The lives of all who have been baptized are built around and supported by him.

Keeping Jesus at the Center of Our Lives

The New Testament has many images for Jesus. Look up each Gospel passage and name the image it uses for Jesus.

John 6:48 _____

John 8:12 _____

John 10:7 _____

John 15:5 _____

Which image helps you remember that Jesus is the center of your life? How does it help you?

_____

_____

_____

_____

_____

_____

_____

_____

Faith Focus

What actions of Saint Peter and the other Apostles helped people become followers of Jesus?

The Word of the Lord

These are the Gospel readings for the Sixth Sunday of Easter. Choose this year's reading. Read and discuss it with your family.

Year A
John 14:15–21

Year B
John 15:9–17

Year C
John 14:23–29

Proclaiming the Good News

You have probably heard the saying, "Actions speak louder than words." What does this saying mean to you?

There are actions that show we are living as Christians. There are also actions that show we are not living as Christians. Jesus invites us to act as he did. He told his disciples to reach out to heal and forgive others. He told them to go out into the whole world and proclaim the good news of God's love.

From the beginning of the Church, Jesus' disciples have done what he asked. Saint Peter and the other Apostles traveled far from their homes to tell others about Jesus Christ. They preached that Jesus had been crucified and died and was raised from the dead.

They wanted everyone to know that God's salvation was to be found in Jesus Christ (Acts 4:5–12). Saint Peter, Saint Paul, and the other Apostles shared with others this good news of God's love.

The Apostles taught that those who wished to follow Jesus were to make a choice and change the way they were acting. Those who changed and were baptized became members of the Church.

We are baptized. We are followers of Christ. By our actions others will know that we are Jesus' disciples. By our actions others will come to know God's great love for them.

Living the Good News

Read and respond to each situation. Describe what you would do and say that shows you are a follower of Jesus.

Mateo tells you that his gerbil died. He is so sad that he can hardly talk without crying.

I will _____

_____.

Yi Min is excited. She tells you her grandmother is finally coming from China to visit.

I will _____

_____.

Your little sister is watching TV. It is time for your favorite show to come on.

I will _____

_____.

Think about your day. What can you do or say today that will show that you have been baptized and are a follower of Jesus?

I will _____

_____.

Faith Focus

How does the story of Saint Stephen, Martyr and Deacon, help us live our faith in Christ?

The Word of the Lord

These are the Gospel readings for the Seventh Sunday of Easter. Choose this year's reading. Read and discuss it with your family.

Year A
John 17:1–11

Year B
John 17:11–19

Year C
John 17:20–26

The Stoning of Saint Stephen. Paolo Ucello (1397–1475), Italian painter.

Giving Witness to Christ

Sometimes we see or hear or read something that makes us stop and think. It becomes so important to us that we cannot stop telling others about it. Saint Stephen the Deacon could not stop talking about Jesus. His faith in Jesus was so strong that he had to share it.

Some people who listened to Saint Stephen became angry with him because he proclaimed that Jesus was truly God and was the Promised One of whom Moses and the prophets had spoken. They insisted that Stephen stop teaching. When Stephen refused, they decided he had to die. After throwing Stephen into a ditch, they kept hurling stones at him until he died.

Since the first days of the Church, Christians have honored Saint Stephen the Deacon as a martyr. The Greek word *martyr* means "witness." Saint Stephen gave witness to his faith in Jesus Christ to the point of dying for his faith.

Saint Paul teaches that all who are baptized into Christ's death and Resurrection are given the grace and vocation to witness to Christ (see Ephesians 2:19). While most Christians will never be faced with dying for their faith as Stephen did, all the baptized must give witness to their faith in Christ.

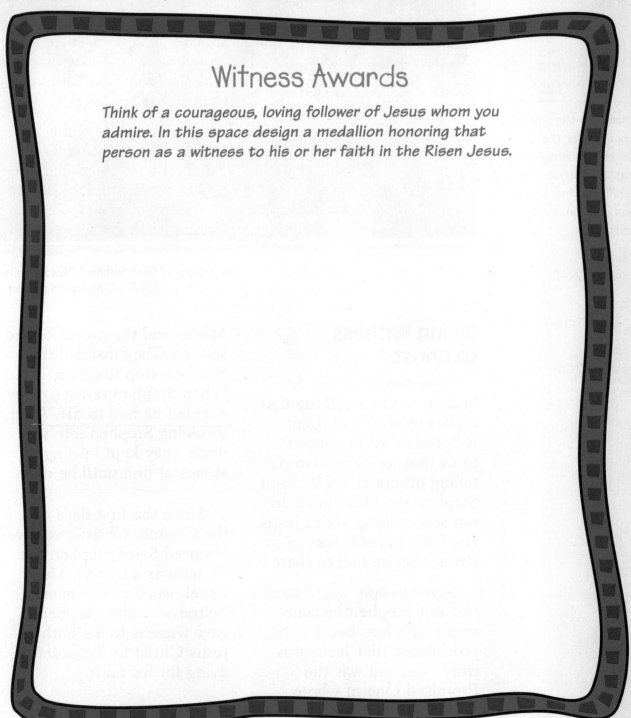

Witness Awards

Think of a courageous, loving follower of Jesus whom you admire. In this space design a medallion honoring that person as a witness to his or her faith in the Risen Jesus.

Pentecost

The Gift of the Holy Spirit

When we play a game, we feel team spirit. That spirit gives us the courage and enthusiasm to do our best. When do you feel a spirit that moves you to be courageous or generous or kind?

After the Risen Lord ascended to his Father in heaven, his disciples gathered in a house in Jerusalem. There, on the Jewish feast of Pentecost, a strong driving wind filled the entire house. Flames as of tongues of fire settled above each of them. This was a sign that the Holy Spirit had come to the disciples as Jesus promised.

Then Saint Peter left the house and preached about Jesus to Jewish people who had come to Jerusalem from many countries. Every one understood Peter in their own language. Many listened and the Holy Spirit moved them to be baptized.

Each year the Church celebrates Pentecost. On Pentecost we stand and sing: Come, Holy Spirit, fill the hearts of your faithful and kindle in them the fire of your love.

GOSPEL ALLELUIA, PENTECOST

Saint Paul tells us that we are Temples of the Holy Spirit. The Holy Spirit lives, or dwells, within us. Each Pentecost we remember that we have received the gift of the Holy Spirit at Baptism. The Holy Spirit fills us with his gifts to live our Baptism.

Living as Temples of the Holy Spirit

Saint Paul the Apostle names nine fruits, or signs, that show we are living a life guided by the Holy Spirit. Read Galatians 5:22–23 to discover these signs. List them in this space.

_____   _____

_____   _____

_____   _____

_____

Describe a situation in which you have seen one or several of these signs in someone else or in yourself.

_____

_____

_____

_____

Catholic Prayers and Practices

Sign of the Cross

In the name of the Father,
and of the Son,
and of the Holy Spirit. Amen.

Signum Crucis

In nómine Patris,
et Fílii,
et Spíritus Sancti. Amen.

Glory Be

Glory be to the Father
and to the Son
and to the Holy Spirit,
as it was in the beginning
is now, and ever shall be
world without end. Amen.

Gloria Patri

Glória Patri
et Fílio
et Spirítui Sancto.
Sicut erat in princípio,
et nunc et semper
et in sæcula sæculórum. Amen.

Lord's Prayer

Our Father, who art in heaven,
hallowed be thy name;
thy kingdom come,
thy will be done
    on earth as it is in heaven.
Give us this day our daily bread,
and forgive us our trespasses,
as we forgive those who trespass
    against us;
and lead us not into temptation,
but deliver us from evil. Amen.

Pater Noster

Pater noster, qui es in cælis:
sanctificétur nomen tuum;
advéniat regnum tuum;
fiat volúntas tua, sicut in cælo,
    et in terra.
Panem nostrum cotidiánum da
    nobis hódie;
et dimítte nobis débita nostra,
sicut et nos dimíttimus
    debitóribus nostris;
et ne nos indúcas in tentatiónem;
sed líbera nos a malo. Amen.

Hail Mary

Hail, Mary, full of grace,
the Lord is with thee.
Blessed art thou among women
and blessed is the fruit of thy
    womb, Jesus.
Holy Mary, Mother of God,
pray for us sinners,
now and at the hour of our death.
Amen.

Ave, Maria

Ave, María, grátia plena,
Dóminus tecum.
Benedícta tu in muliéribus,
et benedíctus fructus ventris
    tui, Jesus.
Sancta María, Mater Dei,
ora pro nobis peccatóribus,
nunc et in hora mortis nostræ.
Amen.

The four prayers on this page are in English
and in Latin. Latin is the universal language
of the Roman Catholic Church.

Apostles' Creed

I believe in God,
the Father almighty,
Creator of heaven and earth,
and in Jesus Christ,
    his only Son, our Lord,

*(At the words that follow, up to and
including* the Virgin Mary, *all bow.)*

who was conceived by the Holy Spirit,
born of the Virgin Mary,
suffered under Pontius Pilate,
was crucified, died and was buried;
he descended into hell;
on the third day he rose again
    from the dead;
he ascended into heaven,
and is seated at the right hand
    of God the Father almighty;
from there he will come to judge
    the living and the dead.

I believe in the Holy Spirit,
the holy catholic Church,
the communion of saints,
the forgiveness of sins,
the resurrection of the body,
and life everlasting. Amen.

Nicene Creed

I believe in one God,
the Father almighty,
maker of heaven and earth,
of all things visible and invisible.

I believe in one Lord Jesus Christ,
the Only Begotten Son of God,
born of the Father before all ages.
God from God, Light from Light,
true God from true God,
begotten, not made, consubstantial
    with the Father;
through him all things were made.
For us men and for our salvation
he came down from heaven,

*(At the words that follow, up to and
including* and became man, *all bow.)*

and by the Holy Spirit
    was incarnate of the Virgin Mary,
and became man.

For our sake he was crucified under
    Pontius Pilate,
he suffered death and was buried,
and rose again on the third day
in accordance with the Scriptures.
He ascended into heaven
and is seated at the right hand
    of the Father.
He will come again in glory
to judge the living and the dead
and his kingdom will have no end.

I believe in the Holy Spirit, the Lord,
    the giver of life,
who proceeds from the Father and the Son,
who with the Father and the Son
    is adored and glorified,
who has spoken through the prophets.

I believe in one, holy, catholic and
    apostolic Church.
I confess one Baptism
    for the forgiveness of sins
and I look forward to the resurrection
    of the dead
and the life of the world to come.
Amen.

Morning Prayer

Dear God,
as I begin this day,
keep me in your love and care.
Help me to live as your child today.
Bless me, my family, and my friends
    in all we do.
Keep us all close to you. Amen.

Evening Prayer

Dear God,
I thank you for today.
Keep me safe throughout the night.
Thank you for all the good I did today.
I am sorry for what I have chosen
    to do wrong.
Bless my family and friends. Amen.

Grace Before Meals

Bless us, O Lord,
    and these thy gifts,
which we are about to receive
    from thy bounty,
through Christ our Lord.
Amen.

Grace After Meals

We give thee thanks, for all thy benefits,
    almighty God,
who lives and reigns forever.
Amen.

A Vocation Prayer

God, I know you will call me
for special work in my life.
Help me follow Jesus each day
and be ready to answer your call.

Act of Faith

O my God, I firmly believe that you are
one God in three divine Persons, Father,
Son, and Holy Spirit. I believe that your
divine Son became man and died for
our sins, and that he will come to judge
the living and the dead. Amen.

Act of Hope

O my God, relying on your infinite
goodness and promises, I hope to obtain
pardon of my sins, the help of your grace,
and life everlasting, through the merits of
Jesus Christ, my Lord and Redeemer.
Amen.

Act of Love

O my God, I love you above all things,
with my whole heart and soul, because
you are all good and worthy of all my love.
I love my neighbor as myself for the love
of you. I forgive all who have injured me
and I ask pardon of all whom I have
injured. Amen.

The Divine Praises

Blessed be God.
Blessed be his holy name.
Blessed be Jesus Christ, true God
    and true man.
Blessed be the name of Jesus.
Blessed be his most Sacred Heart.
Blessed be his most precious Blood.
Blessed be Jesus in the most holy Sacrament
    of the altar.
Blessed be the Holy Spirit, the Paraclete.
Blessed be the great Mother of God,
    Mary most holy.
Blessed be her holy and Immaculate
    Conception.
Blessed be her glorious Assumption.
Blessed be the name of Mary, Virgin
    and Mother.
Blessed be Saint Joseph, her most
    chaste spouse.
Blessed be God in his angels and
    in his saints.

Prayer to the Holy Spirit

Come, Holy Spirit, fill the hearts
    of your faithful.
And kindle in them the
    fire of your love.
Send forth your Spirit and
    they shall be created.
And you will renew the
    face of the earth.

The Angelus

Leader: The Angel of the Lord declared
    unto Mary,
Response: And she conceived of the
    Holy Spirit.
All: Hail Mary . . .

Leader: Behold the handmaid of the Lord:
Response: Be it done unto me according to
    your Word.
All: Hail Mary . . .

Leader: And the Word was made flesh,
Response: And dwelt among us.
All: Hail Mary . . .

Leader: Pray for us, O holy Mother
    of God,
Response: That we may be made worthy of the
    promises of Christ.

Leader: Let us pray.
    Pour forth, we beseech you,
    O Lord, your grace into our hearts:
    that we, to whom the Incarnation
    of Christ your Son was made known
    by the message of an Angel, may by
    his Passion and Cross be brought
    to the glory of his Resurrection.
    Through the same Christ our Lord.
All: Amen.

The Great Commandment

"You shall love the Lord,
your God, with all your
heart, with all your soul,
and with all your mind. . . .
You shall love your neighbor as yourself."

MATTHEW 22:37, 39

The New Commandment

[Jesus said:] "I give you a new
commandment: love one another.
As I have loved you, so you also should
love one another. This is how all will
know that you are my disciples,
if you have love for one another."

JOHN 13:34–35

The Ten Commandments

1. I am the LORD your God: you shall not have strange gods before me.
2. You shall not take the name of the LORD your God in vain.
3. Remember to keep holy the LORD's Day.
4. Honor your father and your mother.
5. You shall not kill.
6. You shall not commit adultery.
7. You shall not steal.
8. You shall not bear false witness against your neighbor.
9. You shall not covet your neighbor's wife.
10. You shall not covet your neighbor's goods.

TRADITIONAL CATECHETICAL FORMULA,
CATECHISM OF THE CATHOLIC CHURCH

The Beatitudes

"Blessed are the poor in spirit,
for theirs is the kingdom of heaven.
Blessed are they who mourn,
for they will be comforted.
Blessed are the meek,
for they will inherit the land.
Blessed are they who hunger
and thirst for righteousness,
for they will be satisfied.
Blessed are the merciful,
for they will be shown mercy.
Blessed are the clean of heart,
for they will see God.
Blessed are the peacemakers,
for they will be called children of God.
Blessed are they who are persecuted
for the sake of righteousness,
for theirs is the kingdom of heaven.

Blessed are you when they insult you
and persecute you and utter every kind
of evil against you [falsely] because of me.
Rejoice and be glad, for your reward will
be great in heaven."

MATTHEW 5:3–12

Corporal Works of Mercy

Feed people who are hungry.
Give drink to people who are thirsty.
Clothe people who need clothes.
Visit prisoners.
Shelter people who are homeless.
Visit people who are sick.
Bury people who have died.

Spiritual Works of Mercy

Help people who sin.
Teach people who are ignorant.
Give advice to people
 who have doubts.
Comfort people who suffer.
Be patient with other people.
Forgive people who hurt you.
Pray for people who are alive and for
 those who have died.

Gifts of the Holy Spirit

Wisdom
Understanding
Right judgment (Counsel)
Courage (Fortitude)
Knowledge
Reverence (Piety)
Wonder and awe (Fear of the Lord)

Cardinal Virtues

Prudence
Justice
Fortitude
Temperance

Precepts of the Church

1. Participate in Mass on Sundays and holy days of obligation and rest from unnecessary work.

2. Confess sins at least once a year.

3. Receive Holy Communion at least during the Easter season.

4. Observe the prescribed days of fasting and abstinence.

5. Provide for the material needs of the Church, each according to one's abilities.

Basic Principles of the Church's Teaching on Social Justice

The Church's teaching on social justice guides us in living lives of holiness and building a just society. These principles are:

1. All human life is sacred. The basic equality of all people flows from their dignity as human persons and the rights that flow from that dignity.

2. The human person is the principle, the object, and the subject of every social group.

3. The human person has been created by God to belong to and to participate in a family and other social communities.

4. Respect for the rights of people flows from their dignity as persons. Society and all social organizations must promote virtue and protect human life and human rights and guarantee the conditions that promote the exercise of freedom.

5. Political communities and public authority are based on human nature. They belong to an order established by God.

6. All human authority must be used for the common good of society.

7. The common good of society consists of respect for and promotion of the fundamental rights of the human person; the just development of material and spiritual goods of society; and the peace and safety of all people.

8. We need to work to eliminate the sinful inequalities that exist between peoples and for the improvement of the living conditions of people. The needs of the poor and vulnerable have a priority.

9. We are one human and global family. We are to share our spiritual blessings, even more than our material blessings.

Based on the *Catechism of the Catholic Church*

Rosary

Catholics pray the Rosary to honor Mary and remember the important events in the lives of Jesus and Mary. There are twenty mysteries of the rosary. Follow the steps from 1 to 5.

3. Think of the first mystery. Pray an Our Father, 10 Hail Marys, and the Glory Be.

5. Pray the Hail, Holy Queen prayer. Make the Sign of the Cross.

2. Pray an Our Father, 3 Hail Marys, and the Glory Be.

4. Repeat step 3 for each of the next 4 mysteries.

1. Make the Sign of the Cross and pray the Apostles' Creed.

Joyful Mysteries

1. The Annunciation
2. The Visitation
3. The Nativity
4. The Presentation in the Temple
5. The Finding of the Child Jesus After Three Days in the Temple

Luminous Mysteries

1. The Baptism at the Jordan
2. The Miracle at Cana
3. The Proclamation of the Kingdom and the Call to Conversion
4. The Transfiguration
5. The Institution of the Eucharist

Sorrowful Mysteries

1. The Agony in the Garden
2. The Scourging at the Pillar
3. The Crowning with Thorns
4. The Carrying of the Cross
5. The Crucifixion and Death

Glorious Mysteries

1. The Resurrection
2. The Ascension
3. The Descent of the Holy Spirit at Pentecost
4. The Assumption of Mary
5. The Crowning of the Blessed Virgin as Queen of Heaven and Earth

Hail, Holy Queen

Hail, holy Queen, Mother of mercy:
Hail, our life, our sweetness and our hope.
To you do we cry, poor banished
    children of Eve.
To you do we send up our sighs,
mourning and weeping
    in this valley of tears.
Turn then, most gracious advocate,
your eyes of mercy toward us;
and after this our exile
show unto us the blessed fruit
    of your womb, Jesus.
O clement, O loving, O sweet Virgin Mary.

Stations of the Cross

1. Jesus is condemned to death.

2. Jesus accepts his cross.

3. Jesus falls the first time.

4. Jesus meets his mother.

5. Simon helps Jesus carry the cross.

6. Veronica wipes the face of Jesus.

7. Jesus falls the second time.

8. Jesus meets the women.

9. Jesus falls the third time.

10. Jesus is stripped of his clothes.

11. Jesus is nailed to the cross.

12. Jesus dies on the cross.

13. Jesus is taken down from the cross.

14. Jesus is buried in the tomb.

Some parishes conclude the Stations by reflecting on the Resurrection of Jesus.

Signs and Symbols of the Catholic Church

From its beginning the Church has used signs and symbols to help us profess our faith. These symbols unite us. They help us understand what Catholics believe.

Cross

The cross is one of the most widely used symbols of our faith. It reminds us that Jesus died on the cross and was raised from the dead. A crucifix is a cross with Jesus' body fixed to it.

Alpha and Omega

Alpha and Omega are the first and last letters of the Greek alphabet. They remind us that Jesus is the beginning and end of everything that is.

Chi-Rho

The Chi-Rho is a symbol for Christ. It comes from the first two letters of the Greek word for Christ.

The Good Shepherd

Jesus is often represented as the Good Shepherd who leads and cares for his sheep. The sheep symbolize those who follow Christ.

Paschal Candle

The Paschal candle, also called the Easter candle, is a symbol of the Risen Christ who is the Light of the world.

The Seven Sacraments

Jesus gave the Church the seven sacraments. The sacraments are the main liturgical signs of the Church. They make the Paschal Mystery of Jesus, who is always the main celebrant of each sacrament, present to us. They make us sharers in the saving work of Christ and in the life of the Holy Trinity.

Sacraments of Christian Initiation

Baptism

Through Baptism we are joined to Christ and become members of the Body of Christ, the Church. We are reborn as adopted children of God the Father and receive the gift of the Holy Spirit. Original sin and all personal sins are forgiven.

Confirmation

Confirmation completes Baptism. In this sacrament the gift of the Holy Spirit strengthens us to live our Baptism.

Eucharist

Sharing in the Eucharist joins us most fully to Christ and to the Church. We share in the one sacrifice of Christ. The bread and wine become the Body and Blood of Christ through the power of the Holy Spirit and the words of the priest. We receive the Body and Blood of Christ.

Sacraments of Healing

Penance and Reconciliation

Through the ministry of the priest we receive forgiveness of sins committed after our Baptism. We need to confess all mortal sins.

Anointing of the Sick

Anointing of the Sick strengthens our faith and trust in God when we are seriously ill, dying, or weak because of old age.

Sacraments at the Service of Communion

Holy Orders

Through Holy Orders a baptized man is consecrated to serve the whole Church as a bishop, priest, or deacon in the name of Christ. Bishops, who are the successors of the Apostles, receive this sacrament most fully. They are consecrated to teach the Gospel, to lead the Church in the worship of God, and to guide the Church to live holy lives. Bishops are helped by priests, their coworkers, and by deacons in their work.

Matrimony

Matrimony unites a baptized man and a baptized woman in a lifelong bond of faithful love to always honor each other and to accept the gift of children from God. In this sacrament the married couple is consecrated to be a sign of Christ's love for the Church.

We Celebrate the Mass

The Introductory Rites

**We remember that we are members of the Church.
We prepare to listen to the word of God
and to celebrate the Eucharist.**

The Entrance

We stand as the priest, deacon, and other ministers enter the assembly. We sing a gathering song. The priest and deacon kiss the altar. The priest then goes to the chair where he presides over the celebration.

Sign of the Cross and Greeting

The priest leads us in praying the Sign of the Cross. The priest greets us, and we say,
"And with your spirit."

The Penitential Act

We admit our wrongdoings.
We bless God for his mercy.

The Gloria

We praise God for all the good he has done for us.

The Collect

The priest leads us in praying the Collect.
We respond, **"Amen."**

The Liturgy of the Word

**God speaks to us today.
We listen and respond to God's word.**

The First Reading from the Bible

We sit and listen as the reader reads from the Old Testament or from the Acts of the Apostles. The reader concludes, "The word of the Lord." We respond,
"Thanks be to God."

The Responsorial Psalm

The song leader leads us in singing a psalm.

The Second Reading from the Bible

The reader reads from the New Testament, but not from the four Gospels. The reader concludes, "The word of the Lord." We respond,
"Thanks be to God."

Acclamation

We stand to honor Christ present with us in the Gospel. The song leader leads us in singing **"Alleluia, Alleluia, Alleluia"** or another chant during Lent.

The Gospel

The deacon or priest proclaims, "A reading from the holy Gospel according to (name of Gospel writer)." We respond,
"Glory to you, O Lord."

He proclaims the Gospel. At the end, he says, "The Gospel of the Lord." We respond,
"Praise to you, Lord Jesus Christ."

The Homily

We sit. The deacon or priest preaches the homily. He helps the whole community understand the word of God spoken to us in the readings.

The Profession of Faith

We stand and profess our faith.
We pray the Nicene Creed together.

The Prayer of the Faithful

The priest leads us in praying for the Church and her leaders, for our country and its leaders, for ourselves and others, for the sick and those who have died. We can respond to each prayer in several ways. One way we respond is,
"Lord, hear our prayer."

The Liturgy of the Eucharist
We join with Jesus and the Holy Spirit to give thanks and praise to God the Father.

The Preparation of the Gifts

We sit as the altar table is prepared and the collection is taken up. We share our blessings with the Church, especially with those in need. The song leader may lead us in singing a song. The gifts of bread and wine are brought to the altar.

The priest lifts up the bread and blesses God for all our gifts. He prays, "Blessed are you, Lord God of all creation, . . ."
We respond,
   "Blessed be God for ever."

The priest lifts up the cup of wine and prays, "Blessed are you, Lord God of all creation, . . ." We respond,
   "Blessed be God for ever."

The priest invites us,
   "Pray, brethren (brothers and sisters),
   that my sacrifice and yours
   may be acceptable to God,
   the almighty Father."

We stand and respond,
   **"May the Lord accept the sacrifice
      at your hands
   for the praise and glory of his name,
   for our good
   and the good of all his holy Church."**

The Prayer over the Offerings

The priest leads us in praying the Prayer over the Offerings. We respond, **"Amen."**

Preface

The priest invites us to join in praying the Church's great prayer of praise and thanksgiving to God the Father.
Priest: "The Lord be with you."
Assembly: "And with your spirit."
Priest: "Lift up your hearts."
Assembly: "We lift them up to the Lord."
Priest: "Let us give thanks to the Lord our God."
Assembly: "It is right and just."

After the priest sings or prays aloud the Preface, we join in acclaiming:
   **"Holy, Holy, Holy Lord God of hosts.
   Heaven and earth are full of your glory.
   Hosanna in the highest.
   Blessed is he who comes in
      the name of the Lord.
   Hosanna in the highest."**

The Eucharistic Prayer

The priest leads the assembly in praying the Eucharistic Prayer. We call upon the Holy Spirit to make our gifts of bread and wine holy and pray that they become the Body and Blood of Jesus. We recall what happened at the Last Supper. The bread and wine become the Body and Blood of the Lord. Jesus is truly and really present under the appearances of bread and wine.

The priest sings or says aloud,
"The mystery of faith."
We respond using this or another acclamation used by the Church,
   **"We proclaim your Death, O Lord, and
   profess your Resurrection until you come
   again."**

The priest then prays for the Church. He prays for the living and the dead.

Doxology

The priest concludes the praying of the Eucharistic Prayer. He sings or prays aloud,
   "Through him, and with him, and in him,
   O God, almighty Father,
   in the unity of the Holy Spirit,
   all glory and honor is yours,
   for ever and ever."
We stand and respond, **"Amen."**

The Communion Rite

The Lord's Prayer
We pray the Lord's Prayer together.

The Rite of Peace
The priest invites us to share a sign of peace, saying, "The peace of the Lord be with you always."
We respond,
   "And with your spirit."
We share a sign of peace.

The Fraction, or the Breaking of the Bread
The priest breaks the host, the consecrated bread. We sing or pray aloud,
   **"Lamb of God, you take away
      the sins of the world,
   have mercy on us.
   Lamb of God, you take away
      the sins of the world,
   have mercy on us.
   Lamb of God, you take away
      the sins of the world,
   grant us peace."**

Communion
The priest raises the host and says aloud,
   "Behold the Lamb of God,
      behold him who takes away the sins
      of the world.
   Blessed are those called to the
      supper of the Lamb."
We join with him and say,
   **"Lord, I am not worthy that you should
   enter under my roof, but only say the
   word and my soul shall be healed."**

The priest receives Communion. Next, the deacon and the extraordinary ministers of Holy Communion and the members of the assembly receive Communion.

The priest, deacon, or extraordinary minister of Holy Communion holds up the host. We bow and the priest, deacon, or extraordinary minister of Holy Communion says, "The Body of Christ." We respond, **"Amen."** We then receive the consecrated host in our hand or on our tongue.

If we are to receive the Blood of Christ, the priest, deacon, or extraordinary minister of Holy Communion holds up the cup containing the consecrated wine. We bow and the priest, deacon, or extraordinary minister of Holy Communion says, "The Blood of Christ." We respond, **"Amen."** We take the cup in our hands and drink from it.

The Prayer after Communion
We stand as the priest invites us to pray, saying, "Let us pray." He prays the Prayer after Communion.
We respond, **"Amen."**

The Concluding Rites
We are sent forth to do good works, praising and blessing the Lord.

Greeting

We stand. The priest greets us as we prepare to leave. He says, "The Lord be with you."

We respond, **"And with your spirit."**

Blessing

The priest or deacon may invite us,
"Bow down for the blessing."
The priest blesses us, saying,
"May almighty God bless you,
the Father, and the Son, and the Holy Spirit."
We respond, **"Amen."**

Dismissal of the People

The priest or deacon sends us forth, using these or similar words,
"Go and announce the Gospel of the Lord."
We respond, **"Thanks be to God."**

We sing a hymn. The priest and the deacon kiss the altar. The priest, deacon, and other ministers bow to the altar and leave in procession.

The Sacrament of Penance and Reconciliation

Individual Rite

Greeting

Scripture Reading

Confession of Sins and Acceptance
of Penance

Act of Contrition

Absolution

Closing Prayer

Communal Rite

Greeting

Scripture Reading

Homily

Examination of Conscience with a litany
of contrition and the Lord's Prayer

Individual Confession and Absolution

Closing Prayer

Act of Contrition

My God,
I am sorry for my sins
with all my heart.
In choosing to do wrong
and failing to do good,
I have sinned against you
whom I should love above all things.
I firmly intend, with your help,
to do penance,
to sin no more,
and to avoid whatever leads me to sin.
Our Savior Jesus Christ
suffered and died for us.
In his name, my God, have mercy.

FROM RITE OF PENANCE

Glossary

A-B

Abba [page 64]
The name Jesus used for God the Father that reveals the love and trust that exist between Jesus, God the Son, and God the Father.

absolution [page 202]
The forgiveness of sins given by God through the ministry of the priest in the Sacrament of Reconciliation.

actual grace [page 257]
The gift of God's presence with us to help us live as children of God and followers of Christ.

Adonai [page 74]
The Hebrew word for "Lord" that the Jewish people use in place of YHWH, the name God revealed for himself to Moses.

Advocate [page 102]
Title or name for the Holy Spirit, which means "one who is at our side," or "one who speaks for us."

almighty [page 62]
Having all power; only God is almighty.

Annunciation [page 40]
The announcement to the Virgin Mary by the angel Gabriel that God had chosen her to be the Mother of Jesus, the Son of God, through the power of the Holy Spirit.

Anointing of the Sick [page 204]
The Sacrament of Healing that strengthens our faith, hope, and love for God when we are seriously ill, weakened by old age, or dying.

Apostles [page 166]
The first shepherds of the Church, the disciples Jesus gave the responsibility and authority to baptize and to teach in his name.

Ascension [page 91]
A word meaning "a going up"; the return of the Risen Christ in glory to his Father.

assembly [page 180]
The Church gathered to celebrate the sacraments and the liturgy.

attributes of God [page 62]
Qualities of God that help us understand the mystery of God.

Baptism [page 152]
The Sacrament of Christian Initiation in which we are first joined to Jesus Christ, become members of the Church, are reborn as God's adopted children, receive the gift of the Holy Spirit, and original sin and our personal sins are forgiven.

Beatitudes [page 242]
The sayings or teachings of Jesus that are found in the Sermon on the Mount that describe both the qualities and the actions of people blessed by God.

bishop [page 214]
A successor of the Apostles; a priest who has received the fullness of the Sacrament of Holy Orders; a member of the order of bishops, or the episcopal college.

breaking of bread [page 188]
A name used for the celebration of the Eucharist.

C-D

cardinal virtues [page 234]
The four virtues of prudence, justice, fortitude, and temperance.

Catholic Letters [page 267]
The seven New Testament letters that bear the names of the Apostles John, Peter, Jude, and James.

chant [page 309]
Plainsong; a simple type of song with only one melody line, using rhythm of the spoken word.

charisms [page 113]
Graces, or gifts, given by the Holy Spirit to build up the Church on earth for the good of all people and the needs of the world.

chastity [page 292]
The virtue that is the good habit of respecting and honoring our sexuality and that guides us to share our love with others in appropriate ways.

chrism [page 153]
One of the three oils blessed by the Church to use in the celebration of the liturgy.

Christ [page 75]
A title for Jesus that states that he is the Messiah whom God promised to send to save his people.

Church [page 122]
The Body of Christ; the new People of God called together in Christ by the power of the Holy Spirit.

communal prayer [page 321]
Praying with others.

Communion of Saints [page 127]
All the faithful followers of Jesus, both the living and the dead, those on earth, in purgatory, and in heaven.

confession [page 202]
The telling of sins to a priest in the Sacrament of Reconciliation.

Confirmation [page 156]
The Sacrament of Christian Initiation that strengthens the graces of Baptism and in which our new life in Christ is sealed by the gift of the Holy Spirit.

conscience [page 232]
The gift of God that is part of every person and that guides us to know and judge what is right and wrong.

consecrate [page 145]
> To set aside for a holy purpose.

contrition [page 202]
> Sorrow for sins, which includes the desire to make up for the harm our sin has caused.

Covenant [page 27]
> The solemn agreement that God entered into with people, promising that he would be their God and they were to be his chosen people.

creeds [page 42]
> Statements of beliefs; professions of faith.

Crucifixion [page 91]
> The event of Jesus' saving death on the cross.

deacon [page 214]
> A baptized man who has received the Sacrament of Holy Orders; a member of the order of deacons, or the diaconate; a coworker with bishops and priests.

disciples [page 50]
> People who learn from and follow the teachings of another person.

Divine Revelation [page 15]
> God making himself and his plan of creation and salvation known over time.

E-F-G-H

epistle [page 189]
> A type of formal letter found in the New Testament.

eternal [page 63]
> Always living, without beginning and without end.

Eucharist [page 176]
> The Sacrament of Christian Initiation in which we share in the Paschal Mystery of Christ, receive the Body and Blood of Christ, and are joined most fully to Christ and to the Church, the Body of Christ.

evangelist [page 98]
> A word meaning "one who announces good news."

Evangelists [page 98]
> The writers of the four Gospels in the New Testament—Matthew, Mark, Luke, and John.

evangelization [page 169]
> The Church's responsibility to care for and share the Gospel with all people "so that it may enter the hearts of all men and renew the human race."

faith [page 19]
> A supernatural gift and power from God inviting us to know and believe in him and our free response to that invitation.

Gospel [page 30]
> The Good News of God's love revealed in the life, death, Resurrection, and Ascension of Jesus Christ.

Gospels [page 30]
> The first four books of the New Testament that pass on the faith of the Apostles and the early Church about the life, death, Resurrection, Ascension, and teachings of Jesus Christ.

grace [page 114]
> The gift of God's life and love that makes us holy and helps us live holy lives.

holiness [page 254]
> The quality, or condition, of a person who is living in communion with and in the right relationship with God, others, and with all of his creation; being in the state of grace.

Holy Orders [page 214]
> The Sacrament at the Service of Communion through which a baptized man is consecrated to serve the whole Church as a bishop, priest, or deacon.

Holy Spirit [page 101]
> The third Person of the Holy Trinity, sent to us by the Father in the name of his Son, Jesus Christ.

Holy Trinity [page 38]
> The central belief of the Christian faith; the mystery of one God in three divine Persons—God the Father, God the Son, God the Holy Spirit.

I-J-K-L

Incarnation [page 76]
> From the Latin word meaning "putting on flesh," to have a real body; the Son of God "putting on flesh," or becoming human, while keeping his divinity.

inspiration of the Bible [page 27]
> The Holy Spirit guiding the human writers of Sacred Scripture to faithfully and accurately communicate God's word.

Israelites [pages 17]
> The Old Testament people to whom God revealed himself and with whom he made the Covenant.

justice [page 294]
> One of the moral, or cardinal, virtues; the good habit of giving to God and to all people what is rightfully due to them.

Kingdom of God [page 126]
> All people and creation living in communion with God at the end of time when the work of Christ will be completed and he will come again in glory.

liturgical year [page 142]
> The Church's yearly cycle of seasons and feasts that celebrate the mysteries of Jesus' birth, life, death, and Resurrection.

liturgy [page 140]
> The work of the Church, the People of God, of worshiping him through which Christ continues the work of Redemption in, with, and through his Church.

Lord [pages 74 and 75]
A word that translates the Hebrew word *Adonai*, which the Israelites used for God; a title for Jesus that states that he is truly God.

Lord's Day [page 282]
The name Christians give to Sunday, the day of the Lord's Resurrection.

M-N-O

Magnificat [page 325]
Mary's canticle of praise to God.

Marks of the Church [page 124]
One, holy, catholic, apostolic; the four signs, or essential qualities, of the Church founded by Jesus.

Mass [page 179]
The main sacramental celebration of the Church at which we gather to listen to God's word and share in the Eucharist.

Matrimony [page 216]
The Sacrament at the Service of Communion that unites a baptized man and a baptized woman in a lifelong bond, or covenant, of faithful love to serve the Church as a sign of Christ's love for the Church.

Messiah [page 75]
A title that means "Anointed One"; Jesus, the Anointed One of God, the Messiah, the Savior of the world.

miracle [page 54]
An occurrence that goes beyond the laws of nature and invites us to deepen our faith in God.

moral decisions [page 230]
The decisions and choices we make to live as children of God and followers of Jesus Christ.

moral virtues [page 234]
Spiritual powers, or habits, that give us the strength to do what is right and good and to live holy lives.

mortal sin [page 259]
A serious failure in our love and respect for God, our neighbor, creation, and ourselves. Three things are necessary for a sin to be mortal, namely, (1) the thing we do or say must be gravely wrong; (2) we must know it is gravely wrong; (3) we must freely choose it.

Mother of God [page 78]
Mary, the Mother of Jesus, who is true God and true man.

Mount Sinai [page 332]
One of several mountain peaks in the Sinai Peninsula in Egypt, also called Mount Horeb, on which God revealed himself to Moses.

Nicene Creed [page 42]
A creed, or brief statement of the faith of the Church, written in the fourth century.

obey [page 290]
To follow the commands of others who have rightful authority in our lives and who are helping us live according to God's laws.

original sin [page 67]
The sin of Adam and Eve by which they and all people lost the state of original holiness, and death, evil, and suffering entered the world.

P-Q

Paschal Mystery [page 88]
The "passing over" of Jesus from life through death into new and glorious life; the Passion, death, Resurrection, and glorious Ascension of Jesus.

Passover [page 87]
The Jewish feast celebrating the sparing of the Hebrew children from death and the passage of God's people from slavery in Egypt to freedom in the land God promised them.

penance [page 202]
Prayer or act of kindness that shows we are truly sorry for our sins.

Pentateuch [page 17]
Word meaning "five containers"; the first five books of the Old Testament.

pentecost [page 114]
A word meaning "fiftieth day."

Pentecost [page 164]
The feast and holy day on which the Church celebrates the coming of the Holy Spirit on the disciples.

personal prayer [page 321]
Spending time alone with God.

prayer of adoration [page 322]
Acknowledging that God alone is the Creator and source of all that is.

priest [page 214]
A baptized man who has received the Sacrament of Holy Orders; a member of the order of priests, or the presbyterate; a coworker of the bishops.

prophets [page 28]
People chosen by God to speak his name.

Psalms [page 309]
The prayer songs found in the Old Testament Book of Psalms, or the Psalter.

public ministry of Jesus [page 50]
The work that God the Father sent Jesus, the Son of God, to do on earth with the help of the Holy Spirit.

R-S

Reconciliation [page 201]
The Sacrament of Healing through which we receive God's forgiveness through the ministry of the priest for the sins we commit after Baptism.

reparation [page 294]
The replacing or repairing of any harm we have caused by our words or actions.

Resurrection [page 90]
The event of Jesus being raised from the dead to a new and glorified life.

reverence [page 192]
The attitude of awe, profound respect, and love.

Sabbath [page 282]
The seventh day of the week, the day Israelites dedicated and the Jewish people today dedicate to God as a holy day and day of rest.

sacraments [page 144]
The seven main liturgical signs of the Church, given to the Church by Jesus Christ, that make his saving work present and make us sharers in the life of God, the Holy Trinity.

Sacraments at the Service of Communion [page 213]
Holy Orders and Matrimony.

Sacraments of Christian Initiation [page 145]
Baptism, Confirmation, and Eucharist.

Sacraments of Healing [page 145]
Reconciliation, or Penance, and Anointing of the Sick.

Sacred Scripture [page 26]
Two words that mean "holy writings"; the writings the Holy Spirit inspired the people of God to write and that have been collected by the Church in the Bible.

Sacred Tradition [page 114]
The passing on of the teachings of Christ by the Church through the power and guidance of the Holy Spirit.

sacrifice [page 177]
Freely giving up something of value out of love for God.

sanctifying [page 256]
A word that means "making holy."

sanctifying grace [pages 155 and 256]
The gift of God's life and love that makes us holy and helps us live holy lives.

Sermon on the Mount [page 242]
The teachings of Jesus that are grouped together in chapters 5, 6, and 7 of the Gospel of Matthew.

sexuality [page 292]
The gift of being male or female—a boy or a man, or a girl or a woman.

sin [page 200]
Freely choosing to do what we know is against God's will or freely choosing not to do something we know God wants us to do.

soul [page 66]
The spiritual dimension of the human person that never dies, or is immortal.

steward [page 338]
One who is given the responsibility to care for what belongs to another person.

T-Z

temptation [page 231]
Everything that tries to move us away from living a holy life.

Ten Commandments [page 278]
The laws of the Covenant God revealed to Moses and the Israelites on Mount Sinai.

theological virtues [page 270]
The virtues of faith, hope, and love (charity); gifts of God that enable us to live a life of holiness, or a life in communion with the Holy Trinity.

Transfiguration [page 310]
The mysterious change in appearance of Jesus in the presence of Peter, James, and John during which Jesus speaks with Moses and the Prophet Elijah; the manifestation of the divinity of Jesus Christ.

trust [page 312]
To know that a person will always do what is good and best for us.

venial sin [page 259]
A sin less serious than a mortal sin; a sin that does not have all the three things necessary for a sin to be mortal.

virtues [page 234]
Spiritual powers or habits or behaviors that help us do what is right and avoid what is wrong.

vocation [page 212]
A call from God to do a special work.

Word of God [page 18]
Jesus, the Son of God; the Bible, which is the inspired word of God.

worshiping assembly [page 180]
The community of the new People of God, the Church, joined with Christ gathered to give praise and thanks to God the Father through the power of the Holy Spirit.

YHWH [page 62]
The four letters of the Hebrew alphabet for the name for God that God revealed to Moses.

Index

Credits